Critical Collaborative Communities

Critical Issues in the Future of Learning and Teaching

Series Editors

Britt-Marie Apelgren (*University of Gothenburg, Sweden*)
Pamela Burnard (*University of Cambridge, UK*)
Nese Cabaroglu (*University of Cukurova, Turkey*)
Pamela M. Denicolo (*University of Surrey, UK*)
Nicola Simmons (*Brock University, Canada*)

Founding Editor

Michael Kompf† (*Brock University, Canada*)

VOLUME 17

The titles published in this series are listed at *brill.com/cifl*

Critical Collaborative Communities

Academic Writing Partnerships, Groups, and Retreats

Edited by

Nicola Simmons and Ann Singh

BRILL
SENSE

LEIDEN | BOSTON

All chapters in this book have undergone peer review.

The Library of Congress Cataloging-in-Publication Data is available online at http://catalog.loc.gov

Typeface for the Latin, Greek, and Cyrillic scripts: "Brill". See and download: brill.com/brill-typeface.

ISSN 2542-8721
ISBN 978-90-04-41096-1 (paperback)
ISBN 978-90-04-41097-8 (hardback)
ISBN 978-90-04-41098-5 (e-book)

Copyright 2019 by Koninklijke Brill NV, Leiden, The Netherlands.
Koninklijke Brill NV incorporates the imprints Brill, Brill Hes & De Graaf, Brill Nijhoff, Brill Rodopi, Brill Sense, Hotei Publishing, mentis Verlag, Verlag Ferdinand Schöningh and Wilhelm Fink Verlag.
All rights reserved. No part of this publication may be reproduced, translated, stored in a retrieval system, or transmitted in any form or by any means, electronic, mechanical, photocopying, recording or otherwise, without prior written permission from the publisher.
Authorization to photocopy items for internal or personal use is granted by Koninklijke Brill NV provided that the appropriate fees are paid directly to The Copyright Clearance Center, 222 Rosewood Drive, Suite 910, Danvers, MA 01923, USA. Fees are subject to change.

This book is printed on acid-free paper and produced in a sustainable manner.

Contents

Foreword   IX
 Pam Denicolo
List of Figures and Tables   XI
Notes on Contributors   XII
Introduction   XXVIII
 Nicola Simmons

PART 1
Writing Partnerships

1 Cheaper Than Therapy: The Unexpected Benefits and Challenges of an
Academic Writing Partnership   3
 Karen Julien and Jacqueline L. Beres

2 "We'll Do Whate'er We List": Growing, Creating, and Writing Together as
Faculty of Difference   17
 M. Soledad Caballero and Aimee Knupsky

3 Collaboration at a Distance: Exploring History, Communication, Trust
and Socialization   29
 Erik Blair and Georgette Briggs

4 Just Show Up: Reflections from a Motley Writing Group   43
 Janel Seeley, Tia Frahm and Elizabeth Lynch

PART 2
Onsite Writing Retreats

5 Advancing the Writing of Academics: Stories from the Writing
Group   55
 Jennifer Lock, Yvonne Kjorlien, M. Gregory Tweedie,
 Roswita Dressler, Sarah Elaine Eaton and Erin Spring

6 Faculty Writing Studio: A Place to Write   66
 Remica Bingham-Risher and Joyce Armstrong

VI   CONTENTS

7 Campus-Wide, Non-Residential, Five-Day Faculty Writing Retreat:
   Partnerships Lead to a Sustainable Writing Program   78
        Dannelle D. Stevens and Janelle Voegele

8 The Benefits of Writing Retreats Revisited   92
        Geneviève Maheux-Pelletier, Heidi Marsh and Mandy Frake-Mistak

PART 3
Offsite Writing Retreats

9 Something Wicked This Way Comes: Wyrd Sisters, Collaborating
   In-the-Round   109
        Lisa Dickson, Shannon Murray and Jessica Riddell

10 Writing Wild: Writing Partnerships That Fly   121
        Cecile Badenhorst, Sarah Pickett and John Hoben

11 Creating and Sustaining a Community of Academic Writing Practice:
   The Multi-University Residential Academic Writing Retreat Model   136
        *Michelle K. McGinn, Snežana Ratković, Dragana Martinovic and
        Ruth McQuirter Scott*

12 Writing about Writing: Collaborative Writing and Photographic Analyses
   from an Academic Writing Retreat   149
        Kari-Lynn Winters, Natasha Wiebe and Mary Gene Saudelli

PART 4
Collaborative Writing Groups

13 Writing within an Academic Microculture: Making Our Practice
   Visible   171
        *Cheryl Jeffs, Carol Berenson, Patti Dyjur, Kimberley A. Grant,
        Frances Kalu, Natasha Kenny, Kiara Mikita, Robin Mueller
        and Lorelli Nowell*

14 Supporting Writing Collaborations through Synchronous Technologies:
   Singing Our SSONG about Working Together at a Distance   186
        *Michelle J. Eady, Corinne Green, Ashley B. Akenson, Briony Supple,
        Marian McCarthy, James Cronin and Jacinta McKeon*

CONTENTS VII

15 Growing the Canadian SoTL Community through a Collaborative Writing
   Initiative   200
      Elizabeth Marquis and Nicola Simmons

16 Collaborative Writing: Intercultural and Interdisciplinary Partnerships as a
   Means of Identity Formation   212
      Phillip Motley, Aysha Divan, Valerie Lopes, Lynn O. Ludwig,
      Kelly E. Matthews and Ana M. Tomljenovic-Berube

17 An International Interdisciplinary Writing Group: Perspectives on Building
   Partnerships and Developing Community   228
      Barbara Kensington-Miller, Carolyn Oliver, Sue Morón-García,
      Karen Manarin, Earle Abrahamson, Nicola Simmons and
      Jessica Deshler

18 Creation, Critique, Consolidation   242
      Nicola Simmons

Foreword

The survival of the human race depends on co-operation and its alter ego collaboration. We see it as nations combine their resources to cope with natural disasters, when professionals work together to solve a complex challenge and more mundanely at the personal level when partners combine their skills and compensate for each other's disabilities. We even form partnerships with animals, say with dogs and horses for mutual companionship, enjoyment and protection. Yet a stranger or newcomer to academe might be forgiven for perceiving academic work as contradicting that trend.

For students, especially postgraduates, there are pressures to be autonomous learners, while doctoral candidates must demonstrate their abilities as independent researchers making a unique contribution to knowledge. The more public aspects of the day to day work of academics involves their presenting, alone, at the front of a large audience in lecture theatres, while the criteria for promotion, recruitment, research funding and for national reviews of research emphasise lists of personal efforts of publication and research activities, often requiring percentage indicators of personal contributions. What images of a lonely existence are conjured by these descriptions, images that both mask the stimulation of working closely with colleagues and belie the sheer necessity of collaborative engagement to produce truly innovative ideas.

The myth of ivory towers filled with lone scholars beavering away on individual scripts will be totally shattered for readers of this book who will find examples, elaborations, and guidance about writing partnerships to stimulate their curiosity and provide ideas for their practice. They can then anticipate, rather than reflecting on past experience as I do here, to contributing and learning, being energised and reassured, feeling challenged and joyous.

Nearly forty years in Higher Education has taught me that opportunities to gain those experiences should be pro-actively sought rather than occurring by happenstance as they did in my early career. Initially I was honoured when my doctoral supervisor/advisor, Maureen Pope, suggested we wrote a conference paper then a journal article together on my research, not realising at the time that for some doctoral researchers such co-authorship was an obligation rather than an opportunity as I saw it. Nor did I know then that our initial literary forays would herald a life-long writing partnership and the beginning of an enduring friendship. Though passionate about the same topics, we each brought to the team different qualities and realms of experience and expertise. Our early good manners in negotiating changes to text gradually evolved into well-accepted constructive criticism, friendly banter, and even productive debate/argument, each secure in knowing that the final product would be infinitely better than anything we could produce alone.

That pattern of working was one I endeavoured to mimic in some form with my multitude of doctoral researchers with each partnership being unique but with goodwill, inspiration and motivation remaining as common factors. That has remained true when working with other colleagues. Through the good auspices of Maureen, I was introduced to several networks and fellow researchers passionate to develop student learning and academic staff development. One of those was Michael Kompf, many of whose colleagues contributed to this book, who shared the same values so that we enjoyed many years of long-distance writing collaboration, even before the advent of email and Skype. We honed each other's understanding of cultural differences in Higher Education, the English language, and humour, to my unending appreciation. One of our literary adventures was the establishment of the series in which this book is embedded, and I know he would be delighted that we are continuing the adventure despite his passing.

My own academic ventures are now diminishing, but collaborative writing remains a constant in my life with colleagues and students providing both impetus and joy in new article and book writing. I cherish their willingness to tolerate my pedantry and treasure the brilliant ideas they provide and the new ones they stimulate in me. I suggest that you will find such positive experience in reading this book and using the ideas conveyed in your own practice.

Pam Denicolo

Figures and Tables

Figures

1.1   Writing group dimensions (adapted from Haas, 2014).   7

6.1   Faculty writing studio attendance by year.   70

8.1   Structure of the writing mini-retreats.   95

8.2   Number of participants who registered and attended the writing circle between November 2017 and October 2018.   95

8.3   Number of applications to the boot camp between 2016 and 2018.   97

9.1   Marginalia.   117

10.1   La Manche, where we went to write-in-place, 53 km south of St John's, Newfoundland.   123

10.2   La Manche: Visible reminders of other lives on the landscape, we walk where they walked – separated by time but connected.   128

10.3   Lunch overlooking the bay thinking about writing, the past, the here and now, the future.   131

10.4   Walking and talking we find stairs that lead somewhere metaphorically and physically.   133

12.1   Work in progress group.   156

12.2   Nature walk.   159

12.3   Work time.   161

14.1   Screenshot from a ssong meeting, conducted via Adobe Connect®.   192

15.1   Collaborative writing group process timeline.   203

15.2   Factors for successful collaborative writing groups.   208

17.1   Kelly's (1955) stages of personal construct revision.   232

17.2   Thematic interrelationships.   233

18.1   Elements of successful collaborative writing groups.   249

18.2   Collaborative writing process: Creation, critique, consolidation.   250

Tables

8.1   Features of the writing mini-retreats.   94

12.1   Photo analysis framework.   155

12.2   Photo analysis of work in progress.   157

12.3   Photo analysis of nature walk.   160

12.4   Photo analysis of work time.   162

13.1   Example collaborative writing strategies that can be used at various stages of the writing process.   181

17.1   Author demographics.   231

Notes on Contributors

Earle Abrahamson
is a senior lecturer and programme leader in sports therapy at the University of East London, UK. He is a Principal Fellow of the Higher Education Academy (PFHEA). Born and raised in Johannesburg, South Africa, Earle gained qualifications and expertise in physical education and soft tissue therapy, clinical psychology, and educational practices. He currently co-chairs the ISSoTL multi-national teaching fellows interest group. His pedagogical research centres around writing development, student learning and experiences, and pedagogies for impact and change. He is co-founder and editor of the *Journal for Impact Cultures*, which foregrounds student partnerships and co-creations.

Ashley B. Akenson
met her co-authors at the annual ISSoTL conference in October 2016. Her research interests include mindfulness, program planning and evaluation, influence of perceptions and unexamined bias, marginalized and underserved populations, transformative learning, learning transfer, collaboration, and quantitative and qualitative research methods. Ashley earned her Ph.D. in Exceptional Learning with a concentration in Program Planning and Evaluation in 2018.

Joyce Armstrong
is the Assistant Director for The Center for Faculty Development at Old Dominion University where she is designing and delivering professional development activities and consulting services related to teaching and learning improvement and providing teaching and learning consultation related to effective teaching practices. She is a reviewer for the *Journal of Excellence in Teaching* and four Higher Education Conferences. She has received the Certification of Appreciation by the Naval Science Department and the Massachusetts Horace Mann Teaching Award.

Cecile Badenhorst
(Ph.D., Queen's) is an Associate Professor in the Adult Education/Post-Secondary Program Education at Memorial University, Newfoundland, Canada. As a researcher, her interests are doctoral education, doctoral writing, graduate writing, thesis/publication writing pedagogies, academic literacies and faculty writing. She engages in qualitative, arts-based and post-structural research methodologies. She has written three books in the area of graduate student

NOTES ON CONTRIBUTORS

writing: *Research Writing* (2007), *Dissertation Writing* (2008) and *Productive Writing* (2010). She is a co-editor of *Inspiration and Innovation in Teaching and Teacher Education* (Lexington Books, 2013) and *Research Literacies and Writing Pedagogies for Masters and Doctoral Writers* (Brill, 2016).

Carol Berenson

(Ph.D.) holds a faculty position in educational development in the University of Calgary's Taylor Institute for Teaching and Learning. Experience teaching in sociology and women's studies informs her approach to collaboration, consultation, research, and program development in teaching and learning. Her educational development interests and activities include graduate student teaching development, Instructional Skills and Facilitator Development Workshop programming, research on the flipped classroom, peer observation of teaching programs, teaching controversial issues, and diversity and inclusion in teaching and learning.

Jacqueline L. Beres

is a doctoral candidate in the Faculty of Education at Brock University. Her interests include diversity, student success and wellness, socialization, research methodology, and the Scholarship of Teaching and Learning. She has taught both domestic and international students across numerous post-secondary levels and has previously worked in Student Affairs within post-secondary education.

Remica Bingham-Risher

is the Director of Quality Enhancement Plan (QEP) Initiatives at Old Dominion University (ODU) where she works with faculty to improve student learning through writing by means of faculty workshops. In addition, she teaches in ODU's creative writing program. Her first book, *Conversion* (Lotus, 2006), won the Naomi Long Madgett Poetry Award, her second book, *What We Ask of Flesh* (Etrucan, 2013) was shortlisted for the Hurston/Wright Prize and her third book, *Starlight & Error* (Diode, 2017) won the Diode Editions Book Award.

Erik Blair

is a senior lecturer in the School of Higher Education Research and Development at the University of West London, UK. His research embraces the Scholarship of Teaching and Learning and focuses on the contextualised development of teaching and learning. He has a particular interest in assessment, curriculum development, professional development and interaction within the teaching and learning environment.

Georgette Briggs

is a lecturer in the Faculty of Science and Technology at The University of the West Indies, St Augustine, Trinidad and Tobago. Her main area of research is in developmental plant biology, where she focuses on crops of high regional agronomic importance (cocoa, pigeon pea, sugarcane, cassava) in the context of food security. Georgette also has a keen interest in Biological Education; her educational research focuses on curriculum development, technology usage in the classroom and academic role identity.

M. Soledad Caballero

is professor of English at Allegheny College. Her work in British Romanticism focuses on travel writing, empire, and gender studies; she is also a poet. Together with Aimee Knupsky, she explores interdisciplinary connections among emotion, affect, and literature through research, teaching, and scholarship. Their first article, "Sharing Contagion: Sympathetic Curiosity and Social Emotion Regulation in Joanna Baillie's DeMonfort" was published in *Romantic Circles*. They were awarded a National Endowment for the Humanities Connections planning grant focused on the application of ethical interdisciplinarity to bolster the humanities in interdisciplinary programs and student experiences at Allegheny College.

James Cronin

is a College Lecturer in Teaching and Learning Enhancement in CIRTL UCC. James coordinates the postgraduate modules in Teaching & Learning and co-teaches the accredited programmes in continuing professional development for university staff and the international visiting scholars programme. Since 2007, James has been researching the Scholarship of Teaching and Learning (SoTL). He has published on integrative learning and applications of constructivist learning theory for the study of Information and Media Literacy. His current SoTL research focuses on integrative learning, formation of disciplinary identities, and fostering student resilience through the arts and humanities.

Jessica Deshler

is an Associate Professor in the West Virginia University (WVU)Department of Mathematics where she is also the Graduate Teaching Assistant Coordinator and a Faculty Associate for both the WVU Center for Women's & Gender Studies and the WVU Teaching and Learning Commons. She spent the 2016–2017 year as a Provost's Fellow in the WVU Office of Graduate Education and the 2015–2016 year as a US Fulbright Scholar at Central European University in Budapest, Hungary. Her research is in undergraduate mathematics education,

NOTES ON CONTRIBUTORS

specifically focusing the professional development of graduate students and the intersection of gender & mathematics.

Lisa Dickson

is an Associate Professor in the Department of English at the University of Northern British Columbia. As a 3M National Teaching Fellow (NTF), she occupies mentoring roles at UNCB, and, nationally, is the current project leader for the 3M NTF Mentoring Network. She is engaged in several collaborative teaching and scholarly projects, including an article on compassionate pedagogy co-authored with Tracy Summerville (UNCB), forthcoming in the *Journal of Perspectives in Applied Academic Practice* and a book on teaching Shakespeare and critical hope, co-authored with Shannon Murray (UPEI) and Jessica Riddell (Bishop's University), forthcoming from U of T Press.

Aysha Divan

is an Associate Professor and Director of Student Education at the Faculty of Biological Sciences, University of Leeds, UK. She teaches undergraduate and Masters students and oversees student education initiatives within the Faculty including academic innovation. Pedagogical interests include curriculum development, internationalization, and professional development.

Roswita Dressler

is an Assistant Professor, Werklund School of Education, University of Calgary. She also holds an academic appointment as Director – Teaching Across Borders. Her research is in the area of second language teaching and learning in a variety of contexts include K-12, post-secondary, and informal learning. Her interests in writing include understanding reflective writing for second language study abroad sojourners, examining instructor and peer feedback in research writing courses, and improving her own academic writing through writing group participation, co-writing, reading, and, of course, practice.

Patti Dyjur

has a Ph.D. in Educational Technology. She is currently an educational development consultant with the Taylor Institute for Teaching and Learning, University of Calgary. She works with faculties and departments as they map, review, and assess their programs to identify strengths and areas for improvement, which she finds to be interesting and challenging work. Currently, she supports more than two dozen groups that are undergoing review. Her research interests include the process and impact of curriculum review and the effectiveness of a micro-credentialing program for faculty and graduate students involved in professional learning opportunities.

Michelle J. Eady

(Ph.D.) is a senior lecturer in Professional Studies in the School of Education at the University of Wollongong, Australia. She is a HERDSA fellow, a senior fellow of the HEA and holds a national teaching citation for her work in quality teacher preparation. Her research interests include SoTL, Distance Learning/Synchronous Technology, Aboriginal Studies and other current issues in Education. Dr. Eady has had the pleasure of speaking at conferences worldwide and looks forward to collaborations with colleagues who have a passion for teaching and learning.

Sarah Elaine Eaton

is a faculty member at the Werklund School of Education at the University of Calgary. Her area of specialization is educational leadership, policy and governance. Her particular research interests focus on academic integrity and ethics. She also engages in research in the Scholarship of Teaching and Learning (SoTL), working to situate academic integrity research within SoTL.

Tia Frahm

(Ph.D.) began her teaching career as an instructional coach and elementary and middle school teacher for eight years, focusing on the connection between reading and writing with students and teachers. During her Ph.D. program she was able to research this connection further through her work with the National Writing Project and her dissertation titled, "Teachers as Writers: Tracing Writing Identity Development of Teachers in a Summer Professional Development Program." Dr. Frahm continues her research in the area of professional learning in writing instruction and coaching contexts as an assistant professor at Northern Arizona University.

Mandy Frake-Mistak

is an educational developer at the Teaching Commons at York University. There she facilitates a number of courses and workshops including the Instructional Skills Workshop, the Education, Curriculum, and Teaching Excellence course (EduCATE), as well as assisting with the graduate student program. Having a research background in critical policy studies in higher education, her role includes leading courses, teaching and contributing to the Scholarship of Teaching and Learning (SoTL). She is also an Instructional Skills Workshop Trainer.

Kimberley A. Grant

has a Ph.D. in Curriculum and Learning and holds a faculty position in educational development at the University of Calgary's Taylor Institute for

NOTES ON CONTRIBUTORS

Teaching and Learning. In this role, Kim collaborates with colleagues as they review and develop curriculum and also leads the Graduate Student Certificate in University Teaching and Learning.

Corinne Green

is a Ph.D. Student at the University of Wollongong, Australia, as well as a Lecturer and Tutor in teacher education. She is currently researching school-university partnerships in initial teacher education programs.

John Hoben

is an Assistant Professor in Memorial University's Faculty of Education. A former practicing lawyer, in 2007 he was awarded a Canada Graduate Scholarship (Doctoral) from the Social Sciences and Humanities Council of Canada to conduct a study of teacher censorship. He is also an award-winning poet (i.e., provincial & university-level) who researches how poetry and narrative can be used to provide insights about culture and identity. John has authored publications on a wide range of topics including: critical research and literacies, education and the imagination, the law, cultural memory and loss, free speech, and democratic education.

Cheryl Jeffs

holds an Ed.D. in Educational Leadership and is an educational development consultant and faculty member at the University of Calgary's Taylor Institute for Teaching and Learning, and the editor of *Papers on Postsecondary Learning and Teaching*. Cheryl is committed to excellence in teaching and learning through a range of research-informed educational programs and initiatives, workshops, consultations, and collaborative projects. With a diverse background in professional and educational development, Cheryl's research interests include formative feedback for teaching development and graduate student teaching development.

Karen Julien

is working on her Ph.D. in Education at Brock University. Prior to her return to higher education, Karen enjoyed a career as a classroom teacher and as an educational researcher. Her current research centres on the intersecting roles of metacognition, self-regulation, and social support in academic writing.

Frances Kalu

holds a Ph.D. in Curriculum and Learning from the Werklund School of Education, University of Calgary. A faculty member and Educational

Development Consultant at the Taylor Institute for Teaching and Learning, University of Calgary she provides consultative leadership to faculties working on curriculum development and review projects. She also works with faculty and graduate students on projects to enhance teaching and learning in the classroom. Her diverse research interests include identity formation in the academia, the experiential learning continuum, and the scholarship of curriculum practice.

Natasha Kenny

holds a Ph.D. in Land Resource Science and is the Senior Director of the Taylor Institute for Teaching and Learning at the University of Calgary. In her role, Natasha collaborates with faculty, staff, and colleagues across the university to plan programs and initiatives that build teaching and learning capacity. Her research interests include graduate student teaching development, educational leadership, the scholarship and practice of educational development, and the scholarship of teaching and learning.

Barbara Kensington-Miller

is a senior lecturer and academic developer at the Centre for Learning and Research in Higher Education, University of Auckland, New Zealand, with a background in Mathematics and Biochemistry. She is Vice-President for Higher Education Research and Development Society of Australasia (HERDSA) and Chair for the New Zealand branch. Her research focuses on early-career academics, peer mentoring, identity, communities of practice and SoTL. Her co-authored article with Sue Morón-García and Joanna Renc-Roe, 'The chameleon on a tartan rug: adaptations of three academic developers' professional identities' was 2016 article of the year in the *International Journal for Academic Development*.

Yvonne Kjorlien

is an anthropologist by training and Research Facilitator at the Werklund School of Education by day. She is immensely grateful to the academic Writing Group at Werklund for inviting her to collaborate on this chapter, and for treating her as a colleague.

Aimee Knupsky

is associate professor of Psychology at Allegheny College. Her work in cognitive psychology focuses on how we learn and communicate in academic settings. Together with M. Soledad Caballero, she explores interdisciplinary connections among emotion, affect, and literature through research, teaching, and scholarship. Their first article, "Sharing Contagion: Sympathetic Curiosity

NOTES ON CONTRIBUTORS

and Social Emotion Regulation in Joanna Baillie's DeMonfort" was published in *Romantic Circles*. They were awarded a National Endowment for the Humanities Connections planning grant focused on the application of ethical interdisciplinarity to bolster the humanities in interdisciplinary programs and student experiences at Allegheny College.

Jennifer Lock

is a Professor and the Associate Dean of Teaching and Learning in the Werklund School of Education at the University of Calgary. Her area of specialization is in online learning, ICT integration, change and innovation, and educational development in higher education. She has expanded her work to studying experiential learning through making and makerspaces.

Valerie Lopes

is a Professor in the School of Arts and Sciences at Seneca College, an Assistant Professor in the Department of Leadership, Higher and Adult Education at OISE / University of Toronto, and a research consultant with eCampusOntario. Her research focuses on the exploration of emerging technologies and pedagogical practices for effective online and technology-enabled teaching and learning, the use of open education resources, and outcomes-based curriculum and programme design. She teaches courses that explore the social, technological, and epistemological consequences of the explosion of access to information and rapidly changing norms and practices in our digitally mediated society.

Lynn O. Ludwig

teaches professional writing, in the Department of English, at the University of Wisconsin-Stevens Point, Wisconsin, USA. Her approach to teaching business and technical writing is informed by over a decade of experience managing and writing in corporate and government settings. Her teaching interests focus on student acquisition of professional communication and problem-solving skills, workplace conflict resolution strategies, and successful team interactions. She mentors students in experiential learning opportunities within the local community. She also enjoys serving on various department, university-wide, and community advisory boards and committees.

Elizabeth Lynch

(Ph.D.) is an anthropological archaeologist interested in how landscapes become socialized through human interaction, thus anchoring social reproduction processes within an intelligible context. Her research combines oral tradition, with morphometric analysis and 3D modeling to better understand social experience at intensive food processing localities called bedrock ground stone features. Her project area is in the Chacuaco Plateau of southeastern Colorado, USA, although she has worked with photogrammetry and 3D modeling on osteological projects, and at Hell Gap. Elizabeth's teaching philosophy combines student-centered learning approaches with active learning activities to engage students in anthropological practice across disciplines.

Geneviève Maheux-Pelletier

(Ph.D.) has played multiple roles within academia in the last 15 years, with extensive teaching experience at universities in Canada, the United States, and France. An educational developer at heart, Geneviève now serves as the interim director of York University's Teaching Commons. Her work and research focus on experiential education, the scholarship of teaching and learning, and evidenced-based practices in educational development. She also serves on the editorial board for the *Canadian Journal for the Scholarship of Teaching and Learning*.

Karen Manarin

is a Professor of English at Mount Royal University. She teaches both writing and literature courses. In her research, she examines how students read, undergraduate research and academic identity. She served as Vice President (Canada) for the International Society for the Scholarship of Teaching & Learning from 2014–2017. Lead author of *Critical Reading in Higher Education: Academic Goals and Social Engagement*, she has also published in a variety of teaching and learning journals, including *Higher Education Research and Development, Teaching and Learning Inquiry, The International Journal for the Scholarship of Teaching and Learning*, and *Pedagogy*.

Heidi Marsh

is the Director of Scholarship of Teaching and Learning at Humber College's Centre for Teaching and Learning where she is responsible for building and fostering a culture of scholarly inquiry across the institution. In this role, Heidi helps to empower faculty to conduct SoTL research in their classrooms and disseminate their findings. With a background in cognitive and developmental psychology, Heidi's research interests include metacognition, educational development, and learning environments. Currently, Heidi also serves as the Editor-in-Chief for the *Journal of Innovation in Polytechnic Education*.

Dragana Martinovic

is a Professor of Mathematics Education and a Fields Institute Fellow. As a Research Leadership Chair at the University of Windsor (2011–2015), she facilitated her colleagues' participation at writing retreats. For Dragana, academic writing retreats present opportunity to engage with scholars from different disciplines, and to extend and enrich one's writing forms and practices. In her research, Dragana explores ways in which technology can improve teaching and learning of mathematics, and the digital literacy skills needed for a successful learner and worker in the 21st century.

Elizabeth Marquis

is an Assistant Professor in the Arts & Science Program at McMaster University and Associate Director (Research) of the university's Teaching and Learning Institute. She is past Co-President of the International Society for the Scholarship of Teaching & Learning, Senior Editor of the *Canadian Journal for the Scholarship of Teaching and Learning*, and an inaugural co-editor of the *International Journal for Students as Partners*. Beth's SoTL research focuses on the intersections between teaching and learning and questions of equity and justice, student-faculty partnership, and media texts as public pedagogy. She co-developed and currently oversees McMaster's Student Partners Program.

Kelly E. Matthews

is an Associate Professor (Higher Education) at University of Queensland, Australia. Her research explores students' experiences of learning and engaging students as partners in learning and teaching. She co-develops, and teaches into, teaching preparation programs for new tutors and academics, and teaches undergraduate subjects in education. Kelly has collaborated on 24 funded projects worth $2.5 million and publishes extensively. In 2015, she was awarded an Australian Learning and Teaching Fellowship. She is a Vice-President for the International Society for the Scholarship of Teaching and Learning and a co-editor for the *International Journal for Students as Partners*.

Marian McCarthy

(Ph.D.) is the director of the Centre for the Integration of Research, Teaching and Learning (CIRTL) at UCC. She is a senior lecturer in Education, seconded long term to the Teaching and Learning Centre, now CIRTL. Her primary research areas are in the Scholarship of Teaching and Learning (SoTL), Multiple Intelligences (MI) theory and Teaching for Understanding (TFU). She fuses these to provide a disciplinary research and pedagogical framework for staff that teach in university and third level settings. Her primary responsibility is for the Accredited Programme in Teaching and Learning in Higher Education.

Michelle K. McGinn

is Interim Associate Vice-President, Research and Professor of Education at Brock University in St. Catharines, Canada, and a member of the Board of

Directors of the Canadian Society for the Study of Higher Education. Her major scholarly emphases include researcher development, collaboration, writerly identities, and ethics in academic practice for (post)graduate students and established scholars. Her collaboration "Academic Researchers in Challenging Times" explores scholars' careers, practices, and identities in the current research climate. She teaches research methodology, higher education, and writing for publication, and facilitates residential academic writing retreats and scholarly writing workshops. Connect via Twitter @dr_mkmcginn

Jacinta McKeon

(Ph.D.) has worked as a programme designer and a teacher trainer for the Department of Education and Science in relation to the introduction of the common syllabus for modern languages for senior cycle. Her work in the School of Education involves teaching modules on the initial teacher education programme and M.Ed. programme on second language education, second language teaching and learning, theories of learning and developing reflective practice among student teachers. She contributes to the teaching in The Teaching and Learning Centre, UCC and in particular on modules for post-graduate students to support their teaching within the university.

Ruth McQuirter Scott

is a Professor in the Faculty of Education at Brock University where she teaches Junior/Intermediate Language Arts in the Teacher Education program. Ruth's research interests are in the effective infusion of technology in education. She also enjoys writing creative non-fiction, and regularly attends creative writing retreats.

Kiara Mikita

(Ph.D.) is an Educational Development Consultant with the Taylor Institute for Teaching and Learning. This work allows her to combine her social justice-related work with her interest in advancing teaching and learning research in these areas. Kiara's disciplinary training is in criminology and sociology where she specializes in analysis of talk about sexual assault. She is interested in teaching and learning about sensitive or controversial issues, ethics in teaching and learning research, and promoting cross-disciplinary conversation, collaboration, and creativity in teaching and learning practices and research.

Sue Morón-García

is the founding Director of the Centre for Excellence in Learning and Teaching at the University of Central Lancashire in Preston, UK. Sue has over thirty years' experience working in higher, adult, and secondary education, is a teacher at heart and an educational developer by vocation. She has led courses and departments, designed, taught, and examined postgraduate certificates and professional recognition pathways at both research-intensive and newer universities. She has an interest in collaborative writing, the benefits of networks and networking, supporting and mentoring less experienced colleagues, and the use of digital technology in education.

Phillip Motley

is an Associate Professor of Communications at Elon University, North Carolina, USA. He teaches courses in visual communication and interactive media to undergraduate and graduate students. His research interests include pedagogies of design and studio-based learning, and experiential learning, especially service-learning and social innovation. He was just selected as the 2019–2021 Center for Engaged Learning Scholar at Elon University where he will focus on the potential that immersive learning holds for liberal arts education.

Robin Mueller

holds a Ph.D. in educational leadership and is an Educational Development Consultant at the University of Calgary's Taylor Institute for Teaching and Learning. She supports engagement in SoTL, consults with campus partners to help strengthen teaching and learning initiatives, and supports the teaching development of individual instructors. Robin also maintains an active research agenda in three key areas: inquiry-based learning in higher education, SoTL research methodology, and the evolving field of educational development.

Shannon Murray

is a professor of Early Modern English literature and a 3M National Teaching Fellow (2001). She is currently the coordinator of the 3M National Teaching Fellows' program. She has facilitated UPEI's Faculty Development Summer Institute on Active Learning since 2002 and gives workshops and talks on threshold concepts, active learning, capstone experiences, and portfolios. Her publications include work on leadership in higher education, on John Bunyan, and on early children's literature. She is co-writing a book on teaching Shakespeare with Lisa Dickson and Jessica Riddell.

Lorelli Nowell

(R.N., Ph.D.) is an Eyes High Postdoctoral Scholar and Educational Development Consultant at the University of Calgary's Taylor Institute for Teaching and Learning. In her role, Lorelli supports and evaluates the professional learning and development of postdoctoral scholars. Her research interests include mentorship, educational development, mixed methods research, evidence synthesis, knowledge translation, and the Scholarship of Teaching and Learning.

Carolyn Oliver

is a community-based researcher from England who lives on the unceded territories of the Musqueam, Squamish and Tsleil-Waututh Nations in Vancouver, Canada. She is author of the book *Strengths-Based Child Protection: Firm, Fair and Friendly*, University of Toronto Press (2018) and numerous publications related to strengths-based practice, professional identity and SoTL Twenty years as a social worker include teaching for the University of British Columbia and Justice Institute of British Columbia. Carolyn's current work with one of Canada's largest urban indigenous child welfare agencies focusses on restorative approaches to indigenous child welfare and explores ways of intercultural, interdisciplinary and experiential learning.

Sarah Pickett

is an Assistant Professor in the Faculty of Education, Memorial University Newfoundland, a Registered Psychologist and the faculty founder/advisor to the Gender and Sexuality Alliance (GSA) in Education at Memorial. Her research has focused on affirmative sexuality and gender practice and pedagogy in education and healthcare. Dr. Pickett is interested in narrative and autoethnographic methodologies; how researchers may use these methods to engage in evocative conversations about in educational contexts and actively publishes in this area from the position of parent, lesbian/queer, psychologist, educator of educators, counsellor educator and academic.

Snežana Ratković

is Research Officer and Instructor in the Faculty of Education at Brock University, Ontario, Canada. She is a published poet from the former Yugoslavia and an award-winning scholar. Snežana has facilitated academic writing workshops and retreats for faculty members and graduate students since 2005. She is a co-investigator on the research projects "Writing about Writing" and "Exploring Perceptions of Well-Being and Mentorship within Canadian and Croatian Faculties of Education." Her research interests include migration, indigeneity, and reconciliation; transnational and transdisciplinary teacher education; social justice leadership; research education; decolonizing and arts-based methodologies; academic writing and publishing; and knowledge mobilization.

NOTES ON CONTRIBUTORS

Jessica Riddell
is an Associate Professor of Early Modern Drama in the English Department at Bishop's University and the Stephen A. Jarislowsky Chair of Undergraduate Teaching Excellence at Bishop's University. Dr. Riddell is the Executive Director of the Maple League of Universities, the VP Canada on the Board of the International Society for the Scholarship of Teaching and Learning (ISSoTL), and a Board member for the 3M National Fellows Executive Council.

Mary Gene Saudelli
is the Associate Dean of Professional Studies, University of the Fraser Valley, British Columbia, Canada. Mary has specialized in learning and teaching in higher education and international education. Most of her research is in the Scholarship of Teaching and Learning. She has taught in Canada, Qatar, Dubai, Abu Dhabi, Afghanistan, Hong Kong China, and Turkey. She has been awarded numerous scholarly grants and has many peer-reviewed journal publications. Education in the 21st Century' and in February 2019 her new edited book *From Divergent to Convergent: Voices from Far Away Lands* was published with Cambridge Scholars. She is passionate about global civicmindedness, community engagement, integrity and leadership, and engaged learning.

Janel Seeley
received her Ph.D. in Educational Psychology and Research from the University of Tennessee. She is currently the director of the Ellbogen Center for Teaching and Learning at the University of Wyoming and is an associate lecturer in Education, Honors and Social Work. Her primary research interests are the Scholarship of Teaching and Learning (SoTL) and Collaborative Communication. She is on the executive committee of the Action Research network of the America's and is the incoming chair of the POD SoTL SIG.

Nicola Simmons
(Ph.D.) teaches and researches Scholarship of Teaching and Learning, higher education, participatory pedagogy, and adult lifelong learning and identity in Educational Studies at Brock University. She has run several writing retreats and has writing partners around the globe. Nicola is a co-editor of the Brill Sense Critical Issues in the Future of Learning and Teaching series, a Canadian 3M National Teaching Fellow, and holds a Brock Chancellor's Chair for Teaching Excellence. Past roles include VP (Canada) of ISSoTL, VP (SoTL) of STLHE, Founding Chair of SoTL Canada and SoTL Ontario, and Chair of the Educational Developers Caucus.

Ann Singh

(M.Ed., Brock University) is a Project Management Professional (PMP) who is interested in adult education, lifelong learning, and mentorship. Ann teaches courses on project development and management and believes in extending learning beyond the classroom.

Erin Spring

is an Assistant Professor in the Werklund School of Education at the University of Calgary. She received her Ph.D. in Education from the University of Cambridge in 2014. Broadly speaking, her research focuses on young people's texts and cultures. She teaches in the areas of literacy, Indigenous Education, and interdisciplinary learning.

Dannelle D. Stevens

is a professor emerita, faculty in residence for academic writing and facilitates the Jumpstart Academic Writing Program at Portland State University Portland, Oregon. Her degree is in educational psychology from Michigan State. Through working with national and international faculty on the complex tasks associated with balancing teaching, writing, publishing, she developed the key ideas in her fifth book, published this year, *Write More, Publish More, Stress Less! Five Key Principles for a Creative and Sustainable Scholarly Practice*. She conducts workshops and coaches faculty on writing and career-related choices that lead to a successful career in academe.

Briony Supple

(Ph.D.) is a Lecturer in Learning and Teaching Enhancement at the Centre for the Integration of Research, Teaching and Learning (CIRTL). Briony has a wealth of teaching experience which spans over 15 years and includes a variety of countries and contexts. Originally trained in Teaching English as a Second or Other Language (TESOL) she has taught in Japan, China, Vietnam, Ireland, the UK, Chile and Australia. She has extensive experience in the use of learner-centred pedagogical approaches to curriculum and assessment, developing innovative resources for face-to-face and blended delivery modes, and in delivering professional development in higher education.

Ana M. Tomljenovic-Berube

is a part-time Lecturer and Laboratory Instructor for the Bachelor of Technology Program in the W. Booth School of Engineering Practice and Technology at McMaster University in Hamilton, Ontario, Canada. She teaches various courses in their Biotechnology stream, including Biotechnology Regulations and Microbiology. Her research interests pertain to how technology, experiential

NOTES ON CONTRIBUTORS

learning, and other interactive learning strategies can be used to engage STEM students to achieve deep learning and improve learning outcomes.

M. Gregory Tweedie
is Associate Professor at the Werklund School of Education in the area of Language and Literacy. His teaching and research draw heavily upon his experiences as a language teacher and language teacher trainer in East, Southeast and Central Asia, the Middle East, Canada, and his native Australia. Gregory's research interests, in the field of applied linguistics, focuses on the phenomena of the English language as communicative vehicle in international professional contexts, for people from differing first language backgrounds.

Janelle Voegele
has a doctorate in Educational Leadership with a focus on Postsecondary, Adult, and Continuing Education. At Portland State University, she is the Director of Teaching, Learning and Assessment in the Office of Academic Innovation with over 20 years of experience working in higher education educational development. She is pleased to support the growth of the Jumpstart faculty academic writing program as part of that work. Her research focuses on pedagogical assumptions and student learning in partially online courses, the role of academic portfolios in faculty scholarship and professional development, and perceptions of scholarship in the institutional change context.

Natasha Wiebe
has helped to coordinate over 25 writing retreats for faculty and academic support staff since 2012 as Research Coordinator in the Office of Research and Innovation Services at the University of Windsor. Natasha is also Adjunct Professor in the Faculty of Education. For over a decade, she has pursued a research interest in cultural narratives, asking how the stories available to us from our culture can inform our thinking and behaviour. Recent work has explored the popular fictional story of the zombie apocalypse, as well as stories that are prominent within some Canadian Mennonite and Pentecostal communities.

Kari-Lynn Winters
is an Associate Professor at Brock University, where she teaches drama-in-education and language arts to teacher candidates. She holds a Ph.D. from ubc in literacy education and the arts, a teaching degree from University of Toronto, and a B.A. and a certificate in drama/theater from Brock University and the National Theatre School of Canada. Her research interests include: body image, embodied pedagogies, children's literature, drama, and multimodal literacies. Kari-Lynn is also an award-winning children's author, scholar, playwright, and performer.

Introduction

Nicola Simmons

Writing comprises a significant proportion of academic staff members' roles. We write comments on student work, reference letters, emails to colleagues, committee reports – and of course, academic papers. While academics have been acculturated to the notion of 'publish or perish,' there is often a struggle to find the time to accomplish writing papers (Boice, 1990). The result can be a sense of significant stress around the writing process (Seldin, 1987).

Those who participate in writing partnerships extol their benefits, noting how helpful it is to have a critical friend (Carr & Kemmis, 1986) with whom they can discuss work in progress. Others find the notion that someone else is writing addresses their sense of isolation in the writing process. Some point to the support of having a writing group facilitator to keep them on track. In each instance, writers find the partnership provides something that helps them stick with their writing projects to completion (for example, Strange & Merdinger, 2015). Lee and Boud (2003) recommend the use of writing groups as a form of academic development and McGrail, Rickard, and Jones (2006) show writing groups to be a strong support for increasing publications per year for participants.

Background to the Book

Writing partnerships take many forms, from meeting with a trusted colleague on a regular basis to electronically-mediated meetings over significant distances. Partnerships may also comprise larger groups. Writing retreats are typically stand-alone opportunities for people to come together to write even though they may have no ongoing partnership. Retreat refers simply to the notion of getting away from day to day tasks and responsibilities, so sometimes they are on campus in a designated space and sometimes they are offsite. As Stanley, Home, Chu, and Joiner (2017) describe,

> Writing retreat is defined as a prescribed period of time during which one geographically separates oneself from a typical or routine work environment for the distinct purpose of writing (as opposed to work-related activities more broadly) with other like-minded individuals with the same purpose. (p. 250)

INTRODUCTION   XXIX

I have been part of many academic writing partnerships and retreats over my career: While I was doing my Ph.D. I created a writing community "Critical Friends" to provide peer feedback for work in final pre-publication stages. I have co-authored several pieces, including a book. I now write weekly for 3-hour blocks with a writing partner in a local café, I share writing online with another colleague, and I frequently invite critical friends to read early and final drafts of work. I have participated in and led various retreats from a full day to multiple days to bring colleagues together (including offsite retreats at my house and a local spa). I have been involved in leading a national collaborative writing group and as a group facilitator in an international one. What I have learned through each of these is that I am more likely to 'get stuff done' when I work with someone else. It is not always straightforward nor painless, but in most cases, work written in this way seems to proceed more quickly to publication.

These are but a few of the diverse examples of academic writing partnerships and groups. Some scholars, like me, have a single partner with whom they meet regularly, either in person or online to write in real time. Others may choose a less formal structure, designating a person to be their writing mentor for peer coaching on asynchronous writing. More formally, there are various forms of writing groups: some meet for a single day, some have weekly writing meetings, some schedule a retreat over several days. Some join in writing communities, ranging from onsite intra and interdepartmental groups to national boundary spanning collaborative writing groups.

Each of these approaches brings mutual support for its members; each is not without its respective challenges. As authors in *Collaboration Uncovered* (Richards, Elliott, Woloshyn, & Mitchell, 2001) noted, not all collaborations are free from tensions. The purpose of this book is to outline some workable approaches, but to not shy away from issues that may arise. Within these chapters you will find approaches to writing partnerships and groups that interrogate their strengths and limitations as well as propose recommendations for others hoping to the implement the practice.

Themes of the Book

The book is organised into four sections: *Writing Partnerships, Onsite Writing Retreats, Offsite Writing Retreats, and Collaborative Writing Groups.* In each section, authors explore and interrogate how they have negotiated writing with others, what they have learned through the process, and what they recommend for others considering these approaches to scholarly writing.

Part 1, *Writing Partnerships*, focuses on writing pairs. Julien and Beres present an adapted typology of how writing groups vary, against which they frame their own learning through writing in partnership. Caballero and Knupsky write as "women faculty of difference" about how their partnership helped them overcome academic isolation to work together on a project. Blair and Briggs describe how their history, trust, communication, and socialisation have helped negotiate the challenges of engaging in a writing partnership across time zones. Seeley, Frahm, and Lynch outline a three-way partnership that grew from a single writing retreat and how it has affected them as writers.

Part 2, *Onsite Writing Retreats*, explores larger groups that meet onsite at regular intervals. Lock, Kjorlien, Tweedie, Dressler, Eaton, and Spring discuss their intra-department weekly writing group and the reflective practice that impacts their growth as academics. Bingham-Risher and Armstrong explore the importance of having a dedicated place for onsite writing retreats in the form of a faculty writing studio. Stevens and Voegele describe a five-day writing retreat held after the term finishes that flourishes with the support of a university administration: teaching and learning centre partnership. Maheux-Pelletier, Marsh, and Frake-Mistak offer their perspectives analyzing the distinctions between their two institutional approaches to creating writing groups, and the relative success of the one that grew from an off-campus retreat.

Part 3, *Offsite Writing Retreats* focuses on various such formats. Dickson, Murray, and Riddell explore what it means for three humanities scholars to retreat offsite to work collaboratively and how the process has made them more courageous writers. Badenhorst, Pickett, and Hoben describe how they developed author "shame-resilience" through their group and how writing in a chosen 'wild' place off campus matters to their work. McGinn, Ratković, Martinovic, and McQuirter Scott outline a multi-institutional annual writing retreat that seeks to support an ongoing community of writers. Winters, Wiebe, and Saudelli provide a meta-reflection on the writing retreat format outlined in the preceding chapter, using photographic analysis to reflect on the retreat process.

Part 4, *Collaborative Writing Groups*, describes groups that come together over time to work on collaborative projects as a whole or in smaller groups. Jeffs, Berenson, Dyjur, Grant, Kalu, Kenny, Mikita, Mueller, and Nowell write as Educational Developers from diverse disciplines who have created an ongoing writing *microsystem* to support both individual and collaborative projects. Eady, Green, Akenson, Supple, McCarthy, Cronin, and Mckeon also write about creating a "small significant network" – in their case, across multiple continents that has supported their various collaborations. Marquis and Simmons outline the organization of a national evidence-based Collaborative Writing Group (CWG) framework, identifying key timelines and discussing the importance of leadership. Motley, Divan, Lopes, Ludwig, Matthews, and Tomljenovic-Berube write about their International Collaborative Writing Group (ICWG) that began in 2012 at the International Society for the Scholarship of Teaching and Learning (ISSoTL) and is still going strong six years later and the impact this has had on their scholarly identity. Kensington-Miller, Oliver, Morón-García, Manarin, Abrahamson, Simmons, and Deshler, also an ICWG from 2012, explore how their ICWG developed "the coherence and confidence" needed for successful collaboration and note parallels of the group's path to Kelly's (1955) personal construct theory (PCT).

In a synthesis chapter Simmons identifies thematic threads running through the book and takes a lens-within-a-lens view of the collaborative writing process that led to this book.

We offer this volume as a starting point for your own creative collaborations and hope you will benefit from the examples, perhaps creating your own versions. Ultimately, our hope is that you will find the authors' recommendations help you find a way to be less isolated and more creative and productive in your writing efforts.

References

Boice, R. (1990). *Professors as writers: A self-help guide to productive writing.* Stillwater, OK: New Forums Press.

Kelly, G. A. (1955). *The psychology of personal constructs. Volume 1: A theory of personality.* New York, NY: WW Norton and Company.

Lee, A., & Boud, D. (2003). Writing groups, change and academic identity: Research development as local practice. *Studies in Higher Education, 28*(2), 187–200.

McGrail, M. R., Rickard, C. M., & Jones, R. (2006). Publish or perish: A systematic review of interventions to increase academic publication rates. *Higher Education Research & Development, 25*(1), 19–35.

Richards, M., Elliott, E., Woloshyn, V., & Mitchell, C. (2001). *Collaboration uncovered: The forgotten, the assumed, and the unexamined in collaborative education.* Westport, CT: Bergin & Garvey.

Seldin, P. (Ed.). (1987). *Coping with faculty stress.* San Francisco, CA: Jossey-Bass.

Strage, A., & Merdinger, J. (2015). Professional growth and renewal for mid-career faculty. *The Journal of Faculty Development, 29*(1), 41–50.

PART 1

Writing Partnerships

CHAPTER 1

Cheaper Than Therapy: The Unexpected Benefits and Challenges of an Academic Writing Partnership

Karen Julien and Jacqueline L. Beres

Abstract

Academic writing can be a daunting, lonely process. To alleviate what we perceived as the unpleasant aspects of writing and to meet our writing goals, we formed a two-person writing group. Using a self-study action research approach, we reflect on our experiences within our writing partnership according to Haas' (2014) Pick-n-Mix typology of writing group dimensions. While our initial goals for increased productivity were not met, we benefitted from our partnership in unanticipated ways. Our results point to the importance of social support and goal alignment for writing group success. This chapter contributes to the body of knowledge documenting the importance of social support in overcoming the challenges of academic writing. We also offer suggestions for academics wishing to develop their own social support systems for academic writing.

Keywords

writing partnership – writing group – academic writing – higher education – social support – action research – self-study

Productive writing has been described as "painless, efficient, and successful" (Boice, 1990, p. 3). Unfortunately, this sentence is hardly reflective of our own writing experiences, and our frustrations are likely to be shared by others. Consistent with literature (e.g., Sword, 2017), we have heard many academics describe their writing experiences as stressful, frantic, lonely, or worse yet, non-existent (Grant, 2006). To alleviate what we perceived as the unpleasant aspects of writing, and to meet our writing goals, we (Karen and Jacqueline) created a two-person writing group over the course of an academic year. This chapter is the result of our experiences with our writing group, hereafter called a writing

© KONINKLIJKE BRILL NV, LEIDEN, 2019 | DOI:10.1163/9789004410985_001

partnership (Stivers & Cramer, 2013). Drawing upon Haas' (2014) Pick-n-Mix typology describing dimensions along which writing groups vary, we analyze our writing partnership, share what we've learned about writing with others, and provide suggestions for others who may also want to form a writing group.

Why Write with Others?

Academic writing is a demanding activity. When we informally asked attendees at a higher education conference about their impediments to successful writing, we received a variety of answers ranging from difficulty finding (or making) time to write to issues involving confidence about the writing process. These findings resemble the writing issues identified by many academic writers (Cameron, Nairn, & Higgins, 2009; Kamler & Thomson, 2006; Sword, 2017). Helen Sword (2017) conducted one hundred interviews with academic writers and found that even prolific academics reported being challenged by a lack of work-life balance, by external forces dictating a writing style, or by emotional disengagement or discomfort with their writing.

When using an effective and suitable format, writing groups have the potential to address many of these impediments. Writing with others can foster motivation through mutual encouragement, accountability, or healthy competition (MacLeod, Steckley, & Murray, 2012). Discussing writing and publication processes can provide valuable perspectives on disciplinary knowledge and the nature of academic writing (Aitchison & Guerin, 2014; Meschitti, 2018). The emotional support fellow writers can provide to one another may provide connections and help participants to learn the ways of academic life (Aitchison & Guerin, 2014; Faulconer, Atkinson, Griffith, Matusevich, & Swaggerty, 2010; MacLeod et al., 2012; Wilmot & McKenna, 2018). Lending expertise and providing peer feedback can improve the writing quality of the reviewer and the reviewed (Maher et al., 2008). Writing groups can also increase productivity: Cuthbert and Spark (2008) and Fleming et al. (2017), for example, found that writing group participants collectively drafted and submitted numerous journal articles, book chapters, and conference presentations.

In spite of the utility of writing groups, according to Haas (2014), "there is no fixed understanding of what constitutes a 'writers' group'" (p. 31). For the purpose of this chapter, a writing group will be defined as any gathering of two or more people, virtual or in-person, that provides social, editing, academic, or other support or feedback to its members. As one would expect from the name, writing groups may be expected to focus on writing, be that on its improvement or on increasing the quantity of writing produced. However, given the increased awareness of the social (Murray, 2015) and emotional (Thesen, 2014) aspects of writing, writing may not be the only essential element of a writing group.

Our Process

Our writing partnership evolved organically. We initially met at a graduate student orientation event, where we had a pleasant but minimal interaction. Sixteen months later, we discovered we had both enrolled in an advanced, semester-long graduate-level writing seminar offered by our faculty. This course proved to be beneficial for several reasons; it gave us the opportunity to start to get to know each other, and it also provided us with a solid foundation in understanding various writing and academic publishing processes.

At the conclusion of our writing seminar course, we briefly discussed the idea of forming a writing partnership for the upcoming fall semester. We connected over the summer and made plans to begin writing together in September. When we began our writing partnership, Karen was a Master of Education student in her third year of graduate school and Jacqueline was a second-year Ph.D. student with five years of graduate school experience. We bonded over our shared goals of trying to achieve a greater work-life balance and our desire to live healthy lifestyles. Like many academics engaged in collaborative writing efforts, we eagerly began writing together before fully examining the writing group literature (McMurray, 2017).

Over the course of ten months and using an approach similar to that taken by Kitchen and Stevens (2008), we conducted a self-study action research project of our writing partnership. In doing so, we gathered the following data sources: audio files from our meetings together; personal reflections about our experience in the writing partnership; emails, text messages, and other social media messages we exchanged; photographs we took while writing or walking together; goal-setting records we created; and logs monitoring how we used our time.

We adopted a pragmatic approach and moved through the action research cycle several times (Savin-Baden & Major, 2013). For example, and as we describe below, after initially identifying our desire for a writing group (identify concern), we established our writing group goals and our meeting times (plan), and then met for several months (act). We engaged in reflection between these phases and when we realized we were not seeing increased productivity (evaluate), we discussed modifying aspects of our group (plan next action). After further reflection, we sought additional clarification from the writing group literature (e.g., Haas, 2014) and decided to meet at different times of day and in different locations (plan and act).

In order to increase the validity of self-study research, Bullough and Pinnegar (2001) recommended a set of guidelines. For example, they noted that self-study research projects should: enable connections and allow readers to see themselves in the self-study; go beyond description and offer insight and interpretation; and when based on correspondence, help readers understand the researchers' thoughts and feelings. To meet these guidelines but remain within the space constraints of this chapter, we have described our situation in detail so that others may recognize elements of their own writing processes; shared our writing partnership approach, including its formation and progression; and provided excerpts from our correspondence, along with interpretations of how we experienced our writing group, including challenges and triumphs.

Our data analysis processes included qualitative coding and thematic analyses. We first conducted individual analyses of our data sources using a mixture of descriptive and in-vivo coding (Miles, Huberman, & Saldaña, 2014). Karen used a mostly paper-based process, completing the coding by hand, while Jacqueline completed her coding using computer software. We then met to discuss our coding results and completed a collaborative coding session. This session was completed by hand and involved further in-vivo coding. We identified any discrepancies and reached a shared consensus about the codes we had applied.

In order to analyze our writing group, we relied on Haas' (2014) Pick-n-Mix typology, which described 11 writing group dimensions that participants can combine in various configurations to suit their individual and group needs. These dimensions are membership, purpose, leadership, contact, time, place, frequency, length (of meetings), duration (of group), in-meeting activities, and between-meeting activities. As we worked through our analysis, we determined that Haas' (2014) dimensions could be further distilled into seven dimensions, with variables grouped together as shown in Figure 1.1. This framework was an integral part of our analysis and we present our results in accordance with this adapted typology.

Our Observations

As described above, we based our analysis of our experiences in the writing partnership on our adaptation of Haas' (2014) Pick-n-Mix typology presented in Figure 1.1. The balance of this chapter is organized following the dimensions of our adapted typology and is supplemented by a discussion of relevant literature.

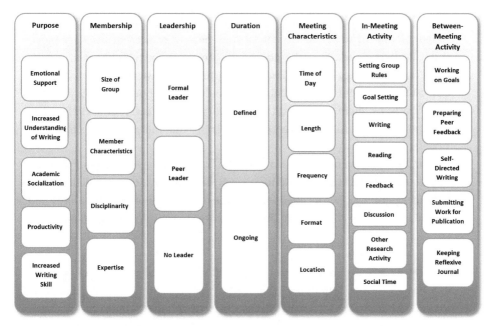

FIGURE 1.1   Writing group dimensions (adapted from Haas, 2014)

Purpose

The initial, primary goal we identified for our writing partnership was increased productivity. Jacqueline emailed Karen with a request to form a writing partnership, writing "when looking towards the fall, I see how much work I have/want to do and unfortunately, just how much of that work centers around writing. It makes me think of our proposed writing [partnership] and how keen I am on having that accountability." After asking about how Karen's summer was going, Jacqueline reiterated her desire for accountability by closing the email with "PS – I am still very serious about a writing group/accountability session. I need that. Badly." Karen responded that she "would love to get together socially and for writing support" and added "I just had several new items added to my already-long to-do list so getting together for mutual support would be wonderful."

During our first meeting, in addition to our focus on increased accountability and productivity, we also decided to incorporate elements of physical activity. We hoped that going for a walk before our writing session would allow us to catch up, socialize, and offset the long stretches of sitting at a desk, so that when we returned from our exercise and began working, we would have increased focus.

Membership

The number of members in a writing group varies considerably. For example, Stivers and Cramer (2013) describe a writing group with only two members.

Others describe engaging in writing groups with varying numbers of participants, and in many cases, not all members were present at every meeting (Cuthbert, Spark, & Burke, 2009; Galligan et al., 2003; Maher et al., 2008). Faulconer et al. (2010) formed a writing group with five members who were consistently present at all meetings, while others reported varying attendance levels; Galligan et al. (2003) had a group of between four and eight faculty members and Aitchison (2009) had a group that ranged from six to twelve people.

Our group contained only two individuals. Although we discussed whether we should open our partnership to others, we ultimately determined that inviting other people to join us might change the open, trusting group dynamic and we did not want to risk altering the supportive environment we had created.

Leadership

Writing groups can adopt one of multiple leadership structures. Groups can have a formal, appointed leader who has expertise in a particular writing-related area and who may or may not also be a participant in the group (e.g., Aitchison, 2009; MacLeod et al., 2012). Groups may have a peer leader, appointed from among the group who remains consistent throughout the group's duration or a group of peers who share leadership responsibilities (e.g., Faulconer et al., 2010). Alternately, groups may be leaderless and thus have no leader at all (e.g., Elbow, 1998). Leaders could be responsible for securing meeting space, facilitating workshops, ensuring the group remains focused and on-task, dividing up peer review tasks, or bringing snacks (Murray, 2015).

Ours was a leaderless writing partnership. Neither of us assumed responsibility for keeping each other on track nor for organizing in-meeting activities. We took turns securing meeting space, though this process was ad-hoc and informal.

Duration

One distinction in the duration of writing groups is whether or not they determine their endpoint in advance (Haas, 2014). Some writing groups intend to meet indefinitely while others set the expected duration at the outset, perhaps meeting to achieve a specific goal and intending to disband when that goal is achieved. The duration of writing groups can vary enormously, with some groups lasting for 10 weeks (Aitchison, 2003), for example, and others spanning 36 months or more (Galligan et al., 2003; Fleming et al., 2017).

Our writing partnership duration was not defined. We met regularly for ten months and the partnership came to a natural conclusion as we went our separate ways for the summer. In this way, no one's feelings were hurt by the withdrawal of the other from the project. We continue to maintain a strong friendship, supporting each other personally and academically, and we come together for the occasional academic or writing-specific project such as this book chapter.

Meeting Characteristics

Haas (2014) presents descriptions of the five meeting dimensions (time of day, meeting length, frequency of meeting, meeting format, and meeting location); we have combined our discussion of these dimensions in this section. The mechanics of the meetings are dependent on the individuals in the group, their schedules, and their preferences, and will therefore be unique to each group.

The timing of writing group meetings may vary to suit their members' changing schedules or may remain fixed at a particular time. Writing group meetings typically last two to three hours (Aitchison, 2003; Cuthbert et al., 2009; Haas, 2011), but an hour-long meeting can be very effective (Faulconer et al., 2010), as can a day-long, or multi-day writing retreat (Grant, 2006; McGinn, Ratković, Martinovic, & McQuirter Scott, 2019; Paltridge, 2016). Authors report meeting weekly (Aitchison, 2003), monthly (Cuthbert et al., 2009; Haas, 2011), or even less frequently, as Galligan et al. (2003) report, with 21 meetings over three years. The frequency of the meetings may depend on how much participants want to achieve between the meetings and whether more frequent meetings help group members achieve greater productivity.

Meetings can take place in person, virtually, or in a hybrid of the two formats, a combination of in-person and online meetings (Haas, 2011). In-person meetings are most prevalent in the literature (Aitchison, 2003; Cuthbert et al., 2009; Faulconer et al., 2010; Silvia, 2007). Common meeting places include public coffee shops, on-campus or other institutional spaces, or members' homes.

We met at various times of day and for various lengths of time lasting between two and four hours, but exclusively in person. We initially started with one meeting per week. After seven weeks, we increased our meeting times to twice per week, where we hoped to have one meeting focused on social support and the other meeting focused on academic productivity. For the first few months of our writing partnership, we met around the lunch hour, and usually in one of two on-campus locations. Approximately four months into our writing partnership, when we found ourselves struggling with productivity during our meetings, we experimented with other meeting times, including various weekday mornings and Sundays at 7pm. We tried meeting off-campus more frequently, alternating among various coffee shops.

In-Meeting Activities

The question of what will occur during the precious time that the group has together is an important decision and should be dictated by the group's goals. Haas (2014) identified four kinds of activities that can go on during group meetings: talking, reading, writing, and tending to the group, which may involve choosing a group name, establishing ground rules (Aitchison, 2009), setting group goals, and updating individual goals (Silvia, 2007).

Writing in the company of others and supporting each other's writing are natural in-meeting activities chosen by some groups. Discussion (Faulconer et al., 2010) and providing peer feedback (Maher et al., 2008) are enhanced when completed in person, as clarifications can be made immediately and the opportunities for miscommunication are limited. During the meetings, short presentations may also occur. These presentations may take the form of writing workshops, resource sharing, or presentation skills, for example.

For the majority of our writing meetings, our sole in-meeting activity was to focus on our individual writing. During the period of time when we were documenting our individual goals, we updated each other on our weekly progress, revising existing goals, updating our shared electronic documents, and setting new ones as necessary. We did not give presentations to each other, and any resources we shared during our meetings were the result of circumstance, such as finding a potentially helpful resource, and not because we planned to cover specific writing topics. When it came time to create conference submissions, we scheduled dedicated meeting times for working on those projects and we did not expect to do any of our individual writing during that time.

In addition to our writing sessions, we often included a non-writing activity before or after our writing time. In nice weather we frequently went for outdoor walks, mixing up our locations to include a quarry, scenic trails along the famed Niagara escarpment, or a local, historic mill. The photos that we captured during these walks show how much fun we were having and as we describe below, these additional, non-writing activities were a key component of the social support that we developed. At other times, our non-writing activities were focused on professional development and included attending events such as a scholarship writing workshop.

Between-Meeting Activities

For most writing groups, the majority of their time will be spent engaging in activities between meetings. Determining the between-meeting activities can be both an individual and a group-mediated decision. Members are likely to engage in self-directed writing between meetings (Haas, 2014), which numerous authors suggest should become a daily practice (e.g. Boice, 1990; Johnson &

Mullen, 2007; Silvia, 2007). The group may decide to prepare peer feedback between meetings (Aitchison, 2003; Cuthbert et al., 2009; Elbow & Belanoff, 2003; Gere, 1987). Reflective journaling may also be beneficial to both the writer and the writing group by capturing emotions, thoughts, and challenges around writing (Elbow, 1998).

Most of our writing was scheduled to occur between meetings. We did not specify the amount or frequency of writing expected outside of our meeting times, and since we were usually working on individual projects, whether one of us met our weekly goals did not impact the other's productivity. At one point in our partnership, in an attempt to improve our productivity, we committed to monitoring how we spent our time throughout the week. Using time-tracking software, we documented the total amount of time we spent writing in a week, along with the focus for each writing session. In addition, we committed to completing regular reflections about our writing partnership as part of our autobiographical self-study.

What We Learned

Overall, the writing partnership was valuable, and we are thankful to have had this opportunity. Surprisingly, we found that we benefited from the writing group in unanticipated ways, and yet we did not fulfill the initial goals that we had each set for this writing partnership. We have also come to recognize the importance of alignment of our goals and activities, and we can identify several dimensions of our partnership where better alignment may have helped us to reach our goals.

As noted above, Jacqueline initially contacted Karen with a request for increased accountability related to her writing. Karen responded with "I'd love to get together socially and for writing support." We assumed our goals were the same, but we have come to realize that there were subtle differences in our understanding. What is interesting about Karen's response is that she is the more introverted member of the partnership, yet she mentioned getting together socially. To Karen, having writing support meant accountability to another person to keep her moving forward, social motivation for meeting her writing goals, and support to develop a deeper understanding of the contexts of writing in academia. In contrast, Jacqueline wrote "I think this is exactly what I need from this writing group – the ability to kick my butt into shape and make sure that I am achieving those goals" as she wanted someone to keep her on track. We have often joked that Jacqueline wanted Karen to 'wield the stick' as she was looking for an external force to be to be the procrastination police. Since we had a leaderless partnership and neither of us ensured strict adherence to a timer, we were often side-tracked and this may have detracted from reaching our productivity goals.

Our between-meeting activities were intended to help us meet our individual goals. However, we found (and still find) writing to be a difficult task, with Jacqueline reflecting "this [writing] needs to get done ... I've just put it off because it's my most unpleasant task, the task I find most anxiety-provoking." Our difficulties focusing on writing were corroborated through our time tracking results, which showed a shocking lack of time engaged in writing outside of our meetings. Therefore, when comparing our espoused goal of increased productivity with the activities we actually completed, it is not surprising that we did not meet our goal of increased productivity. Perhaps we would have achieved better alignment of our goals and activities if we had been more intentional about our goals during the formation of our writing group. However, Karen explicitly noted that "we established priorities for our group" during our first meeting, which shows we thought we had accomplished this important step. Upon further analysis, we wonder whether setting individual goals and setting group goals are two separate activities that we may have conflated.

While we did not identify social support as a key goal for our group, we both agree that it has emerged as a very important outcome. Interestingly, like the productivity goal above, there are some slight differences in our individual interpretations of the social support we offered and received. For Karen, Jacqueline was able to offer elements of academic socialization. Karen noted "for me, the surprise came from a previously unidentified need – I did not realize all the information about grad school that I did not know. As we discussed applications (for awards, funding, and further grad school for me) and opportunities (conference proposals, seminars, etc.), I learned that through maintaining my unintentionally 'aloof' status (i.e., doing what I thought I needed to do to be successful without fully taking advantage of or being aware of the richness of opportunities), I was missing out on a whole layer of grad student existence." Jacqueline does not have an extensive support network in Niagara and Karen was able to offer community connections, such as suggesting a cycling club and restaurant recommendations, and social interactions such as joining Karen's family for lunch or attending one of her children's soccer games.

We also agree that the other has become an invaluable critical friend. Jacqueline shared "I approached Karen with idea of starting an informal writing group so I could gain the accountability I so desperately needed. What I have gained is much more, especially in terms of a critical friend and someone who offers social support." Karen found Jacqueline to be "someone who is able to bring fresh perspective to my work, someone with insight, not willing to give

CHEAPER THAN THERAPY

a reflexive 'yes' but invested and caring enough to bring an honest perspective and ask the sometimes difficult or insight-provoking questions." The critical friend element was an unexpected social and academic benefit that we sincerely appreciate.

We were able to develop this social support through mutual appreciation, by cheering each other on in person and electronically, and through humour. For example, Karen wrote to Jacqueline "How is your week going? I feel like a duckling this week – trying to keep it cool on the surface and paddling my fuzzy fanny off underneath. Looking forward to Friday's walk and talk already." When reflecting on the group, Jacqueline exclaimed "if you [Karen] said all of a sudden that you only have one hour to give this group per week, I want it to be social. That is what has become more valuable for me versus let's go sit in a room and write together." In fact, the shared social support ended up becoming so important, that after one session, Jacqueline exclaimed that she was so thankful for Karen as being able to walk and talk with Karen was so much cheaper than having to pay for therapy!

Our Suggestions

We were successful with our writing partnership in spite of ourselves. Importantly, we discovered that social support is a necessary but not sufficient condition for our success as writing partners. Our support of each other and trust-building was important to us but did not necessarily contribute to our productivity. We therefore suggest that others participating in a writing group be clear about their goals, revisit their goals, and be tenacious about meeting those goals. We suggest that it is crucial to align each aspect of a writing group with its goals, particularly the in-meeting and between-meeting activities.

We also found that our initial goals were not the same as our emergent goals. Our activities were not aligned with our initial goals of productivity, rather we unknowingly aligned our activities with our emergent goals of social support. We therefore suggest that writing group participants be open to the joy of discovering unexpected benefits of their writing group.

Finally, with only two writing partners and no leader, we were free to focus on developing our support system in a way that met our individual needs. However, that was a double-edged sword with regards to productivity. It is possible that having more people in the group would help to increase the accountability and productivity of its members, with less temptation to socialize. We therefore suggest that it might helpful to assign someone – perhaps on a rotating basis – to act as a taskmaster or timekeeper. This becomes particularly important if you are fortunate enough to build a friendship with your writing group members and would often rather chat than write!

References

Aitchison, C. (2003). Thesis writing circles. *Hong Kong Journal of Applied Linguistics, 8*, 97–115. Retrieved from https://www2.caes.hku.hk/hkjal/

Aitchison, C. (2009). Writing groups for doctoral education. *Studies in Higher Education, 34*, 905–916. https://doi.org/10.1080/03075070902785580

Aitchison, C., & Guerin, C. (2014). Writing groups, pedagogy, theory, and practice: An introduction. In C. Aitchison & C. Guerin (Eds.), *Writing groups for doctoral education and beyond* (pp. 3–17). New York, NY: Routledge.

Boice, R. (1990). *Professors as writers: A self-help guide to productive writing*. Stillwater, OK: New Forum Press.

Bullough, R. V., Jr., & Pinnegar, S. (2001). Guidelines for quality in autobiographical forms of self-study research. *Educational Researcher, 30*(3), 13–21. https://doi.org/10.3102/0013189X030003013

Cameron, J., Nairn, K., & Higgins, J. (2009). Demystifying academic writing: Reflections on emotions, know-how, and academic identity. *Journal of Geography in Higher Education, 33*, 269–284. https://doi.org/10.1080/03098260902734943

Cuthbert, D., & Spark, C. (2008). Getting a GRiP: Examining the outcomes of a pilot program to support graduate research students in writing for publication. *Studies in Higher Education, 33*, 77–88. https://doi.org/10.1080/03075070701794841

Cuthbert, D., Spark, C., & Burke, E. (2009). Disciplining writing: The case for multidisciplinary writing groups to support writing for publication by higher degree by research candidates in the humanities, arts and social sciences. *Higher Education Research and Development, 28*, 137–149. https://doi.org/10.1080/07294360902725025

Elbow, P. (1998). *Writing without teachers*. New York, NY: Oxford University Press.

Elbow, P., & Belanoff, P. (2003). *Being a writer: A community of writers revisited*. New York, NY: McGraw Hill.

Faulconer, J., Atkinson, T., Griffith, R., Matusevich, M., & Swaggerty, E. (2010). The power of living the writerly life: A group model for women writers. *NASPA Journal about Women in Higher Education, 3*(1), 207–235. https://doi.org/10.2202/1940-7890.1047

Fleming, L., Malinowski, S., Fleming, J., Brown, M., Davis, C., & Hogan, S. (2017). The impact of participation in a research/writing group on scholarly pursuits by non-tenure track clinical faculty. *Currents in Pharmacy Teaching and Learning, 9*, 480–490. https://doi.org/10.1016/j.cptl.2016.12.004

Galligan, L., Cretchley, P., George, L., McDonald, K. M., McDonald, J., & Rankin, J. (2003). Evolution and emerging trends of university writing groups. *Queensland Journal of Educational Research, 19*, 28–41.

CHEAPER THAN THERAPY

Gere, A. (1987). *Writing groups: History, theory, and implications.* Carbondale, IL: Southern Illinois University Press.

Grant, B. M. (2006). Writing in the company of other women: Exceeding the boundaries. *Studies in Higher Education, 31,* 483–495. https://doi.org/10.1080/03075070600800624

Haas, S. (2011). A writer development group for Master's students: Procedures and benefits. *Journal of Academic Writing, 1*(1), 88–99. https://doi.org/10.18552/joaw.v1i1.25

Haas, S. (2014). Pick-n-mix: A typology of writers' groups in use. In C. Aitchison & C. Guerin (Eds.), *Writing groups for doctoral education and beyond* (pp. 30–47). New York, NY: Routledge.

Johnson, W. B., & Mullen, C. A. (2007). *Write to the top! How to become a prolific academic.* New York, NY: Palgrave Macmillan.

Kamler, B., & Thomson, P. (2006). *Helping doctoral students write.* New York, NY: Routledge.

Kitchen, J., & Stevens, D. (2008). Action research in teacher education. *Action Research, 6,* 7–28. https://doi.org/10.1177/1476750307083716

MacLeod, I., Steckley, L., & Murray, R. (2012). Time is not enough: Promoting strategic engagement with writing for publication. *Studies in Higher Education, 37,* 641–654. https://doi.org/10.1080/03075079.2010.527934

Maher, D., Seaton, L., McMullen, C., Fitzgerald, T., Otsuji, E., & Lee., A. (2008). 'Becoming and being writers': The experiences of doctoral students in writing groups. *Studies in Continuing Education, 30,* 263–275. https://doi.org/10.1080/01580370802439870

McGinn, M. K., Ratković, S., Martinovic, D., & McQuirter Scott, R. (2019). Creating, supporting, and sustaining a community of academic writing practice: The multi-university residential writing retreat model. In N. Simmons & A. Singh (Eds.), *Critical collaborative communities: Academic writing partnerships, groups, and retreats* (pp. 136–148). Leiden, The Netherlands: Brill Sense.

McMurray, C. (2017). A systematic approach to graduate writing groups: Facilitator, first meeting, and feedback structure. *Praxis: A Writing Center Journal, 14*(2), 44–49.

Meschitti, V. (2018). Can peer learning support doctoral education? Evidence from an ethnography of a research team. *Studies in Higher Education.* https://doi.org/10.1080/03075079.2018.1427711

Miles, M. B., Huberman, A. M., & Saldaña, J. (2014). *Qualitative data analysis: A methods sourcebook* (3rd ed.). Thousand Oaks, CA: Sage.

Murray, R. (2015). *Writing in social spaces: A social processes approach to academic writing.* New York, NY: Routledge.

Paltridge, B. (2016). Writing retreats as writing pedagogy. *Writing & Pedagogy, 8*(1), 199–213. https://doi.org/10.1558/wap.v8i1.27634

Savin-Baden, M., & Major, C. H. (2013). *Qualitative research: The essential guide to theory and practice.* New York, NY: Routledge.

Silvia, P. J. (2007). *How to write a lot.* Washington, DC: American Psychological Association.

Stivers, J., & Cramer, S. (2013). Academic writing partnerships: The DIY version. *The Journal of Faculty Development, 27*(3), 30–35.

Sword, H. (2017). *Air and light and time and space: How successful academics write.* Cambridge, MA: Harvard University Press.

Thesen, L. (2014). 'If they're not laughing, watch out!' Emotion and risk in postgraduate writers' circles. In C. Aitchison & C. Guerin (Eds.), *Writing groups for doctoral education and beyond* (pp. 162–176). New York, NY: Routledge.

Wilmot, K., & McKenna, S. (2018). Writing groups as transformative spaces. *Higher Education Research & Development*, 37, 868–882. https://doi.org/10.1080/07294360.2018.1450361

CHAPTER 2

"We'll Do Whate'er We List": Growing, Creating, and Writing Together as Faculty of Difference

M. Soledad Caballero and Aimee Knupsky

Abstract

Through a serendipitous discovery six years ago, we came together to create a collaborative writing partnership that transformed how we work, how we feel about that work, and the directions that work has taken. Before joining forces, we had individual trajectories as a literary scholar of the nineteenth century and as a cognitive psychologist, and we successfully negotiated tenure journeys despite the obstacles facing us as women faculty of difference (Latinx and LGBTQ). Together we pursued a professional development opportunity to explore cross-disciplinary investigations of affect. In this chapter, we share our origin story, position collaborative writing as a place of strength and growth for faculty of difference and share specific suggestions for how to make collaborative writing work in an academic setting with high teaching, research, and service demands. We explore how collaborative writing partnerships can foster self-care and care for each other and keep us focused, energized, and authentically engaged. Overall, we convey both practical nuts and bolts about increasing scholarly output through a writing collaboration and capture the sense of agency, passion, and humor that collaborative writing can provide.

Keywords

collaborative writing – interdisciplinary scholarship – emotion and affect – faculty of difference

Through a serendipitous discovery six years ago, we created a collaborative writing partnership that transformed how we work, how we feel about that work, and the directions that work has taken. Before joining forces, we had individual trajectories as a literary scholar of the nineteenth century and as a cognitive psychologist. We negotiated tenure journeys despite the obstacles facing us as women faculty of difference (Latinx and LGBTQ). With one of us labeled as "prickly" and the other as a "balkanizer" by members of our departments, our explorations became a site of refuge; the source from which we stepped out together to confront the challenges of academe (Cameron et al., 2009; Grant & Knowles, 2000). We were battered and disillusioned by institutional structures that devalued our expertise and experiences; our partnership reignited our curiosity and commitment to engaging in scholarly conversations from a place of strength and solidarity. In this essay, we reflect on the importance of collaborative writing, describe how we became collaborators, interrogate our method, and consider how collaboration disrupts and redefines the emotions we experience when writing.

Collaboration as Solidarity

Academia is constructed around the idea of the "sole genius," of people who think and write and work on their own (Ede & Lunsford, 2001). Often what comes to mind when we think of this prototypical genius scholar is a white, straight, cis-male; he is "competent" while his female counterparts are "nurturing" (El-Alayli, Hanson-Brown, & Ceynar, 2018; Fiske, Cuddy, & Click, 2007; Sprague & Massoni, 2005). Looking at the "artifacts" of academia, we see the solo scholar model writ large from the construction of curriculum vitae, to debates over first author designation, to anxieties of being "scooped," to scoring a single author monograph. The hoops we are asked to jump through for review and promotion require us to prove our individual worth against that of others. It is a zero-sum game that fosters competition rather than cooperation. It is no surprise that the structures and processes of academia do not lend themselves to collaboration or, in some cases, actively discourage it (Lunsford & Ede, 2011). If this "lone wolf" approach is the norm, how much more isolating are the paths of academics who come from underrepresented groups and sometimes find themselves as the "only one" on campus? For individuals like us, from these groups, the lack of a cohort highlights our separateness and increases the feeling of being alone, left to our own devices, with the consequences of any mis-steps magnified.

On the one hand, this isolation is daunting, has been shown to decrease retention, and can lead to serious cases of faculty burn-out and structural gaslighting (Ahmed, 2012; Barnett & Felten, 2016). We discover that our work is scrutinized in ways that others' is not, that we will be asked to negotiate the same "hurdles" for tenure and promotion, while carrying the stigma and

"WE'LL DO WHATE'ER WE LIST" 19

stereotypes about our bodies and our scholarship (LaSala, Jenkins, Wheeler, & Fredriksen-Goldsen, 2008; Seguera, 2003; Turner, 2002). At the end of the day, our work will not be understood or celebrated like that of other colleagues (Gutiérrez y Muhs, Niemann, González, & Harris, 2012). On the other hand, having to make it "on our own" can create a sense of agency. We may lay-down expectations of recognition, let go of the need to "justify" what we do, and try to get on with it. Instead, we can look to find the inherent purpose and joy in our work. We can think about what will sustain us as we navigate departmental and institutional politics, challenges, and inequities. Collaborating means finding people to endure with, commiserate with, and work with. It is a strategy born of necessity and a desire to do more than simply survive. There is a little bit of "we'll show them" to it. It's scrappiness.

We recognize that this is just *one* way to deal with such isolating circumstances, a risky and uncertain one, and one that took us a while to conceive and embrace. For a long time, our instinct was to fight to systematize processes and cultures of academia in order to make them equal. But this "equality" never materializes – even when processes become systematized, there are workarounds, back-room deals, and barriers that sustain the "traditional" trappings and values of academia. Individually we end up reifying an unhealthy system that is an unattainable ideal for most of us. We have discovered that collaborating and pushing our scholarship forward despite these complications is a radical choice. While our dedication to students and service has not changed, resisting inequitable structures of recognition requires that we claim for ourselves the same space and time to focus on our scholarship that our white male colleagues have historically enjoyed. We are able to do this claiming more successfully together and in collaboration than on our own.

Tales of Collaboration

In a moment of re-evaluation on the cusp of tenure and pre-tenure, we pursued a professional development opportunity to explore cross-disciplinary investigations of affect. The *New Directions Grant,* funded through the Great Lakes Colleges Association (GLCA), required faculty to explore a new area of focus. We decided to try the adventure together and embraced the challenge both with a new topic, emotion, and with a new approach, collaboration. This collaboration allowed us to develop an interdisciplinary team-taught course integrating the humanities and sciences in an exploration of emotion, affect, and the passions. Specifically, the course interweaved late 18th century literature and historical texts (e.g., *Sense and Sensibility*, conduct books, and medical treatises) with contemporary psychological and neuroscience experiments and reviews (e.g., of emotion expression and regulation).

Because the topic of the class was new to both of us, the process of preparing to teach it was unlike any other course preparation we had experienced. As we searched for sources, we did not have pre-conceived notions of the "canon," of those authors or works that "must" be included to make the course a rigorous, traditional exploration of the topic. Instead, we were students together – using our expertise to guide each other through our disciplines, but not to "teach" each other about the topic. Purposefully disrupting our own expertise could have been risky given the marginalization faculty of difference, like us, already face in academia. However, we credit this "breaking of expertise" with creating unique and interesting selections and combinations of ideas about emotion and how to teach it. Stepping out of our expert roles also allowed our students to become co-collaborators and explorers with us (Cook-Sather, Bovill, & Felten, 2014). Sharing the floor with our students gave them space to make connections and contributions that were possible because they were not yet entrenched in their disciplinary perspectives.

In fact, when we disrupted the role of "expert" we had inherited throughout our respective disciplinary training, we were able to embrace risk-taking as a new habit of mind; risk-taking became exploration. This resulted in a collaboration that illustrated to us how much more we could accomplish together than apart. Now, by asking questions together, by reading together, and by writing together, we try to escape the pitfalls of knowledge that exist in parallel and disconnected spaces. Doing so prioritizes a bi-directional approach to knowing – where humanists and scientists can confer with one another as they develop novel methodologies and pursue innovative discoveries. Because we reimagined the possibilities of academic space by adopting an interdisciplinary collaboration, when we write together, we are no longer paralyzed by the thought of failure nor crushed by the experience of it. Always, we are left with more questions and ideas for the next project. Our collaboration remains full of curiosity, awe, and discovery (Holmes, 2010), giving us confidence to investigate areas that are of inherent importance to us as teachers, scholars, and writers. We have named our kind of collaboration "ethical interdisciplinarity," calling for scholars to learn with one another rather than to learn about each other in isolation (Caballero & Knupsky, 2018).

Sitting down Together

In many collaborative writing models, individual members are responsible for writing particular sections of a project, and then these are exchanged and

"WE'LL DO WHATE'ER WE LIST"

revised together (Sword, 2017). And this is how we wrote the first draft of our first paper about Joanna Baillie's play *De Monfort* and emotion regulation, with one of us writing the literary analysis section and the other writing the empirical section (Caballero & Knupsky, 2018). However, we quickly realized that this approach did not result in the kind of interdisciplinary synthesis that we modeled and praised in our classroom. It was also not as fun. Since rewriting that first paper together, we have co-written all of our pieces simultaneously, with one of us typing and both of us speaking aloud our ideas for the page. We then switch off and the other types and writes but the talking, out-loud revising, and idea exchange stays the same. Sometimes we find that one of us starts a sentence or thought, gets stuck, and the other one of us finishes it. Sometimes one of us has a vague idea or word but cannot quite think of it and throws out what she's trying to capture, "I'm thinking of something like …," and the other one of us starts the brainstorming process that eventually gets us where we want to be. Sometimes it's hard to keep up with ourselves, but it's always exciting to try. It can be painful, it can be frustrating, it can be exhausting. At the same time, this process and experience of collaborative writing is motivating and exhilarating (Dwyer, Lewis, McDonald, & Burns, 2012). We are often surprised with what we come up with together (Gallant et al., 2014). We write what we want or feel like in the moment knowing we'll go back and make it "pretty" or "make it work" later on. But often times, we've noticed that having two sets of eyes and minds on a page is like having a real-time editor that allows our first drafts to be stronger and more compelling than they would be otherwise. For us, our inner critics are exposed and sometimes silenced when we write collaboratively. We fight those inner demons with each other.

But, of course, there is a method to our madness. Having a partner requires blocking out weekly simultaneous writing time, carefully planning for short and long term writing goals, pushing each other to engage professional networks creatively, making collective decisions about project priorities, and building a "parking lot" of ideas, inspirational readings, and future opportunities. More than anything else, writing productively means carving out time and space for our scholarship in the face of astronomical teaching and service demands (Sword, 2017). We are now experimenting with setting the same offices hours and requesting the same teaching times so that we are able to carve out shared open space to use for collaborative writing. Collaborative writing requires that we incorporate it upfront into our weekly work schedule or else it will simply not happen. As has been said by many experts who discuss writing in academia, we treat it like a class, something that cannot be missed, something that requires us to be present, prepared, and ready (Silva, 2007).

To make the most use of our collective time, we have borrowed from business models that forecast their projects using what is called "a program of work." We have a running list of project types, e.g., conferences, articles, grants, teaching projects, etc. Having these all laid out in one place (we use an excel spreadsheet), allows us to set realistic deadlines, to notice conflicts, to anticipate crunch times, and to revise according to unanticipated life events. While it can be daunting to see all the work in progress and the deadlines together, our program of work also reminds us regularly of how much we have accomplished and is generative in nature since we constantly get excited about adding new projects to it as our work evolves. In addition, seeing the work together allows us to identify themes and connections we might have overlooked. It suggests avenues to pursue with other colleagues. While networking is challenging because we are both introverts and reaching out in these ways is not in our wheelhouse, we are motivated to do it for the sake of the collaboration. We find empowerment in partnership.

As the program of work unfolds, another important point to stress is that we never make decisions about our collaborative writing on our own. It is always a collective decision we talk through and make together about where we should head next, where we should invest our time, and what new challenges and ideas we'd like to explore. Trust is essential here since no decision or obligation is "obvious" or assumed. We talk it all out, consider the ramifications, contemplate potential roadblocks, and then make decisions together. If our collaborative writing is to remain interesting and motivating, we have to be able to decide what *not* to write as well as what to write together. Collective decision-making results in a "parking lot of ideas." This is a folder and list and set of saved Facebook posts that remind us of other fruitful areas of exploration we cannot take on right now but that would move our work forward in intriguing ways. The parking lot is motivation, a promise for more writing and more discovery.

Writing with Emotion

While the nuts and bolts of what make our collaborative writing are important, we have also reflected on many occasions about the role of social emotion regulation in our process. This is not surprising given the long history of research on the relationship between emotion and writing (Brand, 1990; Sala-Bubaré & Castelló, 2018). To some extent, we have been lucky that our scholarship focuses on emotion and affect; it has informed our practice of writing. One area of exploration for our research re-imagines psychological models of emotion regulation. Emotion regulation is a combination of processes through which people maintain, eliminate, increase or decrease their expression and experience of emotion. While many of these models have focused on the individual processes people engage, we are more interested in the approaches that highlight the social nature of emotion (Butler, 2015). In fact, Coan (2011), one of the leading researchers in this area, suggests that individual emotion regulation is a much harder process to engage. When a person tries to regulate on their own, it takes more cognitive control. For Coan, emotion regulation is social by default. We see this play out in our collaborative writing all the time.

In acknowledgement of the affective work writing requires, our partnership fosters self-care and care for each other and keeps us focused, energized, and authentically engaged (Bogad et al., 2007; Neumann, 2006). At the beginning of each writing session we practice a "collaborative clearing of the decks" to create the space for writing. Life is full of crap that, for better or worse, has to be processed in order for us to do our work. We have to give time and attention to what is filling up our psychic space so that we can make room for creativity and inspiration. For example, as unexpected or bad news about a colleague reaches us or as family matters emerge and explode, we are there for each other, and we take the time to stop, acknowledge, and give comfort. Affective research would recognize this as joint regulatory flexibility, the capacity to regulate our emotion by having access to a wider range of regulation strategies (Bonanno & Burton, 2013). Our clearing of the decks is not a long process, but it is a preliminary attempt to manage everyday emotion rather than suppress it so that we can come to the page knowing that real life has not been ignored but is being, for the moment, set aside so that work can continue. In fact, we know that sometimes it's this work that heals, that gives perspective, and that allows us to go back to the real world feeling accomplished and cared for.

But clearing the decks is not the only time that collaborative writing requires social emotion regulation. All aspects of successful writing are about managing and embracing affect (Cameron, Nairn, & Higgins, 2009). When writers comment on the process of writing saying, "it hurts," this is not metaphorical. As Shapiro (2013) asserts, "The page gazes impassively back. It will give us nothing. It will take everything. It isn't interested in how we think or how we feel. It doesn't care if we fill it with words, or if we crumple it up in despair" (p. 43). Getting your ass in a chair takes emotional effort. A partner mitigates that effort. It's the same idea as having a "work out buddy" or having a "wing woman" when we negotiate awkward social situations. Facing a blank page can inspire any number of emotions, most often "negative" ones – fear, frustration, sadness, and even anger (but see Sword, 2017 for alternative emotions). Talking through and laughing at these emotions with a partner helps you break through. When these emotional struggles are shared, more energy and attention are reserved and maintained for the actual work of writing. Of course, emotions do not disappear even when you're in moment of flow (Csikszentmihalyi, 1997). But the beauty of collaborative writing is that it remains a tag-team process: "Let me pull us forward for a minute," and "Now it's your turn to get us to the next place." Social emotion regulation research has shown that simply having someone's hand to hold allows us to more successfully regulate our emotion (Coan, Schaefer, & Davidson, 2006). Successful collaborative writing is always having a hand to hold.

Friendship and Collaboration

Across the years we have been asked if our collaboration works as well as it does because we were friends first. We know that friendship has been stressed by previous collaborators as an important component of making things work (Day & Eodice, 2001; Lunsford & Ede, 2011). We have thought a lot about this question, and our contention is that it's complicated. Friendship provides a potential way in; it might feel safer approaching a friend to start a collaboration. But not all friends can collaborate and sometimes being friends might make it harder because of the honesty and vulnerability required to produce good work. In other words, it would have to be a friendship that could withstand open and honest critiques, a friendship that honors flexibility, careful listening, and that can withstand bruised egos to arrive at valuable compromise. It has to be a friendship capable of prioritizing the success of the partnership. In our case, when one of us is asked to run a workshop or present a paper about our collaborative work, we never respond individually and always make it clear that it's the two of us in this work together. The role of friendship in fostering collaboration is also complicated because it is correlational – we became friends in a new way as we worked together. Did we collaborate because we were friends or did we become better friends because we collaborated?

So, if successful collaboration is not only about friendship, what other ingredients lend themselves to successful partnership? We started with a vision we both believed in, a problem we wanted to engage, specifically the arbitrary distance in undergraduate experiences of the humanities and sciences. We see the importance of this kind of coming together echoed in the work of Day and Eodice (2001) who noted that the collaborators they interviewed "came together because of shared ideologies and interests, friendships, complementary areas of expertise, and a common vision" (p. 65). A common goal was also the impetus for our collaboration. Therefore, we recommend finding someone who shares a framework with you about what matters, someone who will want to explore a shared passion. Because it's the passion that matters, look beyond your department, your institution, your discipline. This might involve networking at professional conferences, talking to colleagues about your interests to see if they know someone with similar passions, and reaching out to scholars doing work that you admire. If you are going out on the collaborative limb, make it count and stretch far even if you don't quite know what will happen or where you'll end up.

That said, it's also important not to expect miracles at the beginning of a collaboration or you risk collapsing under the weight of taking on too much (Nairn et al., 2015). To build trust, start with one problem, one opportunity to explore together and see where it leads. For example, teaching can turn into research which can turn into writing. It's a one-step-at-a-time process, a process that unveils opportunities as your partnership strengthens and becomes prepared for them. These collaborative partnerships build slowly over time, ebb and flow, and can take unexpected routes. In order to give these partnerships the space and time they need to flourish, it is also important to have conversations about priorities and feasibility early in the relationship. Such collaborations will not always be possible at all times and for all scholars. We decided at this point in our careers to choose collaboration over other obligations such as individual teaching innovations, service obligations, and disciplinary engagement. It is a choice with consequences. Beginning a collaboration, especially an interdisciplinary one, is intense and disorienting. For us, we experienced what we called a "brain fog" that enveloped us for a long time as we tried to learn to see across vast topics, literatures, and time periods. This was a physiological sign that we were working in a really new way, and it was a reminder for us about what it is like to learn. Interdisciplinary collaboration requires intentional integration of your work and thinking. It requires constant engagement.

The payoff of these "sacrifices" is an abundance of new opportunities that will seem at first like random coincidences, but what feels like serendipity is actually a changed perspective. Quantum physics has verified that "the everyday world we perceive does not exist until observed, which in turn suggests ... a primary role for mind in nature" (Kastrup, Stapp, & Kafatos, 2018). This is the kind of "constructive perception" illuminated in British Romanticism and later echoed in cognitive psychology (Wordsworth, 1802; Chabris & Simons, 2010). Working together has literally shifted how we see our place of work and our potential contributions to national conversations. Our perceptions changed about what is possible. We have learned to see value in our work beyond institutional recognition (which is illusive) and to see that the sole genius model is not the only way to succeed or to measure worth. We have moved beyond embracing a deficit model, moved beyond trying to assimilate. Our new perceptions show us that faculty of difference bring unique insights and skills that could potentially change how we define and think about academic work and worth. Ours in not an additive but integrative model that centers collaboration as the way forward.

We hope this essay has conveyed both practical advice about increasing scholarly output through collaborative writing, and also captured the sense of agency, passion, and humor that it can provide. Collaborative writing requires intense presence, careful listening, and a willingness to go where your partner leads. It requires trust and vulnerability. We have created empowered lives of inquiry as we continue to learn, read, and write together.

References

Ahmed, S. (2012). *On being included: Racism and diversity in institutional life.* Durham, NC: Duke University Press.

Barnett, B., & Felten, P. (Eds.). (2016). *Intersectionality in action: A guide for faculty and campus leaders for creating inclusive classrooms and institutions.* Sterling, VA: Stylus Publishing.

Bogad, L., Cook, J. S., Darcy, M. G., Johnson, J. D. Patterson, S. K., & Tillitson, M. E. (2007). Finding our way as WAC-y women. *Across the Disciplines, 4.*

Bonanno, J. A., & Burton, C. L. (2013). Regulatory flexibility: An individual differences perspective on coping and emotion regulation. *Perspectives on Psychological Science, 8,* 591–612.

Brand, A. G. (1990). Writing and feelings: Checking our vital signs. *Rhetoric Review, 8,* 290–308.

Butler, E. A. (2015). Interpersonal affect dynamics: It takes two (and time) to tango. *Emotion Review, 7,* 336–341.

Caballero, M. S., & Knupsky, A. (2018, May). Sharing contagion: Sympathetic curiosity and social emotion regulation in Joanna Baillie's De Monfort. *Romantic Circles Praxis, Romanticism and Affect Studies.* Retrieved from http://www.rc.umd.edu/praxis/affect/praxis.2018.affect.caballero-knupsky.html

Cameron, J., Nairn, K., & Higgins, J. (2009). Demystifying academic writing: Reflections on emotions, know-how, and academic identity. *Journal of Geography in Higher Education, 33,* 269–284.

Chabris, C., & Simon, D. (2010). *The invisible gorilla: How our intuitions deceive us.* New York, NY: Crown Publishing Group.

Coan, J. A. (2011). The social regulation of emotion. In J. Decety & J. T. Cacioppo (Eds.), *Handbook of social neuroscience* (pp. 614–623), New York, NY: Oxford University Press.

Coan, J. A., Schaefer, H. S., & Davidson, R. J. (2006). Lending a hand: Social regulation of the neural response to threat. *Psychological Science, 17,* 1032–1039.

Cook-Sather, A., Bovill, C., & Felten, P. (2014). *Engaging students as partners in learning and teaching: A guide for faculty.* San Francisco, CA: Jossey-Bass.

"WE'LL DO WHATE'ER WE LIST" 27

Csikszentmihalyi, M. (1997). *Creativity: Flow and the psychology of discovery and invention*. New York, NY: Harper Perennial.

Day, K., & Eodice, M. (2001). *First person squared: A study of co-authoring in the academy*. Logan, UT: Utah State University Press.

Dwyer, A., Lewis, B., McDonald, F., & Burns, M. (2012). It's always a pleasure: Exploring productivity and pleasure in a writing group for early career academics. *Studies in Continuing Education, 34*, 129–144.

Ede, L., & Lunsford, A. A. (2001). Collaboration and concepts of authorship. *PMLA, 116*, 354–369.

El-Alayli, A., Hanson-Brown, A. A., & Ceynar, M. (2018). Dancing backwards in high-heels: Female professors experience more work demands and special favor requests, particularly from academically entitled students. *Sex Roles, 79*, 136–150.

Fiske, S. T., Cuddy, A. J. C., & Glick, P. (2007). Universal dimensions of social cognition: Warmth and competence. *TRENDS in Cognitive Science, 11*, 77–83.

Gallant, M., Brown, L., Bell, C., Bridges, N., Gale, K., Hung, Y. L. et al. (2014). Retreating out of ourselves: Sharing and spilling the lifeblood of collaborative writing. In J. Wyatt & J. Speedy (Eds.), *Collaborative writing as inquiry* (pp. 13–22), Newcastle upon Tyne, UK: Cambridge Scholars Publishing.

Grant, B., & Knowles, S. (2000). Flights of imagination: Academic women be(com)ing writers. *International Journal for Academic Development, 5*, 6–19.

Gutiérrez y Muhs, G., Niemann, Y. F., González, C. G., & Harris, A. P. (Eds.). (2012). *Presumed incompetent: The intersections of race and class for women in academia*. Logan, UT: Utah State University Press.

Holmes, R. (2010). *Age of wonder: The romantic generation and the discovery of the beauty and terror of science*. New York, NY: Vintage Books.

Kastrup, B., Stapp, H. P., & Kafatos, M. C. (2018, May 29). *Coming to grips with the implications of quantum mechanics*. Retrieved from https://blogs.scientificamerican.com/observations/coming-to-grips-with-the-implications-of-quantum-mechanics/

LaSala, M. C., Jenkins, D. A., Wheeler, D. P., & Fredriksen-Goldsen, K. I. (2008). LGBT faculty, research, and researchers: Risks and rewards. *The Journal of Gay and Lesbian Social Services, 20*, 253–267.

Lunsford, A. A., & Ede, L. (2011). *Writing together: Collaboration in theory and practice*. New York, NY: Bedford's St. Martin's.

Nairn, K., Cameron, J., Anakin, M., Juntrasook, A., Wass, R., Sligo, J., & Morrison, C. (2015). Negotiating the challenge of collaborative writing: Learning from one writing group's mutiny. *Higher Education Research & Development, 34*, 596–608.

Neumann, A. (2006). Professing passion: Emotion in the scholarship of professors at research universities. *American Educational Research Journal, 43*, 381–424.

Sala-Bubaré, A., & Castelló, M. (2018). Writing regulation processes in higher education: A review of two decades of empirical research. *Reading and Writing, 31*, 757–777.

Segura, D. A. (2003). Navigating between two worlds: The labyrinth of Chicana intellectual production in the academy. *Journal of Black Studies, 34*, 28–51.

Shapiro, D. (2013). *Still writing: The perils and pleasures of a creative life.* New York, NY: Grove Press.

Silva, P. J. (2007). *How to write a lot: A practical guide to productive academic writing.* Washington, DC: American Psychological Association.

Sprague, J., & Massoni, K. (2005). Student evaluations and gendered expectations: What we can't count can hurt us. *Sex Roles, 53*, 779–793.

Sword, H. (2017). *Air & light & time & space: How successful academics write.* Cambridge, MA: Harvard University Press.

Turner, C. S. V. (2002). Women of color in academe: Living with multiple marginality. *Journal of Higher Education, 73*, 74–93.

Wordsworth, W. (1994[1802]). Preface to lyrical ballads, with pastoral and other poems. In J. O. Hayden (Ed.), *William Wordsworth, selected poems* (pp. 431–459). New York, NY: Penguin Books.

CHAPTER 3

Collaboration at a Distance: Exploring History, Communication, Trust and Socialization

Erik Blair and Georgette Briggs

Abstract

This chapter takes a personal narrative approach to exploring an academic writing partnership. The authors are based in different countries (Erik lives and works in the UK and Georgette lives and works in Trinidad and Tobago) but, through a shared academic history and a mixture of synchronous and asynchronous approaches, they have maintained an academic writing partnership. Collaboration can be difficult in the online context, especially when the partners are located in different parts of the globe where there are differences in time, culture and expectations. In this case, Erik and Georgette also have different disciplinary backgrounds (in the natural and social sciences) and have been 'trained' to privilege certain research methods and styles of writing. In investigating collaboration at a distance, Erik and Georgette examine four key qualities of a successful collaborative relationship: history, communication, trust and socialization. They argue that successful academic writing is a learned behaviour that requires deliberate action and suggest that, when working at a distance, this is maintained through regular contact; setting short term goals and having a critical friend who can push you in joint and solo projects.

Keywords

distance – relationships – history – communication – trust – socialization – personal narrative – Caribbean

This chapter takes a personal narrative approach to exploring our academic writing partnership. We are based in different countries (Erik lives and works in the UK and Georgette lives and works in Trinidad and Tobago) but, through a shared academic history and a mixture of synchronous and asynchronous approaches, we have maintained an academic writing partnership.

© KONINKLIJKE BRILL NV, LEIDEN, 2019 | DOI:10.1163/9789004410985_003

Collaboration can be difficult in the online context, especially when the partners are located in different parts of the globe where there are differences in time, culture and expectations. In our case, we also have different disciplinary backgrounds (in the natural and social sciences) and have been 'trained' to privilege certain research methods and styles of writing. Collaboration for us is a mixture of working together on projects and developing a critical thinking space that allows us both to develop as individuals. We support each other with a joint goal in mind (although part of the partnership is agreeing what that goal is and how we write to it) and, in doing so, we also enhance our individual areas of interest.

Our partnership has changed over time: from face-to-face to online collaboration and this has helped bring specific concepts to the fore. Ponomariov and Boardman (2016) suggest that in many instances, collaboration is a relational, human and satisfying experience. From their work they suggest that a successful collaborative relationship is underpinned by four key qualities: history, communication, trust and socialization. This chapter draws on the four qualities highlighted by Ponomariov and Boardman as a means of examining the impact of distance, academic disciplines, and time on our ongoing partnership. In doing so, we examine how collaboration at a distance can still allow for the development of a writing 'space' that supports both co-authorship and individual academic pursuits. The chapter concludes with our personal reflections and some broader lessons learned about the collaborative writing process.

History

We first started writing together when we were institutional colleagues at The University of the West Indies, Trinidad and Tobago. Georgette was preparing her Masters in Education thesis for publication and soon realized that the possession of a Ph.D. in the natural sciences and a history of published scientific research papers, did nothing to alleviate the uneasiness felt as a biologist publishing in an educational research journal for the first time. Through our pre-established friendship, Erik, as an educationalist, was able to offer periodic involvement in theoretical discussions on Georgette's thesis work and after the thesis was complete we found ourselves undertaking a comfortable transition from colleagues to collaborators. Our earlier conversations had highlighted areas of mutual interest and we decided to explore these. We arranged to meet in 'neutral' territory in the campus coffee bar where we drank milkshakes and pitched our ideas. Initially we discussed some ideas that Georgette had

COLLABORATION AT A DISTANCE   31

generated for her Masters thesis but that had not made it into the final work. Our conversations were free and wide ranging – we would take an initial idea then refine it from our own perspective and pitch it back at the other. Lots of ideas were discarded as they were either 'too scientific' or 'not scientific enough.' But we found common ground in exploring how students engaged with resources; how teaching staff conceptualised themselves, and how academic job roles were constructed. Later we would use meetings to agree our focus; set targets and divide out tasks. This was usually followed by an outline of the proposed work and the establishment of a follow-up meeting in subsequent weeks where we would review our joint work. Thereafter, we would meet almost every two weeks on campus at the coffee shop where we would move straight into task-master mode and set seemingly ridiculous timelines that we both subsequently met. Meeting over milkshakes helped us to create an inviting and comfortable critical thinking space and helped us get to know each other's approach to the writing process. Academic life for both of us was hectic and dominated by teaching and departmental responsibilities that were often at the forefront of our everyday activities. Our scheduled project appointments, although demanding, were a welcome time away from all that hustle and gave us a sense of worth in that we had some time set aside to develop how we approached academic work. Murray and Newton (2009) found that structured writing retreats, where most time was taken up with the act of writing, allowed individuals to see themselves as writers – we were able to generate this sense of identity through our meetings where our interaction helped establish our individual "writerly identity in relation to other academic identities" (p. 550). Our conversations were relaxed, engaging and wide ranging, and we each left with a better understanding of the other's perspective on teaching; conception of research, and approach to academic writing. But the milkshake meetings were not all work and identity formation as it was hard not to be distracted by the lush green grass; the huge spreading trees, and the hot Caribbean sun.

Our personal histories and disciplinary backgrounds imparted pre-established differences between us from the start. However, any anxiety introduced by our socio-cultural and field-specific differences were diffused by our regular meetings which then became a source of positive and elevating interchange between us. A change of jobs meant that Erik relocated to the UK and Georgette remained in Trinidad and Tobago. This move forced the structure of the writing collaboration to change as the Atlantic Ocean and a five-hour time difference now made our collaboration a virtual one. Like any relationship where distance is involved, it helped that our work ethic and overall writing expectations were smoothed out before distance became a factor. Initially our writing partnership suffered during an adjustment period and all projects were optimistically placed on hold. When we mutually agreed to continue writing, we soon realized it was not as easy to return to our already established routine. What appeared as a simple transition from meeting-up on campus to meeting up virtually, would now require a review of our organization and communication practices but, over time, as we began to find a new way of working and we found ourselves moving to a place where the work that we did between meetings became more obvious. Where, beforehand we had wandered off after our meetings and completed tasks separately, we now had to work using shared files and online dropboxes – a process that impacted how we communicated. Our face-to-face collaboration and friendship had set out the parameters of our partnership and addressed most of the qualities that Ponomariov and Boardman (2016) suggest work to underpin a successful collaborative partnership; however, Ponomariov and Boardman did not discuss the benefits of transparent practice which is something we have found to be very valuable when developing a partnership at a distance.

Communication

Having established a way of working as co-authors and collaborators when we were both on the same campus, we had to find a way to maintain our partnership at a distance despite the divergent nature of our cultures and disciplines. Becoming an academic writer can be a process shrouded in mystery (Cameron, Nairn, & Higgins, 2009) but we found that working at a distance meant that the processes that drive collaboration needed to be clearly communicated and that this helped demystify the writing process. Working across time zones meant that we needed to organise our work to maintain the partnership through various modes of interaction, thus communicating how we did things became an important collaborative tool. The value of our friendship carried significant weight in this process but hand-in-hand with that respect comes the pressure of not wanting to disappoint the other. From this position, in maintaining our collaboration going forward, the significance of timely, friendly, supportive (yet challenging) communication comes to the fore.

Communicating over distance and time means that arranging virtual chats at convenient moments is important. Since we are not aware of the day-to-day machinations of each other's lives this can make it difficult to find the right time to talk. But when we have figured it out, the outcomes are always positive, with each conversation presenting an opportunity to refresh and reflex our academic brains. Having a regular meeting time can help motivation, accountability and productivity (Clark, Jankowski, Springer, & Springer, 2000); however, having competing academic cultures, diaries and responsibilities means that arranging interaction can be difficult. To address this we employ a range of strategies. Thus far, our main 'everyday' mode of communication has been email, which allows for quick check-ins. We use this in an informal sense and our conversations are a mixture of chat, support and target setting. Beyond this we have relatively regular online face-to-face conversations that help us solve problems and help us to re-focus. The third tool we use is synchronous collaborative writing where we each pull up the same document on our computer screen and rework it simultaneously: annotating, editing and problematising. These formats not only help to create the space for partnership and give us structure as co-authors, but they also support individual work offering transferable learning where the skills we teach each other are taken outside into our solo projects.

Elbow and Sorcinelli (2006) suggest that there is satisfaction to be found when we find time away from the demands of life by escaping to a "writing place" (p. 2). The forced responsibility of our online partnership means that we each have to find real-world writing places to complete our individual set tasks, and in doing this for our co-authored projects, we start to carve out spaces in our lives where we can do independent projects. Thus, the practicalities of collaboration from a distance can actually lead to a position where developing real-world writing space becomes the norm and the satisfaction of the writing retreat can be found in our everyday lives. The corollary of this is that because we each have busy lives, the writing spaces that we do manage to find tend to be short lived. So where face-to-face collaboration can involve focussed work over a period of hours, virtual collaboration tends to limit these time periods into somewhat smaller chunks. MacLeod, Steckley, and Murray (2011) found that structured writing spaces could be developed when a more strategic approach, including the combination of shorter blocks of writing time and the switching of competing tasks, is utilized and we have certainly found that to be true. Aitchison (2009) reports that, "For most writing groups, 'talk' is the fundamental vehicle by which group members engage in a reflexive practice that connects reading and writing for the building of meaning" (p. 907). The talks that we used to have over milkshakes under the hot sun of Trinidad and Tobago have now morphed into synchronous and asynchronous interactions. The format may have changed but having a focus on supporting one another through clear and regulated communication means that the output is still the same and the process still instigates individual reflexivity and a mutually rewarding experience (Speedy et al., 2010). Thus, communication in the context of our collaboration has two outcomes – first of all we can discuss the project we are involved in and secondly, we can each become academically reinvigorated.

Trust

Our disciplinary backgrounds are rather different and our training as scientists (natural and social) has led us to prefer some data types and some approaches to writing and research. Email messages can sometimes be misread and time-lags in getting replies can be frustrating. All this means that there is potential for conflict. To reduce this possible tension involves developing a sense of trust in each other. We have developed such trust through a balance of personal and professional interaction. Our shared history helps build personal trust as we don't just 'hear' what the other is saying but often, through knowing each other, strive to listen to the significance behind the statements. In our online collaboration we have also built professional trust through challenge and support. The challenge tends to be end-point focussed as it mainly comes from completing tasks and writing to deadlines; however, support is more *ad hoc*. Most of the support we offer each other comes from short emails that offer positive reinforcement. Praise without evidence is not a very effective tool but, when we offer praise and support for insightful comments; the development of helpful graphs, or finding a great piece of literature, then the praise become more powerful as it is based on evidence. So, our critical collaboration is supported by a mutual professional understanding and is nurtured through friendship and efficacy.

Bringing our own perspectives to our collaboration helps create projects that have many dimensions and working in the same space allows for academic cross-cultural learning, where the lived experience of being a biologist in Trinidad and Tobago intertwines with the everyday nature of being an educationalist in the UK. Collaboration and academic writing can lead to 'hard' and 'soft' outcomes (Morss & Murray, 2001). Hard outcomes include journal articles and conference presentations. Soft outcomes include increased confidence and increased self-knowledge. Our collaboration had initially been set up to lead to the development of hard outcomes (and it does) but working together meant that we got to know how we operate as academics and as individuals and this enhanced our personal academic development. We work together on a project but the act of giving ourselves space for academic activity also supports our individual projects.

In many ways our initial writing collaboration model established whilst working on the same campus, presented fewer limiting factors to our interactions at a distance but, considering our new job roles and expectations and the five-hour time difference, our meetings are now even more purposeful. Our casual discussions in a relaxed, out-of-office context, have been replaced by high-value, goal-oriented, online meetings. Through our online communication, we agree on formats, deadlines and responsibilities then we each go off and do our respective work spurred on by the knowledge that the other partner is hard at work on their side of the Atlantic. Working at a distance means there is a greater need to make use of the writing space we have developed and fewer distractions are entertained. This forces us into positions where we need to find time in our separate lives to complete the tasks before our next virtual meeting. However, we were always good at this and our previous milkshake meetings had helped us regulate our writing activities – but now, at a distance, we have learned to trust the other to complete their tasks. The length of time between meetings can have somewhat of a negative impact on our writing output, as the greater the gaps in communication the more likely it is that turnaround dates lengthen. Being out of sight can mean being out of mind and, to counter this, brief check-in emails have helped us maintain the link and remind us both that there is someone out there who is reliant on us doing what we said we would do.

Cross-disciplinary collaboration can be a strength (Galligan et al., 2008) and Ponomariov and Boardman (2016) suggest that the more boundaries that are spanned, the more productive and more diverse the collaboration will be. But being differently situated as academics can also be tricky as what 'matters' to one author might not be as important to the other. O'Malley and Lucey (2008) suggest that writing partnerships succeed when the partners begin to see themselves as scholars and are able to negotiate individual preference – as long as the group goals reflect the interchange of the various individual inputs. This means that collaborators need to be mindful of each other's cultural and epistemological influences and spend time trying to understand these and organise a thoughtful working relationship. Doing this across disciplinary perspectives and across time zones is doubly difficult as the space available for collaboration is reduced, so having a shared history allows us to know what is best for the project we are working on and best for each other. In this way the relational aspects of collaboration underpin the academic aspects.

Socialization

When researchers work in collaboration they begin to develop a set of community values (Ellis, Adams, & Bochner, 2011) and, over time, these values set the tone and direction of the collaboration. These social values work as a support mechanism as they offer guidance when individuals wander off track or are faced with difficult decisions. Maintaining such values is more troublesome at a distance as each partner faces a different set of competing demands. Pasternak, Longwell-Grice, Shea, and Hanson (2009) report that writing together and working in an effective partnership takes negotiation as there are competing assumptions and competing demands. It is hard to replicate the creative interaction of face-to-face writing collaboration in the online environment, especially when one partner is hungry for lunch and the other has just returned home at the end of a long working day. The 'rules' that exist for socialization within physical space collaborations don't quite work in a virtual format. The face-to-face environment offers a format where individuals can switch off external demands and focus on their various projects, but the multiplicity of online activity means that this is not replicable. Where once we met to 'escape' for institutional demands we now meet in a busy online environment. If we were to try to recreate a writing retreat online there would be competing demands – as emails pop up; tabs vie for attention, and pages buffer. To control for all this, the structure of our partnership is reinforced by our community 'values' of meeting deadlines and supporting agency. We understand and accept the demands of each other's lives and find space to collaborate in short and clear bursts in between them.

Sharples (1999) describes three main ways in which authors working in partnership might organise themselves: parallel, sequential and reciprocal. Parallel working involves allocating different jobs to each member so that many tasks can be done simultaneously. Sequential work is where the first person begins a task then passes the semi-complete work on to their colleague. Reciprocal working is a team-based approach where each member constantly negotiates their activities depending on the current activities of their partner. We employ all three of these strategies at various times in the partnership. Early writing is often reciprocal as we try to navigate through initial ideas and respond to each other's areas of interest. After we have formed our plan we move into parallel working stage where we allocate sections of writing. This is then followed by sequential work where we pick up on each other's drafts and add, edit and rework them. Our interactions take different forms through these three stages – at early stages we are often excited and have face-to-face online conversations that spiral off at various tangents. Once we have allocated jobs our interactions tend to be take the form of short email check-ins. Then in the final stages of a project we come together for detailed conversations during simultaneous document editing.

Kempenaar and Murray (2016) suggest that academic settings have several cultures, such as institutional values and history; societal norms and

COLLABORATION AT A DISTANCE

expectations, and political frameworks, and that these various cultures impact upon the way that individuals approach scholarly work. The culture within which an individual is situated underpins their norms, beliefs and actions, and collaboration can bring such individual perspectives to the forefront. Being differently positioned as authors is both a strength and an area of negotiation. When we worked on the same campus we also met socially away from work along with our families and friends. On these occasions we rarely talked about our writing and this gave us valuable opportunities to learn more about each other's personalities separate and apart from our academic settings. Clark, Jankowski, Springer, and Springer (2000) discuss Hollingsworth's (1992) concept of "relational knowing" and report that through their writing collaborations they developed a sense of trust that allowed them to move beyond intellectual support to a position where they could offer emotional and professional support. Forman and Markus (2005) suggest that interdisciplinary collaboration is bounded by institutional and disciplinary constraints and that extra effort is needed in order to be successful. We recognise aspects of this but have also found that such effort can be reduced through the development of social and relational knowing. Since our academic collaboration evolved in parallel to our friendship, we are simultaneously comfortable supporting each other's academic and developmental needs. Kreijns, Kirschner, and Jochems (2003) also suggest that "social interaction is a prerequisite for collaboration and collaborative learning" (p. 340), again highlighting the significance of social relational history in the establishment of writing partnerships such as ours.

Reflections

Being differently positioned and knowing about the other partner is a strength in critical collaborations as this can lead to new insights and ongoing professional development. A writing partnership is not one homogenous concept but the coming together of individuals who are able to share and learn from each other. Here we offer some individual reflections:

Georgette
The driver for our meetings did not change with time or with distance. When we take on projects, we immediately set tasks based on the research area and on our perceived strengths. We still manage to set short deadlines and ensure that assigned roles are specified and agreed upon, with short turn around dates. Meetings and discussions over a cup of tea or coffee are now completely virtual and involve a combination of email correspondence and virtual appointments, the scheduling of which can be quite challenging at times.

Interestingly, the greatest challenge of our writing collaboration is not from our country origins, but our discipline backgrounds and that of writing for the pure sciences compared to education. Erik plays a major role in establishing the writing framework with a wide search of the literature, a process I think he thoroughly enjoys. Independent of his academic expertise, he possesses that ability to survey the vastness of content knowledge that usually serves as a basis for our writing project. From my experience in education research, the value or weighting of different parts of the process is different and I believe I still struggle with this. Erik's approach to writing is very different to mine.

In scientific research writing, the article is built with the results and data analysis at the core and the literature used at the beginning to introduce and justify the study and towards the end to support the discussion. In education research, although the components of the paper are comparable to that of a scientific paper, the construction of the paper, in my experience, is very different. The data analysis and results are not the sole focal points and the literature tends to be rather broad. As a scientist I found this approach a bit difficult especially given my training to be direct and straight to the point. I also found it quite challenging to completely move away from quantitative data and so, almost as a compromise and possibly to the annoyance of Erik, a component of our data sets always require some measure of quantitative data analysis. I think he has embraced this as much as I have embraced the new writing process and this is one of the key proponents of our writing relationships, that quality of embracing new ideas. My writing partnership with Erik has allowed me to advance my scope as an academic, increasing my confidence and knowledge base. Natural scientists, by training, tend to have, at times, a condescending view of research done by social scientists, placing less value on the outcomes of these studies. My writing relationship and collaboration with Erik has allowed me to gain a greater appreciation and grasp for the body of work done by social scientists.

So far, we have individually brought new writing projects to the table, thus by default, the writing lead was established. With regards to our writing, our relationship is also different from my other research collaborations in the pure sciences. Collaborative projects come to the table with the goal of data generation from experiments that may or may not meet prescribed deadlines, increasing the pressure on partners involved. This pressure significantly impacts on the dynamics of mutual respect across lines of gender, culture and academic lineage. I have tried to transition our approach of tight deadlines, role allocation and assigning of tasks to other collaborative projects with mixed success. The strict goal setting has allowed my research projects, especially with students I supervise, to progress more efficiently as my confidence in this area has increased. Unfortunately, the success of this approach has not translated into my other local or

COLLABORATION AT A DISTANCE

international collaborators. Upon reflection, although there are many shared commonalities with my collaborators, both home and abroad, my collaboration with Erik has many unique facets that have provided a solid foundation for our writing partnership.

Erik

Collaboration from a distance has helped me develop new skills as an academic and our writing partnership has helped formalise my approach to writing. Face-to-face collaborations can become informal over time as time together can lead to more and more casual chat. When we used to meet over cold milkshakes in the hot sun of Trinidad and Tobago, it was easy to become distracted as our usual place was in a shady nook overlooking one of the central areas of the campus. It was a nice spot and our conversation would often meander. This was a bit of a two-edged sword as the milkshake meetings became a place where we could generate new ideas but could just as easily find ourselves chilling out and enjoying the day. We are both driven by deadlines and work hard but it is easier to digress when you know that, if a meeting isn't very productive, you can always meet again the next week. Having the capacity to meet at any time and working on the same campus may actually have been a less productive way for us to work so I have found that writing from a distance, for me, adds format and rigour. I am 'forced' to find time in my life to complete my tasks before the next scheduled deadline and this can help regularise my writing pattern.

Working from a distance can be tough because questions are not instantly answered. If I have a problem I send an email but her various responsibilities and real-life commitments mean that Georgette can't be expected to answer straight away. Emails can also be tricky as they don't have the nuance or subtext of conversation, so what I think is a clear question might seem like utter nonsense to her. This makes our skype chats so valuable. We might digress a little but we can clarify any grey areas and we can share online artefacts – tables, graphs, drafts etc. – and really examine things in a more thoughtful way. Of course, scheduling these discussions is tricky because of competing schedules, time differences and the great number of public holidays enjoyed in Trinidad and Tobago.

Georgette adds rigour to my writing through her disciplinary focus and through her personality. We write on education, which is a field I have been involved in my whole academic life, but, as someone who has spent less time working in this discipline, Georgette questions everything and this helps me to question some of the disciplinary assumptions that I hold. She also has the capacity to say, "No" to things and has a clarity to her thinking. This means that when I am writing I am asking if she would like what I am saying or whether she would find it all a bit flowery – preferring that I cut to the chase. This has helped with my other writing projects, as even though she is not around or involved, I find myself asking some of the questions that I think she would ask. So, our collaboration has given me a new critical voice – even when Georgette is not physically or virtually present. Knowing that I have a writing partner, whether we are actually involved in a specific project or not, helps me feel more academic as I feel there is a space in my life that is for writing and being scholarly.

Collaborating at a Distance – Concluding Thoughts

Collaboration is not just about working together or creating working places it is also about developing critical writing partnerships that give space and structure to joint and solo projects. Cameron, Nairn, and Higgins (2009) highlight how academic writers rarely consider the full picture in regard to the process of writing as "they see only the finished product of other academics' work and not the process by which that work came to be" (p. 281) but working in partnership allows individuals to glimpse behind the curtain and share the mechanics of academic writing. When we were both on the same campus we met, set targets and went off to complete our various tasks but our collaboration at a distance has allowed us to learn more about how academic work is produced. We share artefacts and have joint access to online folders so we can see the processes behind each other's efforts. We see many drafts and everything is done in a transparent manner.

Collaboration through communication and partnership humanises the writing process. Sharing disciplinary codes and norms also helps open our eyes to 'new' approaches and this is further supported by having a range of methods of communication and embracing everything from online email messages to detailed synchronous discussions on full drafts of work. For Forman and Markus (2005, p. 95) interdisciplinary collaboration is a politically negotiated activity where "collaborators from different disciplines cannot be separated from the receptivity of each discipline to borrowing from other fields" but this position gives agency to the discipline rather than the academic within the discipline. As situated academics we find that we can personally negotiate disciplinary differences through our shared history; our range of communication strategies; our trust in each other, and our collaborative values. There are conceptual and methodological differences between us as collaborators; however, we find that these are overcome through personal engagement. In this way, successful collaboration is the product of knowing your partner and learning from them. Kempenaar and Murray (2016, p. 941) suggest that successful academic writing is a learned behaviour that requires "deliberate action" and we have found that, when working at a distance, this particular behaviour

COLLABORATION AT A DISTANCE
41

is maintained through regular contact, setting short term goals, and having a critical friend that can push you in joint and solo projects.

References

Aitchison, C. (2009). Writing groups for doctoral education. *Studies in Higher Education, 34*(8), 905–916.

Cameron, J., Nairn, K., & Higgins, J. (2009). Demystifying academic writing: reflections on emotions, know-how and academic identity. *Journal of Geography in Higher Education, 33*(2), 269–284.

Clark, W. M., Jankowski, P. J., Springer, M., & Springer, N. P. (2000). Moving beyond nouns and verbs. *Journal of Feminist Family Therapy, 11*(2), 49–54.

Elbow, P., & Sorcinelli, M. D. (2006). The faculty writing place: A room of our own. *Change: The Magazine of Higher Learning, 38*, 1–7.

Ellis, C., Adams, T. E., & Bochner, A. P. (2011). Autoethnography: An overview. *Forum: Qualitative Social Research, 12*(1), 1–18.

Forman, J., & Markus, M. L. (2005). Research on collaboration, business communication, and technology: Reflections on an interdisciplinary academic collaboration. *The Journal of Business Communication, 42*(1), 78–102.

Galligan, L., Cretchley, P., George, L., McDonald, K., McDonald, J., & Rankin, J. (2003). Evolution and emerging trends of university writing groups. *Queensland Journal of Educational Research, 19*(1), 28–41.

Hollingsworth, S. (1992). Learning to teach through collaborative conversation: A feminist approach. *American Educational Research Journal, 29*, 373–404.

Kempenaar, L. E., & Murray, R., (2016). Writing by academics: A transactional and systems approach to academic writing behaviours. *Higher Education Research & Development, 35*(5), 940–950.

Kreijns, K., Kirschner, P. A., & Jochems, W. (2003). Identifying the pitfalls for social interaction in computer-supported collaborative learning environments: a review of the research. *Computers in Human Behavior, 19*(3), 335–353.

MacLeod, I., Steckley, L., & Murray, R. (2011). Time is not enough: Promoting strategic engagement with writing for publication. *Studies in Higher Education, 37*(6), 641–654.

Morss, K., & Murray, R. (2001). Researching academic writing within a structured program: Insights and outcomes. *Studies in Higher Education, 26*(1), 35–52.

Murray, R., & Newton, M. (2009). Writing retreat as structured intervention: Margin or mainstream? *Higher Education Research & Development, 28*(5), 541–553.

O'Malley, G. S., & Lucey, T. A. (2008). Promise and possibility: Building collegial opportunities for scholarship. *Academic Leadership Journal, 6*(3), Article 16. Retrieved from https://scholars.fhsu.edu/alj/vol6/iss3/16/

Pasternak, D., Longwell-Grice, H., Shea, K., & Hanson, L. K. (2009). Alien environments or supportive writing communities? Pursuing writing groups in academe. *Arts & Humanities in Higher Education, 8*(3), 355–367.

Ponomariov, B., & Boardman, C. (2016). What is co-authorship? *Scientometrics, 109*(3), 1939–1963.

Sharples, M. (1999). *How we write: Writing as creative design.* London: Routledge.

Speedy, J., Bainton, D., Bridges, N., Brown, T., Brown, L., Martin, V., Sakellariadis, A., Williams, S., & Wilson, S. (2010). Encountering 'Gerald': Experiments with meandering methodologies and experiences beyond our 'selves'" a collaborative writing group. *Qualitative Inquiry, 16*(10), 894–901.

CHAPTER 4

Just Show Up: Reflections from a Motley Writing Group

Janel Seeley, Tia Frahm and Elizabeth Lynch

Abstract

In this chapter we reflect on our cross-disciplinary writing group, specifically on our increased productivity and writing self-efficacy. Our writing group has provided an outlet for both developing and sharing our work over the past two years. This has allowed us to develop our self-image as writers and provide mutual support as we navigate our various responsibilities within the academy. We use an autoethnographic approach to explore the inner workings of our writing group and its impact on our writing lives. We also provide insight to how our writing group experience facilitated our publication portfolios across academic fields. Drawing on relevant writing group research (Gray, 2015; Pajares, 2003; Sword, 2016) our group encourages the practice of sustained writing and accountability. In agreement with Guerin's (2012) research, as a cross-disciplinary group, we have also been able to expand our writing to a broader audience.

Keywords

cross-disciplinary – auto-ethnography – sociocultural theory

Our motley, cross-disciplinary, writing group consists of three members: Elizabeth, an academic professional lecturer in the anthropology department; Janel, an educational developer with the university's center for teaching and learning and associate lecturer in education and social work; and Tia, a recent doctoral graduate transitioning into a tenure-track assistant professor appointment in education. Although Tia and Janel have backgrounds in education, we are not in the same field of study. Janel's research is focused in the Scholarship of Teaching and Learning (SoTL) and Tia's focus is in writing instruction and professional learning. We perceive this as a benefit allowing us to look at each other's work from fresh perspectives, providing an awareness of audience and ensuring that our writing is clear and concise.

Two years ago, our College of Education's three endowed chairs hosted a half day workshop by Tara Gray entitled "Publish and flourish: Becoming a prolific scholar." The goal of the workshop was to provide full-time faculty and graduate assistants with specific tools for managing their success in publishing among hectic academic obligations. In many ways this was our blind date, amounting to a random draw or opportunity of change, introduction to the writing group.

The workshop setting resembled a formal banquet hall with round tables where we all gathered for the sold-out event. We were drawn by the promise of help with publishing, and the offer of hands-on help during the workshop. Armed with chunks of our articles or dissertation drafts, we were able to work along with Gray's lecture to identify (or not) our thesis and key sentences. Most important to our writing group though was that we were able to receive constructive feedback on how to organize our time and re-prioritize writing objectives.

After our initial meeting, we individually drew upon different tools provided during the workshop as we began to form as a writing group. Elizabeth immediately began using writing logs to track her daily writing and even sent her daily word count for accountability. Janel was encouraged by having an initial structure, locating key sentences in each paragraph, to revise her writing. Tia sought to join a writing group that would meet weekly to hold herself accountable to write daily. Collectively, we began to meet at a designated time and place weekly, during the fall and spring academic semesters with email check-ins during the summer. The inner workings of our group have evolved over two years; these specifics are later addressed. But first we provide a review of related literature on writing groups with a focus on multi-discipline academic writing groups. In this chapter, we draw upon sociocultural theory to explore the success of our group, followed by the methodology we employed. We provide our researcher backgrounds, focus on our writing group, and share our current writing stories. The chapter closes with a discussion on the three themes gleaned from our autoethnography that include: the impact of just showing up, regular writing group meetings, and the importance of bringing something to the table, with concluding thoughts on the future of our writing group.

Related Literature

Literature on productive writing offers a variety of strategies and techniques for success. Many authors provide specific guidelines and structures for productive writing (i.e., Blecher, 2009; Gray, 2015; Silva, 2007). However, productive writing is about finding your style and building emotional support rather than spartan like rigidity (Sword, 2016). Most research supports the notion that one's beliefs about writing will determine success levels, or at least give one the confidence to overcome obstacles/challenges (Pajares, 2003). Writing groups are one way to acquire emotional support and confidence.

Writing groups can provide individual self-efficacy as a writer by developing confidence and helping members overcome obstacles (Pajares, 2003). Research does show that doctoral students in particular still consider themselves learners rather than experts, even when participating in writing groups (Guerin, 2013). Even though many writers still view themselves as learners, productivity can still increase.

Interdisciplinary writing groups in particular can provide advantages to writers as they develop both their identity and their productivity. By having access to information beyond one's own circle of colleagues, writers can think more critically about their work, communicate with broader audiences and connect to broader learning (Guerin, 2013). Creating spaces to share work, learn from one another, and hold one another accountable can be invaluable to new and experienced writers alike (Lamont, 1994).

Exploration of Theory

Sociocultural theory provides a backdrop to the work of our writing group. Initially, the purpose of the writing group was to provide feedback on our individual writing. However, through consistent feedback we began learning about ourselves as academic writers, as well as the rules of academic writing within our respective fields. Therefore, we situate our writing group experience within sociocultural theory. We focus on the social interactions within sociocultural theory and draw on Vygotsky's (1978) observation that learning occurs within social interactions within communities of practice. Learning within these communities of practice takes place through apprenticeship, observation, sharing information, developing relationships, and providing mutual support (Lave & Wegner, 1991). The feedback we were able to provide each other during our weekly meetings proved to be invaluable to our growth as academic writers but would not have occurred had we not established relationships with each other and created a safe social space for writing.

Gray (2015) provided the framework for the workshop that launched our writing group. In the beginning, we focused on the key sentences in a few pieces of writing that we would print and bring to each meeting. However, around week four, we noticed that our needs shifted from key sentences to idea development. The needs of our community of practice had shifted. Since the focus of the group was to meet our academic writing needs, we were able to broaden our focus to include overall organization, idea development, and writing related to conference presentations.

Methodology

We employed an autoethnographic approach (Ellis, 2004) that includes our personal histories related to academic writing and our experiences related to writing within this group. Autoethnography as a narrative approach to research is "an important way in which people try to understand and make sense of their world/s" (Daspher, 2015, p. 513). By confronting our own experience as writers while minimizing our biases towards our emotional attachments to academic writing, we were able to provide a rich description of our shared experience in this particular cross-disciplinary writing group.

It was not until we sat down to discuss what a chapter about our writing group would look like that we began to examine what we do with and for each other week after week. It was important for us to capture our writing histories and what brought us to the half-day workshop, which we share in our researcher backgrounds. We then examine how the outside demands of our respective positions caused the structure of the group to change over time. Next, we individually share our stories about what the group has meant for each of us as we have developed our group into a format that works for us. Finally, we examine themes in our reflections that define the key components for our group.

Our Reflections

In this section, we share our reflections on what drew us to Tara Gray's workshop, the evolution of our writing group, and then reflect on how this writing group has impacted our lives as academic writers. Our individual stories are written through a first-person narrative approach. We chose to tell our stories in this way in order to give readers a sense of our individual journeys as academic writers.

Where We Began
Elizabeth
When I joined the writing group, I had just completed my dissertation, but still needed to publish my work. My background in business, cultural resource

JUST SHOW UP

management, and biological anthropology meant that my writing was a bricolage of styles ranging from marketing plans and business analysis to cultural
resource management reports. The result was insecurity about how my writing style would fit into my new role as an anthropology academic. Would I be
able to efficiently navigate the debates in our discipline at a professional level?
I joined the writing group in hopes that a support network would both minimize my nervousness about my writing style and help me to develop a style of
my own. At the same time, I needed the discipline of writing daily, so having a
group to meet with weekly held me to a standard of accountability. However,
my secret hope (secret because I hated to admit just how fearful I was of the
peer review process) was the supportive group would help me cope with comments from reviewers so that I would not give up on publishing my work.

Janel

When I joined the writing group, I had just completed my dissertation the previous year. After twenty plus years of being a practitioner in both social work and
education, the writing process did not necessarily come as easy as other professional activities. Once my dissertation was finished, I described myself as having
post-traumatic stress syndrome from that experience. I knew I needed to change
my attitude if I was ever going to write anything again. As an instructional designer
and academic lecturer, my job does not require many publications, but I knew it
certainly would be looked upon favorably, especially if I wanted to advance my
career in the future. I had a vita a mile long of national and international conference publications, but no journal publications. It was time to challenge myself.
I ordered a book on writing effectively and signed up for the workshop. The idea
of a writing group to keep me accountable sounded like a good idea.

Tia

I had just started my third year in the literacy doctoral program when I joined
the writing group. Up until my third year, my academic writing experience
included papers for doctoral courses, solo and co-authored conference proposals, and co-authored manuscripts. My previous writing experience included
teaching English Language Arts at the elementary and middle school levels,
co-directing an affiliate site of the National Writing Project, along with personal and practitioner writing that focused on the teaching of writing. I joined
the group with the intent of receiving feedback on my writing, specifically outside of my discipline to ensure that my writing could be clearly understood by
an audience outside of education. As I transitioned to a more research-based,
academic approach to my writing, I knew the accountability and support of a
writing group would be invaluable.

How Our Group Evolved

We decided to meet the same day and time each week. We met in a café on campus with large tables and comfortable seating; often we ate lunch or sipped coffee while we met. We scheduled our meetings for an hour and a half in order to give each of us 30 minutes to share. With the exception of summer and winter break, we have kept to this schedule even when one of us could not attend or even when we do not all, or occasionally none of us, have any writing to share. Our motto was to just show up.

When our group formed in August of 2016, we followed Tara Gray's (2015) *Instructions for Writing Groups.* These included instructions on "what we needed to do before we started, establishing ground rules, reading and searching for key sentences, discussing key sentences, the positive round, and hints for successful writing groups" (p. 106). As we progressed however, we realized that we needed more than this one exercise. Although identifying key sentences was useful, sometimes we needed something different.

We began to send each other our work a day or two ahead of our meeting time, along with specific requests. Sometimes these requests involved editing, occasionally they included considering research questions or thesis structure, and often requested help on thinking through format and flow. Our work soon grew to be more than academic journal submissions.

As we became more familiar with one another, we began sharing conference and grant proposals, job application materials, course syllabi, and other written materials. Sometimes in reviewing these documents, we would share resource materials that the others might find useful. These included book chapters, articles, or websites on writing, style manuals, resources for organizing projects, and more.

In addition to sharing resources and writing support, we came to be social, motivational, emotional, and academic support. We cheered one another on through job interviews and article or proposal submissions and consoled one another through article and proposal rejections. If we did not have much writing to review on some weeks, we shared personal stories and supported one another through personal matters and work challenges. We offered advice on health and wellness and recreational activities around town. We also practiced presentations and interviews with each other. We not only kept each other accountable for writing, but for sticking to other personal and professional goals as well. Eventually our support evolved beyond our weekly meetings, to emails, text, and occasional phone calls throughout the week as well. In this way our writing group developed into a valuable community of practice where sharing our writing promoted significant learning.

Where We Are Now as Writers
Elizabeth

In contemplating the value of our writing group, my first thought goes to how the group has helped me mature as an academic writer over the past two years. When we began meeting, although a little conventional at first, sticking close to the tools provided by Gray's workshop, we soon became comfortable with each other. My primary anxiety (and hindrance to effective publishing) was how to effectively engage with reviewers and their comments. Although Gray's workshop had provided several stories illustrating how our work was part of a broader dialogue, actually living that experience is something quite differ- ent. Tia and Janel were so easy going and such enthusiastic writing partners that I soon began to develop my own voice. Dealing with reviewer comments became like grist for the mill; I looked forward to our writing group meetings so I could relate my stories (successes and failures). It was fun being able to laugh about how I engaged with reviewers, but they also helped me make sure I was reading the comments, not projecting myself on to the comments. This, more than anything, helped me break the cycle of procrastination that seemed to plague some of my publications. The first year of our meeting I published three articles. This second year has been more challenging with a full-time teaching load, finding any time to write is a challenge.

Janel

The significance of this group has evolved for me over the past two years. When we first began to meet it felt rather formal, yet helpful to have account- ability to keep plugging away at my writing, even when I did not want to. I initially thought I needed to use this group for big article submissions and to have them review my writing only. Eventually, I began to share conference proposals, grant proposals, marketing flyers, and a variety of other written documents. At first, I just wanted feedback on the writing and editing of these documents. Eventually, however, as we got to know one another and feel more comfortable, we all began sharing and advising each other on research ideas, teaching ideas, and occasionally even personal issues (sharing recipes for healthy eating, offering advice on vacation plans, suggestions for organizing clutter, etcetera). Even when I had nothing for the group to review, I always looked forward to our meetings. Sometimes as academics we get isolated in our research or our departments. Having these colleagues from other depart- ments to share aspects of my practice was beneficial to expanding my thinking and writing, along with providing encouragement and support both personally and professionally.

Although I feel as though I have plenty of room to grow, I now view myself as a writer. Since being part of this group, I have published articles, have more under review, have been awarded three grants, and several peer-reviewed conference presentations. The group helped me prepare for an invited keynote speech and review materials for various workshops and programming. With my budding confidence as a writer, I even agreed to teach a graduate course on writing a dissertation prospectus (the first three dissertation chapters); this group helped me develop the syllabus for the course.

Tia

As I reflect back on the roughly two years of this writing group, the most valuable take-away, for me, has been the accountability the group provided. For me, the practice of daily writing was instilled as I was working on the completion of my doctoral program and finishing my dissertation. However, the writing I primarily brought to the group was related to writing either for course work, presentations, and/or publications. This writing was very content specific as it related to literacy research, specifically writing instructional and professional learning. The feedback this writing group was able to provide was focused on ensuring the writing was clear and concise, and readable by an audience not familiar with my research. This group also provided accountability, regardless of what else was going on in my week, I knew that two hours of it were devoted to meeting with the group. There were weeks when I did not bring any writing, but would talk through job applications, research presentations, and teaching demonstrations. This was not specific to my academic writing, it was related to the work of an academic. So, for me, this group evolved into my academic support system and advanced my writing.

Discussion

Our individual reflections have helped us realize our self-efficacy and productivity as writers. When reviewing our reflections as a group, the following themes emerged: just show up, meet regularly, and bring anything. We offer these suggestions to others interested in forming writing groups.

Show Up

For the three of us, the act of just showing up to the writing group had a profound effect on our academic writing production. For Elizabeth, the act of showing up meant that she was continually engaging with her writing by updating us on her progress or talking through tough parts of her writing. For

JUST SHOW UP   51

Janel, the accountability of weekly meetings helped keep her focus and motivation on writing, any writing.

Meet Regularly

Our group made the decision to meet weekly and scheduled our meeting time early enough in our semester so that we would not have any other scheduling conflicts. Establishing a weekly meeting meant that we would try to send our writing in advance for review. This schedule allowed us to establish a routine where we consistently produced writing.

Bring Anything

Every week we agreed to bring something to work on, no matter how small and regardless of how busy our schedule became. This included anything from academic manuscripts, to job applications, to conference presentations. If we did not have anything ready for review, sometimes we would just think aloud about upcoming projects. Even when we did not bring our own writing to the table, remaining part of the conversation about writing kept us engaged with our writing community of practice. We still contributed to thinking about writing and writing processes, by supporting each other's efforts.

Conclusion

Reflecting on our time together brought to light how our group evolved over the past two years to a format that worked for us. Committing to just show up to our writing group on a regular basis, whether or not we had work to review, provided to be beneficial to our self-efficacy as writers. Being part of a writing group allowed us to view ourselves as writers as well as encourage one another to keep working. Additionally, reviewing each other's work helped us to think further about our own writing. The support and encouragement we gained not only in our writing, but in our academic, professional, and even personal lives proved valuable to our overall well-being.

We have all produced more writing since the group's inception, bolstering our self-confidence and motivation as writers. We realize that our group provided much more support than just in our writing, expanding to include encouragement on job searches, conference and grant proposals, and sometimes personal issues.

Our group continues to evolve; Tia has taken a new position at another university and Elizabeth is currently seeking a tenure-track position. Therefore, we are considering what our group may look like in the future. Perhaps phone calls, emails, video conferences, and road trips? Regardless, we will continue to just show up to our writing group meeting in whatever format it evolves into.

References

Belcher, W. L. (2009). *Writing your journal article in 12 weeks: A guide to academic publishing success*. Los Angeles, CA: Sage.

Dashper, K. (2015). Revise, resubmit, and reveal? An autoethnographer's story of facing the challenge of revealing the self through publication. *Current Sociology, 63*(4), 511–527.

Ellis, C. (2004). *The ethnographic I: A methodological novel about autoethnography*. Walnut Creek, CA: AltaMira Press.

Gray, T. (2015). *Publish and flourish: Become a prolific scholar* (2nd ed.). Albuquerque, NM: Starline Printing.

Guerin, C. (2013). Rhizomatic research cultures, writing groups, and academic researcher identities. *International Journal of Doctoral Studies, 8*, 137–150.

Lamont, A. (1994). *Bird by bird: Some instructions on writing and life*. New York, NY: Cambridge University Press.

Pajares, F. (2003). Self-efficacy beliefs, motivation, and achievement in writing: A review of the literature. *Reading & Writing Quarterly, 19*(2), 139–158.

Silva, P. J. (2017). *How to write a lot: A practical guide to productive academic writing*. Washington, DC: American Psychological Association.

Sword, H. (2016). Write every day! A mantra dismantled. *International Journal of Academic Development, 21*(4), 312–322.

Vygotsky, L. S. (1978). *Mind in society*. Cambridge, MA: Harvard University Press.

PART 2

Onsite Writing Retreats

CHAPTER 5

Advancing the Writing of Academics: Stories from the Writing Group

Jennifer Lock, Yvonne Kjorlien, M. Gregory Tweedie, Roswita Dressler, Sarah Elaine Eaton and Erin Spring

Abstract

In today's higher educational context, an increased focus on accountability and impact factors brings with it a greater expectation for academics to publish. Within the scholarship of teaching and learning, academic writing is a complex act that requires attention. Academics with strong expectations to be productive may nonetheless experience the writing process as isolating, lonely or overwhelming. In this chapter, we examine models and structures that foster a culture of academic writing within a post-secondary context. We then describe the evolution of our writing group's community of practice approach – one in which academics engaged in various forms of writing spanning the spectrum from reporting for academic and scholarly journals to writing for the general public and social media. Drawing from Schön's (1983) reflection-in-action and reflection-on-action model, we illustrate through current members' experiences and insights how the writing group has – and is – impacting their writing and professional growth as academics. Through the analysis of our narratives, we identified factors that influenced the success of several cycles of our writing group, as well as the conditions required to support both individuals and the collective. Recommendations for writing group practices emerge from our findings.

Keywords

academia – collaboration – knowledge dissemination – peer review – reflection-in-action – reflection-on-action – writing group

In today's higher educational context, an increased focus on accountability and impact factors brings with it a greater expectation for academics to publish.

© KONINKLIJKE BRILL NV, LEIDEN, 2019 | DOI:10.1163/9789004410985_005

Academics need to disseminate their work in top-tier journals and mobilize knowledge beyond the academic realm. Within the scholarship of teaching and learning, academic writing is a complex act that requires attention. Academics with strong expectations to be productive may nonetheless experience the writing process as isolating, lonely or overwhelming. Our purpose with this chapter is threefold. First, we examine models and structures that foster a culture of academic writing within a post-secondary context. Second, we describe the evolution of our writing group's community of practice approach – one in which academics engaged in various forms of writing spanning the spectrum from reporting for academic and scholarly journals to writing for the general public and social media. Third, we draw from Schön's (1983) reflection-in-action and reflection-on-action model to illustrate through current members' experiences and insights how the writing group has – and is – impacting their writing and professional growth as academics. Through the analysis of our narratives, we identified factors that influenced the success of several cycles of our writing group, as well as the conditions required to support both individuals and the collective.

Literature Review

> Managing time in the life of the academic is very important, especially to create a space for research within the work-plan of the academic. (Moodley, 2017, p. 114)

The work life of academics involves research, teaching, and service. Academic and professional writing is an integral component of this work. Yet, being an academic does not necessarily equate to being a master writer. A misleading assumption "is that all academics know how to write for publication and do it exceptionally well" (Olszewska & Lock, 2016, p. 133). Academics' writing evolves over time and through access to various degrees of support in developing their writing capacity as they move from graduate school through the ranks of academia.

Publication "flourishes when it receives serious institutional attention, and skilled support from ... [those] who understand academic writing as complex disciplinary and identity work" (Kamler, 2008, p. 284). A foundational component to developing writing capacity is scheduling regular (e.g., daily or weekly) time for writing. "Writing requires physical engagement with dedicated writing time and space" (Moodley, 2017, p. 111). Academic writing output may be facilitated by implementing various strategies including participation in "writing courses and workshops; writing groups; writing mentoring and coaching; PhD bootcamps; and writing retreats" (Castle & Keane, 2016, p. 74). Within this list, writing groups can be understood as individuals coming together regularly to meet, talk, and write.

Writing groups tend to be situated within a contextual practice "of supporting individuals' motivation to write, to continue writing, and to finish a piece of writing" (Castle & Keane, 2016, p. 82). In these collegial and collaborative environments, the writing process is nurtured with a goal of increasing productivity. The group provides a space for talking through ideas, working through writer's block and/or receiving peer feedback (Grant, Munro, McIsaac, & Hill, 2010; Steinert, McLeod, Liben, & Snell, 2008). This "positive interdependence" among academic writers allows them to support and help each other (Moore, 2003, p. 335). Writing groups may be led by a facilitator or leadership may be shared among the members (Grant et al., 2010). In their study of writing groups, Olszewska and Lock (2016) report that participation, engagement, and commitment impact the success of academics in both their individual ability to successfully publish and their ability to foster capacity as part of the group. Writing groups require time "to gel" (Castle & Keane, 2016, p. 89). Members need time to become comfortable sharing ideas. Participants view the lack of support for creative writing or writing that is critical in nature, as well as writing being "invisible in the institution" as challenges (Castle & Keane, 2016, p. 89). Despite challenges, writing groups provide an organized context for success in academic writing.

A writing retreat can be a natural extension of the supportive environment of a writing group. In a writing group cycle that culminated with a retreat, the latter "impacted how academics develop an understanding of writing and publication as an intrinsic part of their roles and identities as writers and academics" (Olszewska & Lock, 2016, p. 134). Writing retreats "provide dedicated time and space to write on or off camps, foster productive writing, develop synergies within a department or group, and develop writing 'know how' in a group" (Castle & Keane, 2017, p. 90). In Moodley's (2017) study of academics' experiences with writing retreats, these retreats provided a "redirected focus on research, beneficial uninterrupted time, and improved writing abilities" (pp. 116–117). Some challenges of a retreat may be cost, group dynamics, and the reluctance of members to share their writing (Castle & Keane, 2016). Additionally, measurable outcomes of writing retreat success are difficult to establish as the number of publications (outputs) is an unrealistic measure given the time it takes to see writing emerge as a publication (Grant, 2006). Paxton, Garraway, and Bozalek (2017) called for "a rethinking of our pedagogies and sharing of ideas ... focused critically on the complexities of teaching and learning to write" (p. 2). It is in this space of 'rethinking' that our chapter is focused. As members of a writing group who have engaged in one or more years of participation, we reflected on our experience and practice to tease out the attributes of a successful writing group and determine what has an impact on academic writing capacity.

Our Writing Group

Through a collaborative initiative led by the Offices of Teaching and Learning and Research in a Faculty of Education, the writing group has evolved over five years, who invite new members through monthly newsletters and word of mouth. The originally stated purpose was "to provide structure, support, and allocate time to formally hone scholarly writing skills" (Olszewska & Lock, 2016, p. 136). A critical premise was the development and fostering of a community of practice (Lave & Wenger, 1991; Wenger, 1998). This community of practice was "defined by peer learning, peer trust, and peer critique" (Olszewska & Lock, 2016, p. 135). Two people facilitated the evolution by providing leadership and structure for the writing group over two semesters per year in order to foster a "supportive peer network within the community of practice" (Olszewska & Lock, 2016, p. 136).

The main structure of the writing group involved meeting once a week for eight to ten weeks each fall and winter semester. The meetings began with 30 to 40 minutes of presentation or discussion focused on a specific theme or topic. The remaining 80 to 90 minutes were to be dedicated to individual or group writing. "Participation in the writing group was a *gift of time* that participants were giving themselves, one that allowed them to become immersed in writing during a busy day" (Olszewska & Lock, 2016, p. 136). As the group evolved, we found greater attendance in the fall semester, as compared to winter. Often people were challenged to attend given teaching schedules and other commitments. Over the years there had been additional writing support activities that included a week-long writing challenge and an annual writing retreat.

Research Design

The six authors, all members of the writing group for one year or more, shared their individual experiences and insights on how the writing group has – and is – impacting their writing and professional growth as academics. Two of the six authors have co-facilitated the writing group for two and five years,

ADVANCING THE WRITING OF ACADEMICS   59

respectively. Three authors have been members of the group for three to five years, with one having only been a member for a year. The majority of the authors have been consistent in attending both fall and winter semesters. This range of experience provided a variety of perspectives.

According to Schön's (1983) reflection-in-action and reflection-on-action, reflection is conducting "an experiment which serves to generate both a new understanding of the phenomenon and a change in the situation" (p. 68). For our "experiment," we provided seven guiding questions for the authors to frame written reflections on their experiences with the writing group. Reflection-in-action (Schön, 1983) is focused on the experience of what is occurring during the activity of a writing group, whereas reflection-on-action (Schön, 1983), the main focus of this chapter, involves the reflections after this year's writing group. This reflection-on-action is the deep thinking about what happened over the year(s) in terms of our own members in the group. We investigated why we participated in this writing group, how it influenced or changed our group and evolution as writers and academics, how well the structure worked or not and what we want for the next cycles.

The questions that guided our inquiry for this chapter were:

1. How long have you been a member of the writing group?
2. What written work have you engaged in as a member of the writing group? Please list work that may or may not be completed.
3. In 100 words or less, what would be your elevator pitch about our writing group?
4. Why do you participate in the writing group?
5. How has the writing group influenced/changed your growth/evolution as a writer and academic? What has changed?
6. To help you evolve as an academic writer, what are three things a writing group needs to do?
7. Other thoughts or comments about the writing group.

Through our reflections, we have gained new understandings of what factors impact the development of our own writing capacity within the structure of the writing group, as well as what conditions impacted the individual and the collective in relation to academic writing.

Discussion of Reflection-on-Action

Each of the authors began the process of writing this chapter by responding to a series of questions regarding the writing group. The responses were collated and the data were thematically analyzed. Two members of the participant-research team engaged in a process of collaborative analysis. We employed Saldaña's (2016) two-stage thematic coding process for qualitative data. This involved reviewing the narrative responses to identify codes (Stage 1), followed by refining codes into themes (Stage 2). Other team members then reviewed and validated the themes, giving feedback to refine the themes further.

Four key themes emerged and we explore them in this chapter: (1) the value of writing socially/collaboratively, (2) learning with and from each other, (3) time and the prioritization of writing, and (4) the future of writing group.

The Value of Writing Socially/Collaboratively

A consistent theme that emerged within the author reflections was the social and collaborative nature of the writing group. While academic writing is often seen as a task done in isolation, the writing group provided a space where we came together as a diverse cohort of scholars, at varying stages of our careers, to share in the writing process. One author commented that, "writing, like running, is ultimately a solitary pursuit – no one has ever won a race by being carried across the finish line. Yet, an observable reality is that most runners seek out a community of practice ... to perfect their craft." Another author shared that "writers need to feel like they are not alone in their writing journey." A third author, a new scholar to our faculty, explained that writing group provided "a new network of colleagues who are supporting me as I transition into my new role." All three quotes point to the social and collaborate nature of the writing group experienced by these scholars.

The reality of our work is that each of us face similar pressures to publish and disseminate our work widely and efficiently. The writing group allowed us to support each other in this process. As a result of "connecting with other scholars," as one author put it, the task of writing feels less isolating. In taking us out of our offices, the writing group not only fosters a generative space where new ideas are visualized and produced, but new friendships and mentorships are formed. Many new writing and research partnerships emerged out of our writing group. One author commented that "there is an undercurrent of positive influence that we share with one another that helps propel us forward, even when we are writing alone." The collaborative and social nature of writing group clearly reached beyond our regular meetings. People worked in teams, participated in writing retreats and reported cultivating a more regular writing practice as a result of attending meetings.

In relation to the theme of collaboration, the authors reflected on the importance of the writing group fostering a safe space where ideas and concerns could be shared freely. One wrote, "We need to be able to share our vulnerabilities and feel like we can ask questions without the fear of being ridiculed." The

ADVANCING THE WRITING OF ACADEMICS 61

safety of our writing group space challenged us to work and think in new and exciting ways; we took risks because we felt safe to do so. An author explained that, "writing group needs to challenge us. We need to be encouraged and nudged to try new things and aim higher with the kinds of writing projects we undertake." Indeed, sharing our writing – "talking about it, learning to do it, sharing tips, and reading each other's drafts for specific feedback" – is what moved our work in exciting new directions – directions that might not have otherwise been possible without the collaborative nature of this shared space.

Learning with and from Each Other

The writing group provided an opportunity to learn *with* and *from* each other. As mentioned previously, we came to the writing group at varying stages of our careers and with diverse research programs of study. One author shared that "writing group provides us with an opportunity to reflect on our practice while hearing about the successes and struggles of each other. In sharing our writing practices with one another, our own finished products are inevitably changed." Another noted that "within this place and space of writing group, we learn with and from each other, as well as bring others in to share expertise to help us develop our academic writing skills [and] understand where and how to mobilize our scholarly work." Reflecting on the writing process in conversation with colleagues, one participant commented: "I am now more alert to possibilities to undertake writing projects, [to] mobilizing knowledge in new (even experimental) ways. I still focus intently on writing peer reviewed scholarly articles and book chapters, [but also] open access works." In addition to the influence of members, the writing group participants learn from the guest speakers brought in on a regular basis. One author recounted how "in one session, we each shared our work on a [large computer monitor in the room] and the senior scholar along with the group did editing of that section. It was an excellent learning experience." Learning with and from each other in different ways encouraged and challenged us to take our writing in new directions.

Time and the Prioritization of Writing

The third theme that emerged from the data was the importance of prioritizing the craft of writing through scheduled time. While the writing group provided a space for collaboration and conversations, it also was intended to provide scholars with individual blocks of time for writing. One author explained the schedule as such: "the two-part of the writing group day, provides 30 to 40 minutes to learn from an expert or learn from colleagues. The other 60 to 90 minutes is designed to be my writing time." One person commented that this particular time frame was useful because it offered "an opportunity for networking and discussion, while also providing time for quiet writing." The writing group typically occurred in the mornings, which some participants appreciated. "It is a great way to start a day .... It also communicates that it is a priority to allocate time at the start of the day for writing, rather than tagging it on later in the day."

Adding to this notion of prioritizing, another member of the writing group explained, "it is giving me time in my calendar during a busy week to have time for writing during the day. Scheduling dedicated writing time after our group meetings meant that I had time to write and submit [an] article within two terms." The dual intention of writing group – split into shared conversation followed by individual writing time – was an effective strategy. It allowed our group to be collaborative and social, and at the same time, prioritize a scheduled block of time for individual writing.

The Future of the Writing Group

Within their responses, the writing group members made recommendations for the future, including both things they wanted to change as well as those they wanted to remain the same. A consistent desire for future writing group cycles was a renewed focus on peer feedback, a concentration which seems to have dwindled over the years that writing group has been in practice. One person described peer feedback "where each semester people worked in pairs or triads in sharing components of the work for feedback." This participant went on to say "It is good to receive feedback. It also helps colleagues to formulate feedback. It is a commitment."

Similarly, another person talked about how meeting and talking about our writing "fostered a sense of commitment and accountability" with peers. She went on to say, when working with peer editing, "it was critical for me to have my writing completed to share and for me to commit to providing feedback on my colleagues' work."

In addition to peer feedback and editing, a desire for collaborative writing emerged, linking back to the theme of writing as a collaborative and social practice. One member noted, "it would be good to see various groups work together in writing. Also to see people from the writing group writing together." One person specifically noted the need for writing group to evolve in terms of membership ("new blood") in order for them to evolve as a writer. "It would be easy to rest on our laurels and stay the (relatively) closed group that we have become." This person noted that if the group wanted to expand, "we/the organizers need to: (a) revisit whether the gift of time motto/commitment works for all potential members; (b) find alternative (possibly technological) means to connect potential members with the group; and (c) onboard new faculty

ADVANCING THE WRITING OF ACADEMICS

members to be immediately included in writing group." As participants gained experience with writing group, they developed a sense of what would keep the writing group moving forward.

Recommendations for Practice

Drawing from our collective experience, we, the authors and members of a writing group, offer these four recommendations for developing a sustainable and productive writing group.

Set the Tone

As we reflected on our experience, we recognized that having a supportive environment is needed for members to ask questions, share stories, and expose vulnerabilities. There is a need to create a safe space for members to learn and grow. In our case, having designated facilitators who were consistent from one academic year to the next provided a sense of continuity to the group. The facilitators were largely responsible for setting the tone, which members then maintained throughout the process.

Include Peer Feedback

Our members reported that one of the most valuable aspects of the group was engaging in peer feedback with one another. After a safe space had been created, members develop a deep sense of trust where they feel comfortable asking for and receiving feedback on their writing in progress. This is a concrete activity that keeps members accountable for producing writing in time to be reviewed by fellow members. This practice further enhances the likelihood that writers will produce writing as a result of their involvement with the group.

Actively Recruit New Members

Our results showed that members felt colleagues could have benefitted from writing group, but also that new members added a sense of energy and vitality. It may not be enough to advertise the group meetings in e-mails, posters, or newsletters. It may also require the regular members to take on the responsibility of actively recruiting new colleagues to join by reaching out on a personal level.

Elicit Feedback to Inform Practice

Facilitators ask participants for feedback on the structure of the group and what worked. Facilitators then use this feedback to develop a structured program for the next semester. For example, one semester, the group focused on writing for impact. Participants review the program structure for each semester and agree to the overall plan as a group.

Celebrate

We recognized that the writing group members have busy lives with a variety of demands on their time. Although the writing group helped us to be more productive, the results of connecting on a regular basis also included developing a sense of camaraderie and community. This in turn helped us to keep a balanced view about producing scholarly outputs and growing together as scholars. Scheduling a celebration provides an opportunity to conclude the academic year on a high note and provide an opportunity to reflect on successes. It is about taking time to acknowledge our good work and time together as writers.

Conclusion

After situating the role of writing groups in fostering a culture of writing within the heightened expectations of today's post-secondary environments, this chapter recounted the authors' own experiences as writing group participants, utilizing Schön's (1983) reflection-in-action and reflection-on-action model as a framework for understanding the experiences. Thematic analysis of the authors' reflective narratives affirmed the value of writing socially and collaboratively, with the writing group providing opportunities to learn both from and alongside colleagues. What we described as our experiences contrasts with traditional images of writing as a solitary activity. The value of peer feedback on writing drafts emerged as an additional benefit of this collegial learning. The narratives highlighted the role of the writing group in supplying authors with a regular, fixed, blocked time for writing, which was seen as key to prioritizing writing among the often competing demands of academic work.

Drawing upon their collective experience as writing group participants, the authors attested to the importance of fostering a group climate of collegial trust and support. They acknowledged the role and opportunity for constructive peer feedback being offered and received as part of growth as academic writers. Further, they noted the central role of group leadership in consistently creating and nurturing such an environment for new and experienced scholars in the field. As part of their next steps, the authors appreciated the need for widening the circle of membership as well as continuing with celebrations of participants' achievements for maintaining a vibrant, productive and sustainable writing group which can continue to facilitate the ongoing development of academics' writing capacity.

References

Castle, J., & Keane, M. (2016). Five writing development strategies to help academics flourish as writers. *South African Journal of Higher Education, 30*(6), 73–93. doi:10.20853/30-6-721

Grant, B. (2006). Writing in the company of other women: Exceeding the boundaries. *Studies in Higher Education, 31*(4), 483–495. doi:10.1080/03075070600800624

Grant, M. J., Munro, W., McIsaac, J., & Hill, S. (2010). Cross disciplinary writers' group stimulates fresh approaches to scholarly communication: A reflective case study within a higher education institution in the North West of England. *New Review of Academic Librarianship, 16*(Sup 1), 44–64. doi:10.1080/13614533.2010.509481

Kamler, B. (2008). Rethinking doctoral publication practices: Writing from and beyond the thesis, *Studies in Higher Education, 33*(3), 283–294. doi:10.1080/03075070802049236

Lave, J., & Wenger, E. (1991). *Situated learning: Legitimate peripheral participation.* Cambridge: Cambridge University Press.

Moodley, P. (2017). Open spaces: The new frontier for academic writers. *South African Journal of Higher Education, 31*(2), 108–123. doi:10.20853/31-2-1342

Moore, S. (2003). Writers' retreats for academics: Exploring and increasing the motivation to write. *Journal of Further and Higher Education, 27*(3), 333–342. doi:10.1080/0309877032000098734

Olszewska, K., & Lock, J. (2016). Examining success and sustainability of academic writing: A case study of two writing-group models. *Canadian Journal of Higher Education, 46*(4), 132–145.

Paxton, M., Garraway, J., & Bozalek, V. (2017). Problematising writing retreats for academic staff in higher education. *South African Journal of Higher Education, 32*(2), 1–3. doi:10.20853/31-2-1349

Saldaña, J. (2016). *The coding manual for qualitative researchers* (3rd ed.). Thousand Oaks, CA: Sage.

Schön, D. (1983). *The reflective practitioner: How professionals think in action.* London: Temple Smith.

Steinert, Y., McLeod, P., Liben, S., & Snell, L. (2008). Writing for publication in medical education: The benefits of a faculty development workshop and peer writing group. *Medical Teacher, 30*, 280–285. doi:10.1080/01421590802337120

Wenger, E. (1998). *Communities of practice: Learning, meaning and identity.* New York, NY: Cambridge University Press.

CHAPTER 6

Faculty Writing Studio: A Place to Write

Remica Bingham-Risher and Joyce Armstrong

Abstract

This chapter investigates the importance of a separate place for faculty to leave their offices and go to a place on campus to write. Drawbacks of writing in one's office and at one's home are examined. A faculty member needs to be separated from daily tasks and interruptions to concentrate on the business of writing and a Faculty Writing Studio meets this need. Collaboration is also available for faculty who wish to discuss writing, projects, and grants. The dedicated space for writing and research is an outward show of an institution's support to the faculty's writing. Both quantitative and qualitative data are presented.

Keywords

place – writing – faculty writing – academic writing – writing spaces – writing groups – collaboration

Amid the mounting emails, student papers, department meetings and university service – not to mention home life – where and how do faculty find time to be productive participants in their chosen disciplines? When and where do they process information and synthesize it, so that it begins to gel into new insights to add to the collective field of information in their discipline? For many, the pressures of research and writing for promotion and tenure mean that their productivity is linked to job security, and this added weight can make the difficult task of writing a more daunting, even crippling, one. So, how can institutions support faculty in their writing endeavors, especially since those endeavors are part of their required university life? And where should a faculty member write to aid in their productivity? Should they write in their campus office, at home, in a library, or some other place? Is solitude important, or does finding a writing group have tangible benefits?

© KONINKLIJKE BRILL NV, LEIDEN, 2019 | DOI:10.1163/9789004410985_006

Virginia Woolf, a modernist writer and early feminist, in her essay *A Room of One's Own* suggests the importance of finding a particular *place* where one is able to write. For faculty, place is certainly not the only but often one of the most difficult parts of the writing equation. Trying to write in their office on campus presents constant challenges, as the campus office is not designed for writing; instead, it is designed as a site for office work not necessarily a place for creativity (Jensen, 2017). When faculty glance around their offices, they see notes from the latest committee report, calendars filled with things that must be accomplished, students in need of immediate attention, the ringing telephone, all manner of messages that must be answered, papers that need to be graded and a myriad of other distractions that make writing in the office during office hours nearly impossible. The idea that, at some institutions, faculty need to be observed in their office, always visible and working constructively, adds to the frustration of finding a place to write.

Of course, when a faculty member decides to write at home, other complications arise. The dream of fashioning a perfect writing space might quickly disintegrate into a makeshift place of clutter and storage for other projects filled with its own interruptions – hungry or harried children and partners, the dog barking, laundry that needs to be done, or ever unfinished projects around the house. So where can anyone write successfully?

Current research details the importance of writing groups as a means to encourage faculty members. Houfek et al. (2009) write about the barriers to academic writing, such as intrapersonal characteristics, faculty role complexity, and time constraints, while Burns (2010) describes how the pressure to publish in higher education is eased when faculty work together in a writing group. An article describing how to support academic publications (Richard, McGrail, Jones, O'Meara, Robinson, Burley, & Ray-Barruel, 2009) stresses the importance of a writers' group to offset some of these challenges (Elbow & Sorcinell, 2006).

Old Dominion University's Faculty Writing Studio

These were guiding questions at Old Dominion University (ODU) – a large liberal arts college with nearly 30,000 students and over 800 full-time faculty members – several years ago after the successful launch of a new faculty development initiative on campus. In 2012, ODU's Quality Enhancement Plan, *Improving Disciplinary Writing*, was launched as a means "to improve upper division undergraduate students' disciplinary writing – that is, writing that demonstrates a reasoning process supported by research and reflection on a problem, topic or issue – through two faculty development and engagement initiatives." *Improving Disciplinary Writing* is made up of two faculty initiatives: (1) Faculty Workshops and (2) Action Projects (internal grants). While these initiatives focused on improving writing pedagogy, faculty began thinking more about the importance of the writing process and their own practice in the field, many shared their exasperation about the lack of space and time to work on their own writing, as well as to help teach and improve students' writing in their courses. Moreover, ODU faculty were in need of a dedicated, physical space that allowed them to work individually or collaboratively on writing research and pedagogy along with developing and honing the best practices highlighted in the IDW Faculty Workshops and Action Projects.

As a means of supporting faculty, a Faculty Writing Studio (FWS) was created by the Executive Director for Academic Enhancement and the Director of Writing and Faculty Development and housed in a permanent room on the second floor of the university's Student Success Center in the Fall 2014. The approach to improve faculty writing partnerships on our campus was based upon the idea of an FWS developed by Elbow and Sorcinelli (2006) at the University of Massachusetts-Amherst. An FWS is a dedicated space to allow faculty to do their own writing in conjunction with one or more team members. This space (FWS) needs to be maintained with writing equipment and resources for faculty to be most useful. ODU's Faculty Writing Studio was designed to serve as: (1) an external work space for faculty who are completing writing and research projects and (2) a meeting space for faculty interested in working collaboratively on writing or improving a disciplinary writing. Our FWS is fairly small – the tables have seating for eight, there's one comfy armchair and two computer nooks with seating, so a maximum of 11 people can work comfortably together. In addition to workstations and spaces, the FWS includes a writing library with resources to assist with various facets of the writing process, developing writing ePortfolios, writing pedagogy, and multidisciplinary collaboration. The FWS is open to any faculty member who wishes to take advantage of a quiet, stress-free atmosphere in order to write.

After the launch of ODU's Faculty Writing Studio, focused workshop sessions were developed to help draw faculty into the space. In 2014, before the launch of these workshops, a committee of campus constituents who had some investment in faculty writing and research considered several factors when creating workshops to be offered in the FWS, such as: Does this topic address a gap in ODU's writing/research agenda? Who (which faculty member on campus who has some expertise in the area) can we get to teach this workshop? Which faculty groups can we target to participate in this workshop? How can we best

FACULTY WRITING STUDIO   69

market this workshop? With these ideas in mind, the original FWS workshops covered a wide range of topics including: IMRAD (Introduction, Methods, Research [and] Discussion) research writing, Dissertation Boot Camp, End-of-Semester Wrap-Up & Reflect, Poets and Creative Writers Working Group, Diverse Faculty: Meeting the Challenges of Academia, and Writing-intensive "W" Course Brown Bag Sessions. The sessions generally met weekly for four to six weeks, with each session scheduled for one to two hours (with the exception of the Dissertation Boot Camp which was offered in four-hour blocks). In 2016, an *Improving Capstone Courses* Workshop was designed and held in the FWS. During the *Improving Capstone Courses* sessions, leveraging the same workshop model used for ODU's Quality Enhancement Plan, five faculty members worked to re-design or create new capstone (i.e., a senior thesis, seminar or internship) courses by focusing on the following themes: integrative learning (based on the Association of American Colleges & Universities outcomes rubric), course and curriculum mapping, reflections and metacognition, and project-based learning/real-world experience. Our objective was to create and offer unique programming that touched on as many areas of interest as possible, in hopes of peaking the interest of as many faculty members as possible and getting them to head to the FWS. To promote the workshops and the FWS itself, an open house event was held in the space as soon as it was available and open to all faculty on campus. An online survey response system was used to gauge interest in workshop topics and track requests for scheduling the FWS for writing sessions.

The faculty who were early adopters of the FWS tended to request the space repeatedly and, by 2015, even began forming their own writing groups. Many were faculty who previously participated in the ODU QEP: *Improving Disciplinary Writing* Workshops, and this common ground helped link multidisciplinary faculty and aided in the creation of FWS groups. As FWS attendance increased, more faculty seemed solely interested in the space as a dedicated, physical space for working individually or collaboratively on their own writing and research than a space that facilitated that writing by means of workshops overseen by others, and attendance began to increase even without the creation of new theme-based workshops that might respond to faculty needs. What faculty needed and valued most was imminently clear: physical space and time to do the work without interruption, and a few other colleagues alongside them in the space to help ensure accountability.

In 2015, ODU had 830 full-time instructional faculty (ODU, n.d.). By the end of 2014, 113 workshop attendees had taken part in FWS workshops (though that number was bolstered by the many faculty who came to preview the space during the open house event). With the launch of the workshops, by the end of 2015, 72 attendees had taken part in FWS sessions. By the end of 2016, three

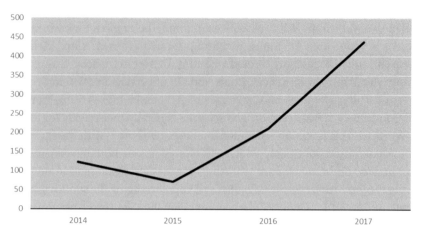

FIGURE 6.1   Faculty writing studio attendance by year

times as many attendees used the FWS as in 2015, as 212 faculty and staff members utilized the space. By the end of 2017, even though no pre-designed workshop sessions were offered, more than twice as many attendees had come as in 2016, as 438 faculty and staff members used the FWS space for writing, research and collaboration.

Thematic Responses from the Survey

In 2017, to gauge how faculty used the space and why they valued it, the most frequent users and writing group leaders were asked to respond to two open-ended reflection questions: *How has the Faculty Writing Studio helped with your own writing and research? Why is having a space like this at ODU beneficial for all faculty?* The authors analyzed the qualitative data by reading the reflective questions, then coding the responses. We coded the reflections by writing memos capturing the categories that emerged after several readings. As analysis, we compared codes and organized the codes into themes that could be confirmed by the data set. After coding the reflection responses, three major themes emerged (research and personal advancement, distance from distractions, and collaboration) along with several other recurring ideas (stress-free environment/safe space, helping faculty feel less alone in a solitary task, and the FWS as an acknowledgment of university support).

Research and Personal Advancement
When we compared the responses from our sample, the first pattern we observed was linked to research and personal advancement. All (5/5) of the

FACULTY WRITING STUDIO   71

respondents noted that the FWS contributed to their field research, promotion and tenure work, and/or their personal advancement. In academia, faculty feel an immense pressure to publish. Decisions are made about hiring, tenure and promotion based on publication rates (Burns, 2010); the phrase "publish or perish" isn't just an empty idiom, in academia, it is the truth (Burns, 2010). To that end, in their reflection one faculty respondent commented that the FWS helps with the "daunting progression [of moving] towards big goals such as tenure or manuscript production" (R3). When promotion committees meet one of the first questions that the committee asks is what is the history of publication? Are there peer reviewed articles, books, is the person the first or second author on an article and are they consistent in their publication output? The answer to these questions could make or break a faculty member. "Failure to publish within the expected norms established by a college or university can result in a faculty member's termination" (Burns, 2010, p. 1). If the tenure and promotion committee is not satisfied, then a faculty member could be denied promotion and/or terminated. A third respondent went so far as to list the types of research that the FWS has helped facilitate both for the writing group on the whole and individually:

> We've generated numerous successful grant proposals, book chapters, manuscript submissions, and journal articles. For me personally, in the last nine months, I have written three successful research grant proposals, as well as three accepted journal articles, all written in the Faculty Writing Studio. (R5)

Another respondent called the FWS "a physical space which facilitates dedicated focus and attention to scholarly writing activities" (R4).

Distance from Distractions

The second theme that all (5/5) of the faculty respondents mentioned was that the FWS helped with writing because of its distance from distractions, particularly that of the campus office space. Elbow and Sorcinell (2006) wrote that the purpose of a faculty writing place is to "provide a quiet [space], free of the distractions of office or home" (p. 18). One radical solution to the problem of space was presented by Murray and Newton (2009). The structured place they describe is an hour's drive from their university, with no network coverage (Internet or mobile phone signal) our FWS certainly differs here, as it is on campus, linked to all of the university's online networks and online collaboration is encouraged. Items needed for writing had to be loaded onto laptops or brought on a memory stick. Although this is extreme, the structured place

Murray and Newton (2009) wrote about brought positive comments from participants. Emulating this idea but adding convenience by making it a space on campus might be the silver bullet to many faculty members' writing woes. One of the ODU respondents notes, "Faculty need a place to process things and work through writing challenges without interruptions" (R1). Another reflection notes, "It is beneficial because it offers faculty a physical space which limits distractions, unexpected interruptions, and a place which helps maintain time dedicated specifically to writing tasks" (R4). A third explains:

> The space also provides location that is far enough from my office that I can come here to work and really manage my distractions. No office phone, no colleagues stopping by to chat, no one coming by to ask questions outside of office hours ... this is a place where I come to write ... Because of this it helps to set the tone, if you will, that now is the time to work. (R2)

Collaboration

Collaboration also emerged as a major theme in the reflections, as 4/5 of the respondents mentioned that the FWS fostered their working with others to complete writing projects. Writing collaboration is a complex process that can be defined in many ways. For instance, the collaboration could be co-contribution (multiple authors give ideas), co-authorship (two or more authors write and edit a single piece), co-writing (two or more people sit down and compose the piece at the same time) or co-existence (two authors are writing in the same place but their article is not related to each other) (Sword, 2017). The FWS facilitates multi-faceted collaboration in various ways. One faculty member explained that the way the FWS space is organized helps facilitate collaborative writing sessions for all: "The FWS has helped my collaborators and I work more effectively together .... Having a space like the writing lab is beneficial for all faculty (even lecturers) because it is designed to be a productive space. The space and arrangement of furniture facilitates collaboration and productivity (e.g., plug-ins for laptops, projectors, whiteboard/wall, desktop computer, teleconference capability)" (R2). After commenting on how the FWS helps faculty focus on scholarly writing, another respondent remarked, "More importantly, it creates the opportunity to network with other tenure track faculty whose drive, techniques, and simple compassion have been invaluable to maintaining the focus and momentum necessary to finish projects" (R4). As professional identity is also tied to publication, Henderson and Buchanan (2007) report that faculty believe in the importance of scholarship as part of their professional identity as it contributes to the health of the academic community in

FACULTY WRITING STUDIO

general. Echoing this idea, one faculty member noted that collaboration that began in the FWS has extended well beyond the space and to more than just scholarly support:

> The Faculty Writing Studio has been an amazing space for our faculty writing group. We presently have 14 regular writers, and we meet both in the Writing Studio as well as virtually .... What cannot really be expressed in words is the camaraderie that the space has fostered for our group. As we have met there in person and continued our conversations in our online forum, the support has been tremendous. We have weekly challenges and check-ins, and when we have encountered difficulty, we have lifted each other up. This summer, we listened to each other when we had writer's block; we challenged each other to find work life balance during the summer months and semester; we set goals that included writing as well as mental and physical health; we helped edit each other's work; and we encouraged each other when we were feeling defeated. (R5)

Recurring Ideas

While not emerging as major themes, 3/5 of the reflections touched on the ideas that the FWS is a stress-free environment/safe space; it helps faculty feel less alone in an often solitary task and that having the FWS on campus is an acknowledgment of support from the university.

When faculty have the opportunity to meet in a safe, quiet, comfortable working place apart from distractions, they are able to focus on their writing (Elbow & Sorcinelli, 2006). "Safe" in this instance means a space away from the eyes and ears or more senior faculty, department chairs, deans, etcetera, but also a space free from the routine onslaught of distraction. Often other faculty who are trudging away at the same kinds of writing tasks are just looking for peers who can relate to the difficulties they encounter along the path to publication, tenue or both, and the FWS provided that "safe" space in many instances. A respondent noted of the FWS:

> Personally, it has been a safe quiet space for me to work through the tenure requirements. I have been able to ask questions on my interpretation of things and use the computer and screen to show what I was thinking then discuss why it is accurate or not. I feel like it is a stress-free environment with no judgment. (R1)

A second respondent mentioned that the FWS even encourages faculty from different disciplines to work together, "The space has been really important to us for two reasons. First, it has given us a quiet space with ample room to spread out. This may seem insignificant, but there is nowhere else on campus where we can regularly gather without distraction to write. Second, the space has enabled us to join together across colleges to form our group. From the College of Engineering to Arts and Letters, we have nearly all of the colleges represented in our writing group. Having a space that is in a 'neutral' location makes it easier for us to find new members who don't think that it is a college specific group" (R5).

Several respondents mentioned how daunting a task writing can be, especially when tied to personal advancement. For some, the FWS helped them feel less alone. One respondent said: "It is also fostering a sense of community among those of us who use it, building in accountability and helping us feel less alone in what is often a solitary task .... Feeling good about writing produces better and more writing!" (R3). Elbow and Sorcinelli (2006) report about how a writing space should be focused on opportunity not remediation: "Sometimes there's a palpable feeling of concentration in the air – and attention and involvement ... it can contribute to a faculty member's sense of self and public image as a serious writer" (p. 20).

Lastly, the majority of respondents also noted that the FWS itself is an acknowledgment of university support, as there are few resources or spaces on campus that support faculty productivity and research outside of their office. "ODU has such scant resources for research, especially for humanities faculty, that any extra support is welcome. A dedicated space for writing is at least an acknowledgment that we do need such support, be it material, financial, or psychological" (R3), noted one colleague. Since academic publication is crucial to a faculty member's advancement, a FWS is one way an institution can offer support to help them navigate this process. Likewise, Moore (2003) adds that support of a faculty member's writing represents a valuable professional development opportunity provided by a university.

Recommendations

At ODU, the creation of our FWS has helped faculty be more productive writers. There are several general recommendations we can share about how an institution might design their own space for writing.

Designate a Physical Space
All of our faculty noted that just having a physical space on campus set aside for writing enhanced their productivity. To find a space, we put together a

FACULTY WRITING STUDIO 75

committee of campus partners who were invested in writing and research to help think through some of the obstacles that might be involved in launching a new initiative. Our FWS was an unused double-sized office with a door that at one time housed several cubicles for graduate student tutors – we took out the cubicles, put in tables and chairs that can be rearranged, painted the walls a bright color, added computer workstations, floating shelves and a large collaborative computer. We also added overhead lights and found lamps that could be used as alternate lighting to accommodate individual lighting preferences. We wanted the space to be bright and inviting (similar to a bookstore nook) but also wanted to ensure that there was plenty of table space for spreading out with papers, laptops, etc. When creating a physical space, you don't have to have lots of room, just having any room designated for writing may be enough to get faculty interested. Another important caveat was that our FWS was not placed in any of the traditional academic buildings that would have made certain disciplines feel like it was "their" space. We chose a central location away from most faculty offices, so that all faculty would feel like it was a bit of an escape from the traditional settings of their offices and/or departments.

Publicize the Space

There is generally so much going on campus at our institution that it is sometimes difficult to not feel like you are siloed. Part of the reason our FWS has been successful is because we set out to publicize it in various ways. When creating your space, make certain to get the word out to faculty. Utilize campus announcements, mass emails, flyers and send out invitations to an open house (make sure to offer refreshments and some will come just for the brownies!) to get faculty into and acquainted with the space. While they are there, have them respond to a one or two question survey about the types of workshops they would like to see offered or about how they would most like to use the space. Soon after, send out an email to all who came to remind them of specific workshops that link to their interests or just have them email the person who is designated to oversee the space to reserve it (e.g., faculty send an email requesting use of the space, their writing time is blocked off on a digital FWS calendar and a confirmation is sent).

Share Accomplishments with the Academic Community

To help engender continuous buy-in from faculty, encourage others to visit and to get administrators and gatekeepers onboard, find ways to share faculty accomplishments and feedback about the FWS with the campus community. At ODU, we have added highlights about journal publications, conference presentations and book chapters to our *Improving Disciplinary Writing* ePortfolio that can be linked directly to time spent in the FWS. In addition, we've reported about the growing number of faculty using the FWS and created presentations that highlight their feedback about the usefulness of the space which we have presented at university leadership (i.e. Provost's Council, Deans Retreats, etc.) meetings each year. Once faculty begin coming to the FWS on your campus, note who the 'writing leaders' are and ask them to reflect on how the space has helped them be productive. If there are regular forums to highlight faculty accomplishments or innovative strategy or research on your campus, find ways to link your own FWS to those high-profile events, as a means of helping to ensure others know the value of an FWS on campus.

Conclusion

One needs to be separated from daily tasks and interruptions to concentrate on the business of writing. An institution should provide a space – aside from faculty offices – for faculty to come together to write because of the importance of writing (i.e., in the journey to promotion, advancement of knowledge in one's field, cross-disciplinary collaboration, and personal success) for each faculty member. Providing a dedicated space for faculty writing and research is an outward show of an institution's being as supportive as possible of these endeavors. When faculty have a 'room of their own,' the space can create a much-needed support system for the arduous road to tenure, living life as an academic, and adding to the ever-growing body of scholarly thought.

References

Burns, B. (2010). Working together to ease the pressure to publish in higher education. *Academic Leadership: The Online Journal, 8*(4), Article 80.

Cameron, J., Nairn, K., & Higgins, J. (2009). Demystifying academic writing: Reflections on emotions, know-how and academic identity. *Journal of Geography in Higher Education, 33*(2), 269–284.

Elbow, P., & Sorcinelli, M. D. (2006). The faculty writing place: A room of our own. *Change: The Magazine of Higher Learning, 38*(6), 17–22.

Henderson, B. B., & Buchanan, H. E. (2007). The scholarship of teaching and learning: A special niche for faculty at comprehensive universities. *Research in Higher Education, 48*(5), 523–543.

Houfek, J. F., Kaiser, K. L., Visovsky, C., Barry, T. L., Nelson, A. E., Kaiser, M. M., & Miller, C. L. (2010). Using a writing group to promote faculty scholarship. *Nurse Educator, 35*(1), 41–45.

Jensen, J. (2017). *Write no matter what: Advice for academics.* Chicago, IL & London, UK: The University of Chicago Press.

Moore, S. (2003). Writers' retreats for academics: Exploring and increasing the motivation to write. *Journal of Further and Higher Education, 23*(3), 333–342.

Murray, R., & Newton, M. (2009). Writing retreat as structured intervention: Margin or mainstream? *Higher Education Research & Development, 28*(5), 541–553.

Old Dominion University. (n.d.). *Factbook.* Retrieved from http://www.odu.edu/content/odu/about/facts-and-figures/factbook.html

Richard, C. M., McGrail, M. R., Jones, R., O'Meara, P., Robinson, A., Burley, M., & Ray-Barruel, G. (2009). Supporting academic publication: Evaluation of a writing course combined with writers' support group. *Nurse Education Today, 29*(5), 516–521.

Steinert, Y., McLeod, P., Liben, S., & Snell, L. (2008). Writing for publication in medical education: The benefits of a faculty development workshop and peer writing group. *Journal Medical Teacher, 30*(8), e280–e285.

Sword, H., (2017). *Air & light & time & space: How successful academics write.* Cambridge, MA: Harvard University Press.

CHAPTER 7

Campus-Wide, Non-Residential, Five-Day Faculty Writing Retreat: Partnerships Lead to a Sustainable Writing Program

Dannelle D. Stevens and Janelle Voegele

Abstract

More and more institutions are expecting faculty to write and publish their work. Yet, many faculty do not have the tools and strategies that undergird a sustainable and successful writing practice. Some researchers assert that universities should find ways to support faculty as writers. For five years, our university has partnered with the campus center for teaching and learning to sponsor a summer five-day non-residential faculty writing retreat. The purpose of this chapter is to describe the university partnership as well the partnerships among faculty across the campus that have grown out of this retreat program. Besides a full description of the program, we identify four key themes from faculty evaluations of the retreat. Finally, we include suggestions for others who might be interested in creating writing retreats that support faculty success as writers.

Keywords

writing retreat – non-residential writing retreat – institutional partnership – academic writing practice – cross-disciplinary – writing program

One week after the graduates receive fresh bouquets, heartfelt hugs, and cheery congratulations, the university hallways are empty. Yet, at the remotely-located child development centre 18 faculty begin trickling into the five-day non-residential summer writing retreat. Walking past the little cubbies for the 2-year-old "stargazers" and 3-year-old "lilliputs," they find the elevator to venture up to the ever-so-quiet third floor meeting rooms. All faculty members have individual tables with extension cords to keep their devices charged. "Shh-hh" signs abound. The savory scents of breakfast goodies rise from the food and coffee/tea table. Most will be in the room from 9am to 2pm; others will come

© KONINKLIJKE BRILL NV, LEIDEN, 2019 | DOI:10.1163/9789004410985_007

CAMPUS-WIDE, NON-RESIDENTIAL, FIVE-DAY FACULTY WRITING RETREAT 79

earlier and stay later. This is the first of two writing retreats that the centre for teaching and learning has offered each summer for the last five years. The competition for attendance is keen; only about half who apply are invited to participate in the retreat. The aim of this chapter is to describe the partnerships with the university administration and the participants that undergird the retreat's success and its continuation for the last five years. We address three questions: What are the goals and structure of the retreat? How do faculty evaluate the impact of the retreat and its activities on their writing practice during and after the retreat? What do we recommend to others about forming partnerships to build a strong foundation for a successful writing retreat program?

The foundation for this multi-year successful endeavor is two types of partnerships. We define a partnership as a mutually beneficial relationship between two or more entities. The first partnership is between the university administration and the centre for teaching and learning, called the Portland State University Office of Academic Innovation (OAI). The university administration, Office of Academic Affairs, approves the budget and OAI provides advertising, logistics, food, and salary for the facilitator. With the rising expectations that faculty write and publish, the administrative support is clear evidence of its commitment to helping faculty as writers. Even though the mission of OAI is primarily to improve teaching and student learning, the retreat is a demonstration of OAI's underlying philosophy that academic writing and teaching are interdependent activities in the full professional life of faculty. Supporting faculty as writers helps them balance writing and teaching and, for some, integrate new writing strategies into their teaching.

The writing retreat also fosters a second set of partnerships, that is, connections among faculty during the retreat. Various activities encourage faculty to share their daily writing goals as well as their successful practices. One example is that the retreat facilitators (the authors), assign cross-disciplinary faculty buddies who meet every day to discuss writing goals for the next day.

Our faculty writing retreat model responds to the current context of faculty writing and publishing. Writing and publishing expectations are becoming ubiquitous. In national and international contexts, more and more faculty are expected to submit their work for publication (Dickson-Swift, James, Talbot, Verrinder, & Ward, 2009; MacLeod, Steckley, & Murray, 2012; Roberts & Weston, 2014). Yet, most faculty members have not received formal training on the craft associated with being an academic such as teaching and committee work that often compete with writing (Cameron, Nairn, & Higgins, 2009; Hjortshoj, 2001; MacLeod et al., 2012). McGrail, Richert, and Jones (2006) reviewed 17 studies of "structured writing interventions" address faculty writing and publication needs. These interventions had positive outcomes including an increase in publication rates and generating "support, encouragement and motivation" (p. 30). One of the successful structured writing interventions was writing support groups such as writing retreats. Yet, not all writing retreats are the same.

Faculty writing retreats occur in a variety of disciplines and have an array of different structures. According to Stanley, Home, Chu, and Joiner (2017),

> Writing retreat is defined as a prescribed period of time during which one geographically separates oneself from a typical or routine work environment for the distinct purpose of writing (as opposed to work-related activities more broadly) with other like-minded individuals with the same purpose. (p. 250)

The prescribed time is usually between two and five days. Some retreats are residential where faculty leave the campus and stay overnight at a remote spot to focus on writing (Cable, Boyer, Colbert, & Boyer, 2013: Grant & Knowles, 2000; Moore, 2003; Murray & Newton, 2009). Writing retreats are found in different disciplines: public health (Dickson-Swift et al., 2009), psychology (Stanley, Hom, Chu, & Joiner, 2017), medicine (Cable et al., 2013), nursing (Jackson, 2009), and education (Murray & Cunningham, 2011; Murray & Newton, 2009; Roberts & Weston, 2014; Swaggerty, Atkinson, Faulconer, & Griffith, 2011). In addition, the structure of writing retreats can include goal setting, peer support, skill-based workshops, peer feedback on writing, team building, and catered food. Some retreats are the culmination of pre-work among faculty mentors and mentees (Cable et al., 2013); others are a follow-up to a year-long program on writing skills (Roberts & Weston, 2014). Examples of research on writing retreats hail from the United Kingdom (MacLeod et al., 2012; Moore, 2003), Australia (Dickson-Swift et al., 2009; Jackson, 2009), New Zealand (Grant & Knowles, 2000), and the United States (Stanley et al., 2017; Swaggerty et al., 2011).

Writing retreats seem to foster a bevy of positive outcomes for faculty. Several researchers found that the sense of being in a community of writers developed during the retreat (Grant & Knowles, 2000; Roberts & Weston, 2014). Faculty appreciated the dedicated time for writing and feedback from their peers (Dickson-Swift et al., 2009; Jackson, 2009; Roberts & Weston, 2014). Another positive outcome was that faculty incorporated the retreat strategies into their subsequent writing (Murray & Newton, 2009). MacLeod, Steckley, and Murray (2012) noted the value of writing retreats in helping participants manage the emotions of writing and understanding more about the writing process:

> [Faculty] identified [that] the benefits of [writing retreats} were twofold: first, increased confidence from seeing more experienced writers

struggling – like them – but also modeling working through those struggles; and, second, working through their thoughts and difficulties with other writers in a way that reduced anxiety. (p. 648)

Writing retreats helped faculty in a number of significant ways from feeling more connected to a community of writers, incorporating new writing strategies into their skill set, and increasing their confidence as writers.

While writing retreats offer a considerable number of benefits to faculty as writers, we wonder who on campus should be responsible for organizing and offering writing retreats. On one hand, some studies show that departments have successfully sponsored retreats (Cable et al., 2013; Dickson-Swift et al., 2013; Stanley et al., 2017). On the other hand, reaching out to the entire campus, university administrations can play a role in supporting interventions like writing retreats. From their review study, McGrail et al. (2006) concluded with this recommendation:

We recommend that universities support the development of structured interventions for their staff in order to increase their writing for publication. A regular, ongoing arrangement seems to be most beneficial, with a format that can be adapted to meet the needs of the attendees. (p. 34)

Aitchison and Lee (2006) echoed this recommendation, "research writing pedagogies need to become incorporated into 'the way we do things here' in specific institutional contexts" (p. 275). Others have also noted the importance of institutional support for faculty on the path to publication (Moore, 2003; Murray, Steckley, & McLeod, 2012). Involving the institution as partners in supporting faculty writing sends a powerful message that the administration not only views academic writing as an essential aspect of faculty work but also is willing to offer financial support. One place for a university to look for a partner to support faculty writing is a centre for teaching and learning.

Key Issues

To foster better teaching and improve student learning, university administrations create centres for teaching and learning. Often this partnership supports improvement of classroom and online instruction. Even though the university administration expects faculty to have the skills to publish, as noted above, it seems that many centres for teaching and learning do not include support for faculty academic writing in their portfolio of activities (McGrail et al., 2006; Murray, Steckley, & McLeod, 2012).

Partnerships

Two partnerships undergird the sustainability of our writing retreats. One partnership is between the university administration and our centre for teaching and learning, the Office of Academic Innovation. We described some features of that institutional partnership earlier in the chapter. One result of the writing retreat being offered through the centre rather than by a single department is that the retreat is open to all faculty across the campus. The second important but different partnership that seems to sustain the retreat is among the faculty attendees. During the retreat faculty meet others from outside of their departments and build writing partnerships among themselves that might not otherwise happen.

As we (the authors) laid out a plan for our retreat, we identified two key issues related to a five-day retreat. The first issue was that, even though having five days to write and do some activities related to writing was validated in the literature (Grant & Knowles, 2000; Moore, 2003; Stanley et al., 2017), we were worried that faculty might get the message that the only way to write was to wait for large chunks of time. We knew the research on "binge writing" (Boice, 1992) and did not want faculty to believe that the *only* way to write was to attend retreats. We wanted to expose faculty to some strategies and practices that undergird a sustainable writing practice beyond the retreat, like setting goals, being in a writing group, and understanding the rhetorical structures of academic writing. Therefore, we planned activities around the noon hour that would add to their knowledge about writing process and contribute to their repertoire of strategies to incorporate into their writing practice after the retreat. This was an antidote to the tendency of faculty to see "binge" writing as the best solution to getting writing done.

Second, another issue was whether we should offer time for peer feedback on manuscripts, which some other models of writing retreats use (Jackson, 2009; Moore, 2003). Partly because we had a cross-disciplinary group, we decided that the buddy program was not meant for peer editing but for accountability for writing goals. Faculty met and set writing goals for the next day and shared their process in accomplishing those goals. Buddies were not set up for faculty to get feedback from their peers.

Writing Retreat Model and Process

The two summer writing retreats at our university, Portland State University, Portland, Oregon, USA, are five-day (Monday-Friday) events. Portland State is an urban university with 28,000 students and 1700 faculty members.

CAMPUS-WIDE, NON-RESIDENTIAL, FIVE-DAY FACULTY WRITING RETREAT   83

Our centre for teaching and learning, Office of Academic Innovation, offers the writing retreat. Along with a faculty committee in the first two years, the authors of this chapter planned the summer writing retreat. Because we had to choose the participants from the many applicants, we sought to balance new and experienced faculty, to have a variety of disciplines (e.g., humanities, social sciences, science, arts), to have some faculty that are new to the retreats along with those who have come before, and to have a mix of men and women. During the retreat, we strongly encouraged faculty to turn off their email. Because the retreat is on campus at a remote location, we still needed to impress upon faculty that, when they choose to participate, they needed to be considerate of others and not leave the retreat to do errands or go to their offices. We wanted them to experience what they can accomplish when they focus solely on writing for these five days.

Participants committed to five hours (9:00–2:00) with optional writing time (7:30–9:00 am and 2:00–4:00 pm). The five overarching goals for these five-day non-residential retreats were:

1. Faculty will make significant research and writing progress.
2. Faculty will collect writing strategies to continue the momentum begun during the retreat into the rest of the summer and during the school year.
3. Faculty will increase their awareness of the common obstacles to productive and satisfying academic writing practice, as well as strategies to address those obstacles.
4. Faculty will engage in cross-discipline discussions and experience the value of community connected to the practice of academic writing.
5. Faculty will have focused time to work on their writing projects.

We carefully considered all aspects of the writing retreat to create an environment and experience where faculty can achieve these goals. For example, as noted earlier, we hold retreats in a quiet, remote campus location away from most other buildings and offices. Meals, technology and logistical supports were provided, and the schedule for each day afforded opportunity for both extended, uninterrupted writing time and time for building community and writing accountability. The writing retreat schedule was as follows:

7:30 am:	Optional "early-bird" writing time (with coffee and tea)
9:00 am:	Retreat begins/Writing time [with breakfast]/Optional 1:1 consulting times
11:30 am:	Writing "Not-so-Trivia" and Writing Buddy times
12:00 pm:	Lunch [catered]
12.15 pm:	Lunch/Continued quiet writing or lunch with colleagues
1:00 pm:	Optional mini-workshop

2:00 pm: Retreat ends
2:00–4:00 pm: Optional additional writing/consulting time

We asked that participants commit to the 9:00–2:00 hours at a minimum to make progress, to minimize distraction with members coming and going at various times, and to be available for community-building activities. However, some participants also took part in the "early bird" and/or late afternoon optional times, as well as other opportunities for community building. As the writing retreat week went on, we noticed that participants increasingly engaged in cross-discipline conversations at lunch and other times, away from the quiet rooms.

Each day at 11:30 am, just before lunch break, participants gathered in one room for an activity called "Writing Not-So Trivia." This activity asked the faculty to reflect briefly on a question of the day, such as "Can a writer expect to make progress when writing only 30 minutes a day?" "Creativity has nothing to do with academic writing. True or false." "My writing practice has little to do with my teaching practice. What do you think?" Participants wrote their responses on a sheet of paper, which were collected before discussion. Typically, during the discussion, we shared findings from literature on academic writing as well as dispelled some myths (Stevens, 2019). Just as important, however, we also found that faculty shared experiences and perspectives across the group among the faculty themselves. Although perspectives and individual writing styles may vary, most faculty members came away with new insights for their writing practice (for example, "I learned the strategy of making writing appointments with myself and prioritizing those").

After the large group discussion, participants met briefly in "Writing Buddy" dyads, (chosen by facilitators to ensure cross-department exchange), to discuss their writing successes and challenges, and brainstorm ideas for the latter. They concluded by setting writing goals for the upcoming 24 hours, to be discussed at the next writing buddy check-in. Sometimes these discussions spilled over into lunch, where dyads joined others for lunchtime conversation. Although some participants choose to continue their writing over lunch, we have observed that the majority of faculty members enjoy meeting and conversing with new colleagues during lunch.

The afternoon optional mini-workshop session afforded more opportunity for educational development as well as fostering community around academic writing practice. Over the years of conducting this retreat, we have sought feedback from participants about the workshop topics so that we can offer those that are most germane to their practice. A partial list of the topics follows:
– Writing engaging titles and abstracts
– Writing a book proposal

- Selecting a journal and getting articles accepted using a text-structure-analysis strategy
- Writing the narrative for promotion and tenure
- Employing reflective practice strategies to decrease stress and engage imagination
- Writing effective conference proposals
- Making the "argument" for your manuscript in the introduction
- Writing collaborations: Challenges and opportunities

The material for the mini-workshops came from the literature on academic writing (Belcher, 2009; Silvia, 2007; Stevens, 2019). In addition, one author, the Faculty-In-Residence for Academic Writing, offered individual consulting at various times throughout the day. Both the consultations and workshops were offered in a separate space away from (but near to) the quiet writing rooms.

Faculty feedback on the retreat affirmed consistently the importance and impact of a structure that provides both extended writing time and multiple options for the development of a cross-discipline community of practice on academic writing (Voegele & Stevens, 2017). Over time, we have learned a great deal from faculty about the strengths and limitations of the retreat structure, as well as the impact of the retreats on faculty professional lives. In the final two sections, we describe what we have learned and make recommendations for others in creating and sustaining partnerships that support the broader goal of a thriving faculty academic writing community.

Writing Retreat Strengths

Over the past five years, about two weeks after the retreat, we have conducted an online anonymous open-ended survey of faculty participants about the value of the retreat (response rate of 47%). In the survey, we asked respondents to rate the effectiveness of various retreat components, and to comment on the impact of the retreat on their writing progress and on their professional development as writers, to comment on ideas that they applied (or plan to apply) to their writing practice, and to suggest changes or improvements to the retreat. Prior to conducting the survey, we sought and received Institutional Review Board approval to use these evaluation data in this chapter. Because the data were anonymous, the IRB expedited and approved of its use. In addition to learning about which aspects of the retreat participants found most useful, we also learned much about participants' perceptions of their professional growth as writers. Through our qualitative analysis, we identified several common themes, including: feeling less alone in writing struggles, seeing themselves as writers, making connections with others across the campus, and appreciating the dedicated time for writing. Let us look at each of these in turn.

Feeling Less Alone in Writing Struggles

A recurring theme across the surveys was that faculty gained insight into how others write and the recognition that they were not alone. For some, it was a startling awareness that they are not the only one with writing challenges. Their colleagues struggle as well. Their comments follow:

- I always assumed that no one felt like sitting down to write was as hard I as felt it was. Knowing now that others feel this way too has motivated me to join a writing group this year.
- Prior to this week I had no idea about the extent to which my struggles with writing were normal (ie [sic], shared).

The cultural myth is that writers thrive from being isolated from their peers (Grant & Knowles, 2000; Moore, 2003); faculty should write behind their closed office doors. The noontime discussions with writing buddies and our open-discussions with everyone on writing myths and challenges helped faculty feel they did not have to struggle alone and that others also have challenges. Several realized that joining a writing group could decrease isolation and increase accountability.

Seeing Themselves as Writers

The writing retreat seemed to build up the faculty members' view of themselves as writers. As Grant and Knowles (2000) acknowledged, "If through collectively imagining ourselves as writers we can overcome some of our deep resistances, then it is possible that we will have the will to overcome other more pragmatic obstacles" (p. 15). One faculty member summarized this sentiment, "These extended retreats help me take my role as writer seriously."

Making Connections with Faculty across Campus

The value of being in a cross-disciplinary community of writers was evident in the survey responses. The cross-disciplinary writing buddies during the retreat, reinforce the idea that faculty, even outside of their own discipline, can support each other's writing efforts through sharing goals, offering successful strategies, and discussing challenges. Ninety-four percent of the respondents mentioned that meeting colleagues outside of their own department was an important benefit of the retreat. This is how faculty members described their experiences:

- I really enjoy meeting people from across campus and hearing their perspectives on the practice of writing.

CAMPUS-WIDE, NON-RESIDENTIAL, FIVE-DAY FACULTY WRITING RETREAT 87

- I look forward to the chance to meet colleagues from across campus and learn about their work.

The cross-disciplinary writing buddies did not distract faculty participants from meeting their writing goals but fostered a sense of community that enhanced their overall experience as writers and faculty members.

Appreciating the Dedicated Time for Writing

Faculty acknowledged that they get more writing done during the retreat. At the very least, faculty would spend 4 ½ hours a day writing during the retreat. A few would come in an hour early and stay later in the afternoon for another two hours for a total of 7 ½ hours. Their comments indicated the role that this amount of dedicated time played in affecting what writing they did at the retreat but also what they will do for the rest of the summer, and even the year.

- These retreats really are a "jumpstart!" I wouldn't be half as productive the rest of the year without them.
- I get writing done, but I also get a dose of renewed purpose and enthusiasm for why I chose a career that includes writing.
- The time and space to think is such a gift – improves my creativity and gets me into healthy habits for the rest of the summer.

Indeed, it appears that the retreat was meeting our goals of faculty gaining awareness of the writing process, seeing themselves as writers and growing into a community of writers. Furthermore, faculty members valued getting to know more colleagues on campus. Finally, not only do they get their writing done, learn about the writing process, and hear from other writers, they seem to feel energized to continue writing in the summer and throughout the year.

Recommendations

When embarking on the creation of writing retreat, both the literature on academic writing programming (McGrail, Rickard, & Jones, 2006; Moore, 2003; Murray et al., 2012), and our own experiences have taught us that two types of partnerships work together to sustain an effective five-day non-residential summer writing retreat program. Each partner has its set of roles.

- *The university administration and centre for teaching and learning partnership* establishes continuous and reliable support through its financial, logistical and evaluation practices.
- *The partnerships created among faculty from different disciplines* at the retreat develop a community of writers who learn much more about the

writing process together and can use this knowledge to sustain their practice during the year.

Institutional Partnership

We recommend that one of the most important activities early in the establishment of a writing program is the creation of partnerships that can both support and promote the program's growth and impact. Establishing clear roles for each partner clarifies the structure that their support will take. In our case, the program originated with the centre for teaching and learning. The director of the centre had to seek approval for this financial investment from the university administration, the Office of Academic Affairs. Because the mission for the centre was faculty teaching and learning, the Director needed to make the case that focusing on faculty academic writing was an appropriate role for the centre and contributed to faculty teaching and student learning. To do this, the Director shared faculty evaluations of the retreat with the Provost, deans, and department chairs. In addition, if faculty spoke to either of the authors with a lot of enthusiasm about the retreats, and, even how they used the ideas in teaching students to write, we suggested that they casually convey their responses to their department chairs, deans, and the members of the Office of Academic Affairs. These steps actually seemed to work quite well in establishing a positive reputation for the retreats and, thankfully, ensuring continuous institutional support. Our future research needs to investigate how faculty use the strategies learned in the writing retreat in working with their students on academic writing.

Within the centre itself, other roles supplemented the centre's contribution to the partnership. The Faculty-in-Residence for Academic Writing, one of the authors, works in the centre and provides strategic leadership for and research on the program, plans and conducts group and individual writing meetings, and provides oversight and consultation for the summer writing retreats. The centre hosts the academic writing program that includes the summer writing retreats, promotes the program through campus communications, and provides needed event supplies and logistical support.

Faculty Partnerships

Central to our planning for sustaining support was building a strong community-of-practice during the retreat. Based on Wenger's work (1998), Smith (2003) described how a community of practice functions:

> For a community of practice to function it needs to generate and appropriate a shared repertoire of ideas, commitments and memories. It also

CAMPUS-WIDE, NON-RESIDENTIAL, FIVE-DAY FACULTY WRITING RETREAT   89

needs to develop various resources such as tools, documents, routines, vocabulary and symbols that in some way carry the accumulated knowledge of the community. In other words, it involves practice ...: ways of doing and approaching things that are shared to some significant extent among members. (para. 14)

During the retreat, the noon programming encouraged faculty to share their experiences, challenges and insights about the writing process, and offered research-based strategies to address challenges. Thus, they built a "shared repertoire" of understandings about academic writing and some successful practices from the research as well as their peers. Following a somewhat provocative prompt as described earlier, faculty discussed its meaning in their lives as writers. In addition, they worked with buddies to create writing goals for the next day so that they could be accountable, as well as anticipate how much time different writing tasks take. We designed these activities to contribute to building a foundation for a campus-wide community of writing practice.

Conclusion

In universities with financial challenges and increasingly scarce resources, it is remarkable that a non-residential five-day academic writing retreat for faculty survives. As Murray and Cunningham (2011) argue

From this study we conclude that, without support from institutions, experienced colleagues and peers, emerging researchers may make limited progress. Researcher development requires nurturing, and since institutions stand to benefit from researchers' outputs, it makes sense to provide this nurturing in a range of mechanisms, one of which should be a structured, facilitated retreat. (p. 844)

Yet, the two types of partnerships seemed to have led to this success. Partnerships with the university and faculty allowed us to offer a successful and sustainable writing retreat program for the last five years. Our centre for teaching and learning partnership with the university ensured financial support. In addition, the partnerships among cross-disciplinary faculty at the retreat itself brought faculty together to build a campus-wide community of practice as writers who understand and use the strategies that undergird and support a sustainable writing practice. Indeed, we feel fortunate that we can "nurture" the writers among our faculty with the extraordinary help from our partners.

References

Aitchison, C., & Lee, A. (2006). Research writing: Problems and pedagogies. *Teaching in Higher Education, 11*(3), 265–278. doi:10.1080/13562510600680574

Belcher, W. L. (2009). *Writing your journal article in twelve weeks: A guide to academic publishing success.* Thousand Oaks, CA: Sage.

Boice, R. (1992). *The new faculty member: Supporting and fostering professional development.* San Francisco, CA: Jossey-Bass.

Cable, C. T., Boyer, D., Colbert, C. Y., & Boyer, E. W. (2013). The writing retreat: A high-yield clinical faculty development opportunity in academic writing. *Journal of Graduate Medical Education, 5*(2), 299–302. doi:10.4300/JGME-D-12-00159.1

Cameron, J., Nairn, K., & Higgins, J. (2009). Demystifying academic writing: Reflections on emotions, know-how and academic identity. *Journal of Geography in Higher Education, 33*(2), 269–284. doi:10.1080/03098260902734943

Dickson-Swift, V., James, E. L., Talbot, L., Verrinder, G., & Ward, B. (2009). A non-residential alternative to off campus writers' retreats for academics. *Journal of Further and Higher Education, 33*(3), 229–239. doi:10.1080/03098770903026156

Grant, B., & Knowles, S. (2000). Flights of imagination: Academic women be(com)ing writers. *International Journal for Academic Development, 5*(1), 6–19. doi:10.1080/13601440410060

Hjortshoj, K. (2001). *Understanding writing blocks.* New York, NY: Oxford University Press.

Jackson, D. (2009). Mentored residential writing retreats: A leadership strategy to develop skills and generate outcomes in writing for publication. *Nurse Education Today, 29*(1), 9–15. doi:10.1016/j.nedt.2008.05.018

MacLeod, I., Steckley, L., & Murray, R. (2012). Time is not enough: Promoting strategic engagement with writing for publication. *Studies in Higher Education, 37*(6), 641–654. doi:10.1080/03075079.2010.527934

McGrail, M. R., Rickard, C. M., & Jones, R. (2006). Publish or perish: A systematic review of interventions to increase academic publication rates. *Higher Education Research & Development, 25*(1), 19–35. doi:10.1080/07294360500453053

Moore, S. (2003). Writers' retreats for academics: exploring and increasing the motivation to write. *Journal of Further and Higher Education, 27*(3), 333–342. doi:10.1080/0309877032000098734

Murray, R., & Cunningham, E. (2011). Managing researcher development: 'Drastic transition'? *Studies in Higher Education, 36*(7), 831–845. doi:10.1080/03075079.2010.482204

Murray, R., & Newton, M. (2009). Writing retreat as structured intervention: Margin or mainstream? *Higher Education Research & Development, 28*(5), 541–553. doi:10.1080/07294360903154126

Murray, R., Steckley, L., & MacLeod, I. (2012). Research leadership in writing for publication: A theoretical framework. *British Educational Research Journal, 38*(5), 765–781. doi:10.1080/01411926.2011.580049

Roberts, A., & Weston, K. (2014). Releasing the hidden academic? Learning from teacher-educators' responses to a writing support programme. *Professional Development in Education, 40*(5), 698–716. doi:10.1080/19415257.2013.835277

Silvia, P. J. (2007). *How to write a lot: A practical guide to productive academic writing.* Washington, DC: American Psychological Association.

Smith, M. K. (2003). Communities of practice. *The Encyclopedia of Informal Education.* Retrieved from http://www.infed.org/biblio/communities_of_practice.htm

Stanley, I. H., Hom, M. A., Chu, C., & Joiner, T. E. (2017). Increasing research productivity and professional development in psychology with a writing retreat. *Scholarship of Teaching and Learning in Psychology, 3*(3), 249–256. doi:10.1037/stl0000089

Stevens, D. D. (2019). *Write more, publish more, stress less! Five key strategies for a creative and sustainable scholarly practice.* Sterling, VA: Stylus.

Swaggerty, E. A., Atkinson, T. S., Faulconer, J. L., & Griffith, R. R. (2011). Academic writing retreat: A time for rejuvenated and focused writing. *Journal of Faculty Development, 25*(1), 5–11.

Voegele, J., & Stevens, D. D. (2017). Communities of practice in higher education: Transformative dialogues toward a productive academic writing practice. *Transformative Dialogues: Teaching & Learning Journal, 10*(1). Retrieved from http://www.kpu.ca/sites/default/files/Transformative%20Dialogues/TD.10.1.5_Voegele%26Stevens_Academic_Writing_Practice.pdf

Wenger, E. (1998). Communities of practice: Learning as a social system. *Systems Thinker, 9*(5), 2–3.

CHAPTER 8

The Benefits of Writing Retreats Revisited

Geneviève Maheux-Pelletier, Heidi Marsh and Mandy Frake-Mistak

Abstract

In this chapter, we examine examples of writing communities embodied in two writing retreats, the Writing Circle at York University and the Writers' Collective at Humber College. Although similar in aim and structure, one has not succeeded in fostering a community of writers while the other one has – Humber's success being attributed, in part, to an intensive off-campus retreat that fed the Writers' Collective. In our analysis, we discovered that retreat attributes such as protected time and space, community of practice, improved writing competency, intrapersonal benefits, and institutional investment are valuable outcomes in and of themselves, in addition to uncertain and often overemphasized writing productivity. For our communities, characterised by peripheral participation into the writing for publication paradigm, prioritizing relationship building and increased self-efficacy were critically important. We conclude by suggesting that writing communities such as the ones described here can empower an increasingly diverse group of academics such as female scholars, early career academics, contract professors, and college-sector faculty to see themselves as capable writers. For these individuals, institutionalized experiences that foster a sense of community and self-efficacy may be as important as engagement with writing per se. The challenge, then, is to find ways to nurture a sense of belonging, both as a legitimate member of such communities and as a capable writer.

Keywords

writing retreat – writing community – peripheral participation – relationship building – self-efficacy – writing for publication

As educational developers and scholars of teaching and learning, we have witnessed the transformative possibilities that arise when instructors come together to share teaching practices and support one another through change.

© KONINKLIJKE BRILL NV, LEIDEN, 2019 | DOI:10.1163/9789004410985_008

Independently from each other, our respective writing communities at York University and Humber College have emerged from a desire to foster the scholarship of teaching and learning (SoTL) in a collaborative environment. As a starting point, we observe that our initiatives, the Writing Circle at York and the Writers' Collective at Humber, share many characteristics. They were both inspired by best practices as described by Murray and Newton (2009) and aimed to provide protected time and space for SoTL writing in a supportive and distraction-free environment. Yet, York University has not succeeded in fostering a community of writers while Humber College has.

In this chapter, we interrogate why two practically identical writing communities have led to a very different outcome. Our experiences, while lending partial support to Kornhaber, Cross, Betihavas, and Bridgman's (2016) conceptual framework situating the benefits of writing retreats, highlights the importance of prioritizing relationship building and increased self-efficacy for the development of a community of academics poised to establish their sense of identity as writers.

The Purpose of Writing Retreats

As a part of their everyday professional world, academics have the increasing responsibility to write and publish – a somewhat standard indicator of both individual and institutional performance (Cable, Boyer, Colbert, & Boyer, 2013; Grant, 2006; Rickard et al., 2009). Indeed, research dissemination is the most common and valued currency for tenure and promotion in the university system (Kolomitro, Laverty, & Stockley, 2018; Secret, Leisey, Lanning, Polich, & Schaub, 2011), and increasingly research and publication output are a significant source of funding both in the university and college sectors (Fisher, 2014).

Writing retreats are professional development opportunities purposely designed to provide dedicated space and time for participants to attend to their writing (Moore, 2003; Moore, Murphy, & Murray, 2010). They are facilitated and structured, often including goal setting, periods of timed writing, sharing of progress, reflection, free-writing exercises, team building, and large group discussions (Girardeau, Rud, & Trevisan, 2014; Moore, 2003; Rickard et al., 2009). Much of the empirical literature interrogating the value of writing retreats uses metrics such as publication rates and/or perceived increases in scholarly productivity as key indicators of success (Cable et al., 2013; Grant, 2006; Jackson, 2009; Moore et al., 2010; Pololi, Knight, & Dunn, 2004; Rickard et al., 2009).

TABLE 8.1   Features of the writing mini-retreats

	Writing circle at york	Writers' collective at humber
Start/end date	November 2017–October 2018	Fall 2016 and ongoing
Frequency	monthly	bi-weekly
Number of sessions offered	12	10 since January 2018[a]
Overall number of attendees	5	19[1]
Target participants	Anyone with a writing project related to teaching and learning	Anyone with a writing project, from across the college community
Status of attendees	70% contract faculty	30% contract faculty/other academic staff
	30% tenured faculty	70% full-time faculty
Length	4 hours	3 hours
Registration mechanism	Registration encouraged, drop-ins welcome	Registration encouraged, drop-ins welcome
Cost	Low	Low
	Facilitator's time	Facilitator's time
	Space	Space
		Coffee

a Attendance was not formally collected until January 2018. Before that time, anecdotally, there was a group of six faculty who regularly attended (typically with 3–4 attendees at a given session).

The Context of Our Writing Retreats

In the next section, we describe these academic writing mini-retreats – the Writing Circle at York University and the Writers' Collective at Humber College, summarized in Table 8.1.

Both initiatives align with effective practice, as described by Murray and Newton (2009), and are similar in structure, as shown in Figure 8.1.

The Writing Circle at York University

York University employs approximately 1,800 faculty on a contractual basis in comparison to the nearly 1,600 faculty employed full time (OIPA, 2017). In

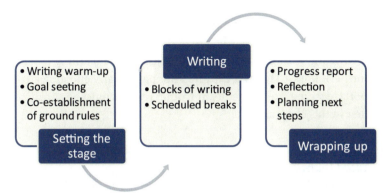

FIGURE 8.1   Structure of the writing mini-retreats

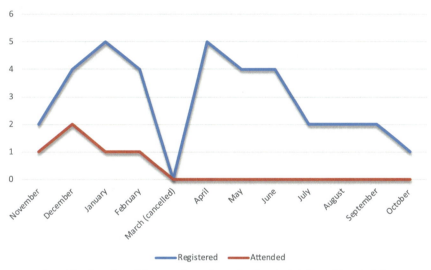

FIGURE 8.2   Number of participants who registered and attended the writing circle between November 2017 and October 2018

addition to the research-oriented tenure track stream, York has another tenure stream characterized by an increased teaching load and no research expectations. These different paths result in a diverse professoriate with divergent agendas, and many do not prioritize or engage in research.

The Writing Circle was a 4-hour mini-retreat facilitated monthly by an educational developer. It ran between November 2017 and October 2018 and was suspended thereafter because of low uptake. As shown in Figure 8.2, the number of registrations improved after the inaugural Circle, but after February none of the registrants attended, coinciding with the beginning of a four-month strike by contract faculty.

We could blame the initiative's failure entirely on the strike, but we recognize that the Circle was never well attended before or after it. We can speculate that another reason for this disappointing outcome is the Writing Circle's focus on writing projects related to teaching and learning – the vast majority of faculty not engaging with the scholarship of teaching and learning (Secret et al., 2011). Furthermore, SoTL is not expected nor particularly encouraged at York, even among teaching stream faculty. Yet, other reasons must be at play, as explored further in this chapter.

The Writers' Collective at Humber Institute of Technology and Advanced Learning

Humber Institute of Technology and Advanced Learning is one of Canada's largest colleges. As a polytechnic institute, its programs range from apprenticeships and diplomas to degrees and post-graduate certificates. Approximately one-quarter of Humber's 2000 faculty are full-time, while the remaining are part-time instructors, and many remain active within their respective industries. Along with this diversity of expertise comes a broad spectrum of experience with research and scholarship, including faculty who have never conducted research, and those that have doctorate degrees and extensive scholarly experience. Regardless, research and publishing are not a formal requirement of employment. Instead, the emphasis is on teaching, with full-time faculty teaching as many as five courses per semester.

The Writers' Collective is very similar in structure to the Writing Circle at York: it has a drop-in format with no advance sign-up required, is facilitated by an educational developer, and available to the entire college community. Writers joining the Collective may work on any piece of writing, regardless of the topic. This is in contrast to York's Writing Circle where the focus was on projects related to teaching and learning. The Writers' Collective at Humber is offered bi-weekly, alternating between Humber's two main campuses, and loosely follows the structure described in Figure 8.1. The Writers' Collective has been relatively better attended, compared to the Writing Circle at York. It has most often been attended by a small critical mass of 6–8 faculty members.

Given the structural similarities between the Writing Circle and the Writers' Collective, their differing levels of success is surprising, at first glance. However, there is one critical difference between the two – the Writers' Collective emerged as a result of Humber's other writing initiative: The Writing Boot Camp. At the end of one of the boot camps, a few faculty expressed an interest in continuing to write together on campus, and thus, the Writers' Collective was born. Although the Writers' Collective is available to the entire college community, it has been attended almost entirely by previous boot camp attendees. As the catalyst of the Writers' Collective, the Boot Camp is examined next.

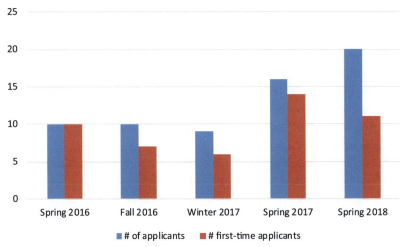

FIGURE 8.3   Number of applications to the boot camp between 2016 and 2018

The Scholarly Writing Boot Camp

The Scholarly Writing Boot Camp is a 3-day, intimate off-campus retreat, in a setting meant to foster a sense of community and manage costs, all covered by the institution. There are limited spaces in each boot camp, with an average of ten spots available at any given retreat. With each iteration the number of applications has increased (see Figure 8.3), with a relatively consistent number of new applicants each time. In total, 48 different faculty members have applied to the retreat at least once, with 50 total attendees (including repeat attendees). Approximately half of the applicants were full-time faculty members, while the remainder were part-time or other academic staff, and these proportions were reflected among the successful applicants that ultimately attended.

The overall structure of the boot camp is similar to the two previously described initiatives (see Figure 8.2). Upon arrival, attendees are given a book on academic writing by Silvia (2007). Articulation and reporting of goals are formalized, with written reflection and revisions at the end of each day. The group co-establishes ground rules, with a shared commitment to respecting the process and its enforcement. Before dinner, the facilitator leads an optional informal conversation on a topic related to scholarship (e.g., how to submit a paper for publication). All meals are shared in a separate area of the resort and provide a chance to chat informally and build connections among attendees. At the end of the third day, attendees complete a comprehensive questionnaire and impact statement on the quality and value of the retreat. They also summarize the progress they made on their writing and set future goals.

Insights from the Writing Boot Camp

In their review of peer-reviewed primary research on academic writing retreats, Kornhaber et al. (2016) found "evidence that writing retreats can facilitate measurable increases in publication outputs" (p. 1213), identifying five key elements contributing to this outcome: protected time and space, community of practice, development of academic writing competence, intrapersonal benefits, and organisational investment.

In what follows, we revisit these five themes with evidence from the Boot Camp at Humber College as a way to inform York University and other institutions wishing to establish and sustain communities of academic writers.

Protected Time and Space

By and large, the Humber participants reported that they found the setting of an academic writing retreat to be particularly productive – both for enabling them to legitimize a chunk of time dedicated to writing as well as for facilitating time on task. As noted by one participant, *"I am so used to being interrupted and having my space disrupted that this physical continuity really helped."* This is consistent with the literature reviewed by Kornhaber et al. (2016). Of the 11 studies reviewed, ten reported on the value of retreats in providing protected time and space. By way of harbouring uninterrupted writing time, the retreat can be a mechanism to legitimise writing and reduce barriers such as competing demands on one's time (Girardeau et al., 2014; Grant, 2006; Moore, 2003; Murray & Newton, 2009; Pololi et al., 2004). Anecdotally, this finding was reported in the Writers' Collective and the Writing Circle too.

Community of Practice

As Lee and Boud (2003) argue, support in academic activities is scarce, and given the increasing diversity of academic staff, "there is a need to help academics identify new goals and desires in the changing climate and to help them locate themselves in a productive relationship to change" (p. 190). In this context, retreats may play an important role in interrupting the habits of writing in isolation, which can be more damaging than productive:

> The price we pay for the practice of solitary writing is that we often doubt ourselves, we feel as if we lack courage or commitment, we find writing lonely and hard, we can't get to it. By refusing the boundaries between individualism and community, between the public and the private, as the retreats challenge us to do, we can learn much about ourselves and our

writing that can make a difference to the experience of writing in general. (Grant, 2006, p. 494)

The notions of having a shared purpose (Jackson, 2009) and collegial support (Girardeau et al., 2014; Grant, 2006; Moore et al., 2010) have been identified in the literature as key factors in increasing motivation and productivity. In fact, ten of the 11 studies reviewed by Kornhaber and colleagues (2016) mention features that foster a sense of community and position those as inherent characteristics of retreats. Furthermore, Moore et al. (2010) suggest that the intense nature of a retreat can encourage writers to engage with others about their writing, a finding reflected in this response from a boot camp participant: "*I wrote and whenever I questioned my thoughts and ideas, I shared them with Heidi or colleagues. The confirmation made me write and press my writing trajectory.*"

A few studies have found that the retreats translate into continuing collaborative research and writing (Grant, 2006; Kornhaber et al., 2016; Rickard et al., 2009). This materialized in the experience of Humber College, where two separate writing communities have emerged from the writing boot camp – a group of three faculty in one school who continued among themselves and the Writers' Collective, which has been attended exclusively by a small critical mass of 6–8 individuals of previous boot camp attendees, with only three exceptions (each of whom came only once). Of the 19 total attendees in the past semester, all but one had been to a boot camp, and most had attended two or more boot camps.

At Humber's boot camp, bonds are forged during the retreat, often among faculty that did not know each other beforehand. This is evident in the following response: "*Foremost, I was provided the opportunity of meeting and bonding with incredible colleagues who came to the boot camp with the same objective of 'writing.'*" When rating the importance of various boot camp features, three of the five most important elements that faculty identified were social support as a scholarly writer, forming collegial relationships, and forming cross-disciplinary relationships.

Improved Writing Competency

Each of our initiatives encouraged best practices informed by scholarly literature. Many boot camp participants commented spontaneously on the impact of the retreat on their writing habits and skills; as observed by one attendee: "*This was a valuable learning experience. It allowed for developing writing skills.*" Additionally, all participants at the most recent boot camp agreed that it had inspired them to change their writing practices. Kornhaber et al. (2016) also found that academic writing competence can be enhanced by participating in a retreat, notably by offering strategies for realistic goal setting.

Intrapersonal Benefits

One unanticipated benefit of the boot camp has been the influence it has had on faculty members' sense of self as writers and scholars. At Humber's most recent boot camp, nearly 90% of attendees reported increased confidence and motivation as scholarly writers, and increased motivation as scholarly teachers. For example, one boot camp attendee reported that "*the boot camp taught me writer's discipline and courage to write.*" The literature identifies increased self-awareness (Moore et al., 2010), confidence (Rickart et al., 2009), and motivation (Grant, 2006; Moore, 2003) as well as decreased writing-related anxiety (Jackson, 2009; Moore et al., 2010; Pololi et al., 2004) as important outcomes associated with writing retreats.

Institutional Investment

Organisational support is needed for the planning, resourcing, and staffing of a writing retreat (Girardeau et al., 2014; Grant, 2006; Swaggerty, Atkinson, Faulconer, & Griffith, 2011). At Humber, there is a clear sense of appreciation for the support the institution demonstrates towards its members by running writing retreats. As noted by one boot camp attendee, "I benefited greatly from knowing that Humber prioritizes my scholarly writing and academic contributions …. This was a generous initiative and has facilitated my development as a scholar." This quotation reveals that the participant is starting to embrace her developing identity as a scholar, also appreciating that Humber supports her scholarly work by funding the retreat.

The Value of Academic Writing Retreats: A Moving Target?

At the core of the model proposed by Kornhaber et al. (2016) is the assumption that writing retreat attributes, namely, protected time and space, community of practice, improved writing competency, intrapersonal benefits, and institutional investment, ultimately serve instrumental goals such as increasing writing scholarship (Cable et al., 2013), writing output (Grant, 2006; Moore et al., 2010), supporting career development (Moore et al., 2010), increasing pace and production (Moore, 2003), and publishing book chapters and refereed journal articles (Jackson, 2009; Rickard et al., 2009). Their model presupposes that the five benefits afforded by writing retreats lead to or serve the goal of increasing productivity, rather than being important outcomes unto themselves.

We do not have data enabling us to decisively gauge whether our writing retreats have led to increased output. We posit, too, that gathering data that can reliably draw a relationship between attendance to a writing retreat and publication outcomes is an empirical conundrum that has not been critically considered in Kornhaber and colleagues' (2016) comprehensive review of the evidence. At Humber, for instance, 44% strongly agreed at the end of the boot camp that they would complete their writing projects within their projected timeline, but we do not know whether they delivered on these anticipated results.

Based on our observations within our own institutional contexts, we venture that our writing retreats and the communities they have helped or failed to sustain depart from this bias towards publication output, in terms of the value they bring. We recognize that Kornhaber and colleagues (2016) offer a compelling case drawn from the available empirical evidence; however, as we reflect on the dissonance between their model and our experiences, we are poised to reposition the fringe benefits associated with writing retreats as core outcomes of our initiatives, with writing output as a valuable but uncertain by-product.

In problematizing academic writing as a highly complex activity that involves "more than simply producing more publications" (p. 548), Murray and Newton (2009) acknowledge that writing for publication is better framed as a developmental process rather than strictly an academic product. They found that the writing process, when set up in a retreat environment, benefits greatly from mutuality of engagement, or "the practice of writing in the same room as other writers for the entire period of retreat" (p. 545). Many of their participants reported being able to initiate a positive shift in their identities as writers after an academic writing retreat. This is reflected in the comments of a boot camp participant when asked to describe the value and impact of the initiative:

> This experience has improved my sense of scholarly community and being a part of that community. It has been VERY motivating. After a very stressful term, I entered this retreat on the verge of demoralized burnout. Now I feel strengthened and reaffirmed. I am motivated to continue.

Murray and Newton (2009) indicate that after the retreat some of their participants were able to fit writing into their job and adopt productive habits such as writing in small chunks or allocating predefined amounts of time for each subtask. Others still struggled to engage with writing as a legitimate professional activity, mainly because of the competing demands on their time as well as a "sense of ambivalence that came with self-identifying as writers" (p. 547). In large part, the authors attribute this conflict to two main factors. Many writers perceived themselves as still learning the process of writing and were engaged in legitimizing their peripheral participation (Lave & Wenger, 1991). In the context of our initiatives, where most of our participants hold academic appointments that do not include publication expectations, peripheral participation may in fact be a salient feature of these communities – that is, a retreat can be a mechanism through which participants gain legitimate access to or status into a community of scholars who write and publish. If this process of self-empowerment is indeed a driving factor, then the fringe benefits associated with writing retreats become core attributes.

This is, in part, demonstrated by a comparison of attendees' articulated goals at the outset of Humber's boot camp and their subsequent reflective impact statements. A fair deal of goal setting by the boot camp participants was around increased output (e.g., number pages to write, sections to complete, etc.), yet attendees reported back on their experience in a more wholesome way, as shown in the impact statement of one attendee:

> This boot camp has positively impacted not only my scholarly research and writing, but also my stress level, my collaborative approach, as well as my teaching strategies. While the writing aspect of the boot camp is rigorous and motivates me to complete the work I have planned, the social and retreat aspect of the boot camp allows me to have informal conversation with colleagues about research and teaching strategies or experiences. As academics, we are often isolated within our own work (...). This boot camp exposes us to colleagues from other departments who use a variety of teaching and writing tools that I find innovative and exciting.

Thus, although output is surreptitiously the goal of the retreats, the other unimagined, less tangible benefits appear to dominate attendees' perceptions after the fact.

Implications for Practice

The Boot Camp requires a significant investment of resources on the part of the College as well as an intense time commitment from the participants. Both highly committed, the institution and the participants enabled long-term success. As we reflect on Humber's success, we note that the socialization process facilitated at the boot camp was helpful for the group to develop into a community. This is not to say that an off-campus retreat is a necessary precursor, but it suggests that investing in relationship building enables meaningful and sustainable communities of practice to flourish. Perhaps a series of writing workshops on campus, where opportunities for repeated attendance and relationship building are offered and encouraged, can provide the necessary context in which a shared experience nurtures a community of writers. Welcoming all writing projects, whether it relates to teaching and learning or not, may also set a more inclusive and encouraging tone contributing to community building.

Concluding Thoughts

Academic writing retreats foster intrapersonal gains such as changes to scholarly identity, confidence, motivation, and legitimization of engagement with scholarship in addition to encouraging writing output. They offer protected time and space for writing as well as a context in which writers learn effective writing practices. In the case of Humber College, an ongoing writing community emerged out of an intensive collective experience around writing financially supported by the organization. At York, the institutional context, with a strike paralysing most academic activities, hindered the development of a community that had no prior shared experience to hold onto.

Writing communities such as those described in this chapter, when viable, embed many strategies empowering an increasingly diverse group of academics, particularly vulnerable individuals such as graduate students (Singh, 2012), early career academics (Girardeau et al., 2014; Pololi et al., 2004), women (Grant 2006; Moore et al., 2010; Rickart et al., 2009; Swaggerty et al., 2011), and peripheral participants such as contract professors and college-sector faculty. For these groups, institutionalized experiences that foster a sense of community and increased self-efficacy may be as important as engagement with writing proper. We learned from York University that writing cannot be the sole motivator for these communities to emerge. At Humber, forging a community through a meaningful collective experience played a critical role for sustaining its writing community in the long term. The challenge, then, is to find ways to nurture a sense of belonging, both as a legitimate member of such communities and as a capable writer.

References

Cable, C. T., Boyer, D., Colbert, C. Y., & Boyer, E. W. (2013). The writing retreat: A high-yield clinical faculty development opportunity in academic writing. *Journal of Graduate Medical Education, 5*(2), 299–302.

Fisher, R. (2014). A conceptual framework for research at Canadian colleges. *Pédagogie Collégiale, 24*, 1–7.

Girardeau, L., Rud, A., & Trevisan, M. (2014). Jumpstarting junior faculty motivation and performance with focused writing retreats. *Journal of Faculty Development, 28*(1), 33–40.

Grant, B. M. (2006). Writing in the company of other women: Exceeding the boundaries. *Studies in Higher Education, 31*(4), 483–495.

Jackson, D. (2009). Mentored residential writing retreats: A leadership strategy to develop skills and generate outcomes in writing for publication. *Nurse Education Today, 29*(1), 9–15.

Kolomitro, K., Laverty, C., & Stockley, D. (2018). Sparking SoTL: Triggers and stories from one institution. *The Canadian Journal for the Scholarship of Teaching and Learning, 9*(1). https://doi.org/10.5206/cjsotl-rcacea.2018.1.10

Kornhaber, R., Cross, M., Betihavas, V., & Bridgman, H. (2016). The benefits and challenges of academic writing retreats: An integrative review. *Higher Education Research & Development, 35*(6), 1210–1227.

Lave, J., & Wenger, E. (1991). *Situated learning: Legitimate peripheral participation.* Cambridge, UK: Cambridge University Press.

Lee, A., & Boud, D. (2003). Writing groups, change and academic identity: Research development as local practice. *Studies in Higher Education, 28*(2), 187–200.

Moore, S. (2003). Writers' retreats for academics: Exploring and increasing the motivation to write. *Journal of Further & Higher Education, 27*(3), 333–342.

Moore, S., Murphy, M., & Murray, R. (2010). Increasing academic output and supporting equality of career opportunity in universities: Can writers' retreats play a role? *The Journal of Faculty Development, 24*(3), 21–30.

Murray, R., & Newton, M. (2009). Writing retreat as structured intervention: Margin or mainstream? *Higher Education Research & Development, 28*(5), 541–553.

OIPA: Office of Institutional Planning and Analysis. (2018). *Contract faculty and teaching assistants headcount.* Retrieved June 27, 2018, from http://oipa.info.yorku.ca/data-hub/quick-facts/quick-facts-contract-faculty-and-tas/

Pololi, L., Knight, S., & Dunn, K. (2004). Facilitating scholarly writing in academic medicine. *Journal of General Internal Medicine, 19*(1), 64–68.

Rickard, C. M., McGrail, M. R., Jones, R., O'Meara, P., Robinson, A., Burley, M., & Ray-Barruel, G. (2009). Supporting academic publication: Evaluation of a writing course combined with writers' support group. *Nurse Education Today, 29*(5), 516–521.

Secret, M., Leisey, M., Lanning, S., Polich, S., & Schaub, J. (2011). Faculty perception of the scholarship of teaching and learning: Definition, activity level, and merit considerations at one university. *Journal of the Scholarship of Teaching and Learning, 11*(3), 1–20.

Silvia, P. J. (2007). *How to write a lot: A practical guide to productive academic writing.* Washington, DC: American Psychological Association.

Singh, J. R. (2012). Promoting writing for research: The "writing retreat" model. *South African Journal of Higher Education, 26*(1), 66–76.

Swaggerty, E., Atkinson, T., Faulconer, J., Griffith, R. (2011). Academic writing retreat: A time for rejuvenated and focused writing. *Journal of Faculty Development, 25*(1), 5–11.

PART 3

Offsite Writing Retreats

∵

CHAPTER 9

Something Wicked This Way Comes: Wyrd Sisters, Collaborating In-the-Round

Lisa Dickson, Shannon Murray and Jessica Riddell

Abstract

This chapter both explores and models a collaboration that three literature professors from three disparate locations have evolved in an effort to write about Teaching Shakespeare. Aside from the usual technological ways academics now work across geographic divides, we have come to depend most on three strategies: writing prompts, prolonged writing retreats, and conversations in the margins of each other's writing. All of these now seem to us organic, mirroring the material we work with and our central concerns. But these strategies emerged from looking through disciplinary lenses to reframe what research into teaching and learning might look like. The method of collaboration we have forged together – one that has transformed our scholarly lives – celebrates our separate voices and resists resolving difference, even when the constraints of our lives, discipline, or publishers insist on a smoothed unity and single confident voice. While the strategies we discuss are not always the most "efficient," we have come to believe that efficiency is not necessarily a helpful virtue in the pursuit of knowledge and creativity. These methods are, for us, generative, supportive, energizing, and ultimately hopeful.

Keywords

writing prompts–freewrites–retreat–marginalia–Shakespeare –collaboration

I'm just going down into the basement and if I'm not back in five minutes, send help.

∴

© KONINKLIJKE BRILL NV, LEIDEN, 2019 | DOI:10.1163/9789004410985_009

We are staying in a quaint, old-fashioned cottage in North Hatley, Quebec. The river wanders lazily at the foot of the property. A cat wanders across the lawn, and chickadees "you-hoo" at each other. It's beautiful and charming, a perfect place for a writing retreat.

Although it's a summer day, the heat is inexplicably blasting in the dining room. Shannon has gone down to the basement to investigate strange noises coming from the furnace. All of us have seen this horror movie before. While Shannon's gone, Lisa is standing at the flip chart paper, marker in hand, trying to capture Jessica's rapid-fire synopsis of the conversation the three of us had while making coffee. What's this article on collaborative writing going to be about? Lisa needs some first principles before she can sit down with her writing prompts. Jessica and Lisa prowl on either side of the dining room table, almost stalking each other as the ideas begin to interlock and connect. It's Improv Games meets tigers from the circus: we pace on our respective sides of the table, pointing emphatically at each other. "Yes! Yes and ...!" Lisa scribbles down line references from *The Comedy of Errors*. "Yes and ..." becomes "but what about ..." and "by contrast ...." More circles and arrows. Having investigated the furnace and escaped death-by-ghost, Shannon emerges from the basement, and we have an animated discussion about ghosts we've met and dreams we've had. Shannon looks at our circles and arrows and says, "Yes, yes this looks good .... But ...." And we rearrange, refocus, reshape.

Act I: The Origin Story

> Anyone who has worked on a collaborative project is aware of the frustrations potentially accompanying such work, which have led more than one scholar to recall that during wartime, 'collaboration' was a punishable offense. (Ede & Lunsford, 2001, p. 363)

A few years ago, the three of us met at a teaching and learning conference. We quickly discovered a deep sense of scholarly kinship: we are all 3M National Teaching Fellows, love teaching Shakespeare, and at the time were deeply unhappy with where we found ourselves in our scholarship. However, our differences became as crucial to our collaboration as the similarities that brought us together: we span three decades; have grown children, small children, no children; represent east coast, centre, west coast Canada; and play different roles within our universities.

> There is something particularly functional about the way we three work together. While we all take up different roles at different times depending

SOMETHING WICKED THIS WAY COMES

upon what we're doing and what we need, it seems to me that we each offer the others something that we can't do on our own. (LD)[1]

As we started to work together on our major project – a book on teaching Shakespeare for critical hope and critical empathy – a model of collaboration evolved. Aside from the usual technological ways academics now work across geographic divides (through Skype, text messaging, Facebook Messenger, email, Google Drive, Dropbox), we have come to depend most on three strategies:
- Writing prompts,
- Prolonged writing retreats, and
- Conversations in the margins of each other's writing.

All of these now seem to us organic, mirroring the material we work with and our central concerns. But these strategies emerged from looking through disciplinary lenses to reframe what research into teaching and learning might look like. The method of collaboration we have forged together – one that has transformed our scholarly lives – celebrates our separate voices and resists resolving difference, even when the constraints of our lives, discipline, or publishers insist on a smoothed unity and single confident voice. While the strategies we discuss below are not always the most "efficient," we have come to believe that efficiency is not necessarily a helpful virtue in the pursuit of knowledge and creativity. These methods are, for us, generative, supportive, energizing, and ultimately hopeful.[2]

Act II: Our Disciplinary Context

In our field, meaning in Shakespeare (and other drama) exists in and is co-created by multiple voices on the stage. As educators, we write about teaching, and teach about (dramatic) writing. It became increasingly clear in our early forays into collaboration that the underlying value that links our discipline, classrooms, and collaboration style is the fundamental role of conversation. Critical hope and critical empathy – defined as the open and thoughtful interaction of multiple perspectives – emerged as theoretical frameworks that challenge (in both form and content) the privileging of the monolithic or singular voice. The classroom experience – which is essentially and necessarily collaborative – was what the three of us loved best in our work. We wanted to bring the dynamism of the classroom into our writing, to overturn the traditional one-way path of knowledge dissemination (research to classroom) and to use the classroom, rather, as our investigative and methodological paradigm. This shift in stance challenges how we understand our identities that, shaped largely by our classroom experience, often feel at odds with the prevailing definitions of more traditionally recognized literary research.

> Before I found my collaborative writing partners, writing alone was an inherently lonely process, and I often felt mired in self-doubt (with swirling questions like, "Is this is fresh intervention?" "Am I overreaching?" "What is at stake?" "Who cares?"). (JR)

Humanities research tends to be solitary, with limited opportunity to develop ideas *with* our peers (as opposed to *at them*). The single-authored article or monograph is the usual means of production. When the possibility of collaboration arises, we often find that we have no training and few models to draw upon. It is striking how many times the word "lonely" appears in our writing about this topic. Additionally, all three of us noted the long delay between the conception of the work, the publication, and any response from the abstract and faceless "critical field."

> I love conference presentations, their immediacy, but hate that so many of my articles were written one year and actually published two or four years later. That seems like a long delay between idea and usefulness, and I hate not being useful. It's like a conversation with delay so long after a statement that, by the time an answer comes, you've already forgotten what you've said. (SM)

Another narrative that emerged in all our writing prompts was the courage and encouragement we get from this collaboration, and the support we needed to risk writing about what matters to us.

> Collaboration makes me wicked. And by wicked I don't mean nasty or violent or dark. I think of wicked as disruptive of norms, both internalized and systematized in the discipline or the institution. The potions we make are far more potent because we all have ingredients that are unique to each of us. Collaboration makes me courageous, gives me new tools for my toolbox, makes me ask questions that I would never have asked on my own, helps me to challenge the limits of my discipline and to launch ideas into practice. (LD)

This sense of productive wickedness has led us to imagine ourselves as Shakespearean "wyrd sisters," the witches of *Macbeth* who live on the margins and disrupt the peaceable order of the centre. (We are even addressed by our editor as "Wyrdos.")

SOMETHING WICKED THIS WAY COMES

From loneliness to companionship, monologue to dialogue, self-doubt to courage. This is the trajectory we follow, hopefully.

We come from a traditionally "agonistic" academic culture (Ede & Lunsford, 2001, p. 357). As Ede and Lunsford observe, "despite vigorous debates over theories and methods surrounding issues of subjectivity and authorship, ideologies of the individual and the author have remained largely unchallenged in scholarly practice" (2001, p. 378). The agonistic paradigm that assumes that one's scholarly credit can best be assured by challenging and overturning the labour and conclusions of others, coupled with a value system that privileges solitary and individualistic effort, creates an environment antithetical to the kind of empathy that our model of inquiry demands. If we are to think about the pedagogy and methodology of critical hope, we have to overturn this idea of agonism and rethink what it means to offer ideas in a scholarly conversation that evolves outside of a zero-sum paradigm of winners and losers. Challenging agonism requires change at the levels of classroom practice, pedagogical theory, and institutional systems of assessment and reward that often do not recognize the value of work that does not conform to the individualist model.

Resistance to such change arises at all levels and stages of dissemination. For example, one way we represent lively engagement is through marginal responses to each other's papers. However, some publishers are not set up for this kind of unconventional representation, especially when there are financial implications and constraints such as in-house style guidelines. When we encounter these systemic barriers we are forced to examine the values that shape our work. Do we compromise our method in order to make some move forward? To push the envelope even a little is a kind of progress. Or, do we stick to our principles and method at the risk of never getting it to print? At what point, if any, do we consider abandoning the wyrd project, or setting it aside until conditions change?[3] Ultimately, we ask;

> So why would we reduce that dynamism to a solo when our subject matter celebrates the choir? (SM)

The answer is: We don't. Instead, we give each other the strength to trust the process, trust Shakespeare, trust our vision.

Act III: Organic Relationship of Subject and Method

The vision arises organically from the convergence of our classroom practice and our experience of Shakespeare, whose dramatic method chimes with our pedagogical commitments. He throws a precept or a problem onto the stage and begins to turn it over and over, looking at it from this side and that.

> Each time a new character appears on stage, a new perspective is introduced, and the complexity, depth and beauty of the idea is increased. Yes but .... Yes and. (LD)

Shakespeare's plays could never work with only one character speaking in soliloquy. Empathy is only possible when there is a multiplicity of selves, each looking at and confirming the reality of the others. And the plays never boil down to a neat statement, even when Shakespeare concludes with an aphorism delivered in rhyming couplets. There remains in the minds of the audience the irreversible, ineffaceable history of many voices, many characters, engaging in the messy process of learning, training us to assess, critique, engage and to be comfortable with complexity. In this way, Shakespeare is a pioneer, anticipating a large body of research into authentic learning and High-Impact Pedagogical Practices (HIPP) that is redefining classrooms all over the world (see for example Herrington & Herrington, 2006; Kuh, 2008). For this reason, we seek to maintain the sound of our distinct voices in our collaborative works; like a Shakespearean play, what we create can only be created as conversation.

Act IV: What We Actually DO

Writing Prompts

Writing prompts allow our pedagogical practice to inform our research methodology. In our classrooms we use writing prompts to increase critical reflection in low-stakes, in-class assignments. We adapt these exercises in our scholarship to propel our thinking and to establish new directions for our work.

> The writing prompts as writing performances are dialogic, informal, playful, curiosity-driven; these pieces can expand to take new shapes and fit purposes yet unimagined. Prompts generate material that we can then excerpt and analyze, often offering us fresh insights and new revelations on old, stale material, even with the most prosaic prompt. (JR)

Prompts are a sensible way of chunking our work, but they are also a way for us to slow down and try something out, to reflect deeply on an idea that we may have been skirting or making assumptions about.

SOMETHING WICKED THIS WAY COMES

> Writing prompts give us the opportunity to do some thinking on our own, as preliminary preparation, to pin down our initial responses and positions with regard to an idea or question, or as a means of synthesizing the joyful messes of our Skype and in-person conversations. (LD)

Querying and writing keeps us honest, and guards against any tendency to be swept away in a pleasing and energetic groupthink. Writing prompts challenge us to see what we're excited about from another perspective, even from the opposite side.[4] So when we find ourselves writing and talking cheerfully about how wonderful critical hope is as a theoretical concept, for example, someone will suggest that we try a writing prompt on the possible dangers in hope. The prompts are exploratory, tentative, even risky, but we generate rich material that way. Revision comes later. The writing prompts function as part of our commitment to the conversation of distinct voices. When we were writing the introduction to our book – or, indeed, writing this article – we were not interested in presenting a monologic "unified" voice that would conform to the disciplinary standard that values individual accomplishment in an agonistic context of competition.

> To maintain the integrity of our project, and to truly put Shakespeare through his paces, we must emulate that model of empathetic inquiry that does not thrive in the echo chamber of the soliloquy, which, in any case, is a myth: in Shakespeare, the soliloquy includes an audience and is therefore never solitary. The audience breathes a few feet away. (LD)

Ede and Lunsford (2001) insist that "Academics who wish to resist late capitalist tendencies of commodification will need not only to critique conventional understandings of authorship but to enact alternatives as well." Our use of writing prompts is one of these enactments.

Retreats

> In order to understand the world, one has to turn away from it on occasion. (Camus, 1980, p. 141)

The collaborative exercise not only demands intervention in writing method, but in how we define "work" within our institutional contexts. As collaboration seems to thrive in an environment of trust and mutual understanding, the "soft" activities that build community – and with it the productive play of delight and rigor in non-traditional spaces and formats – are crucial conditions, if often unacknowledged and practically invisible in the institutional accounting of time and resources. As Ede and Lunsford (2001) ask, "[T]he material conditions that enable most academic work exclude or discourage collaboration. Who, for example, has had a collaborative sabbatical?" (p. 363). We have not yet managed a sabbatical together, but our writing retreats are brief approximations of that kind of intense time.

Our first writing retreat was at a cottage in Nova Scotia, and then extended weekends coinciding with conferences in Calgary and Prince George; these retreats provide us with intense and very productive time together, unencumbered by other responsibilities. Long hours, meals, walks, and naps punctuate talking, sketching, whiteboarding, and writing. It was at our first retreat that our original plan to write a rather more conventional (and ultimately simpler) *How to Teach Shakespeare* book morphed into a complex multivocal approach to hope and empathy.

> Writing together, even on our individual book sections, is a vibrant play of focus and distraction. Even as I write, we are mapping our structure for this article, but we keep veering off to ideas about how to teach together next week and then to managing a shared sabbatical. The distractions and digressions are as important as our "sensible" time on task. Out of these we get the new ideas, the next talk, the next project, and a lot of stuff that gets cut. (SM)

If there is one aspect of our collaboration that we would most recommend to others, it would be this: find excuses to be in the same space together, separate from normal life, preferably with a view and nice walks. Technology is a poor substitute for real time contact, even if that time, like now, means three of us are sitting at a kitchen table typing separate bits, alone together.

Marginalia

> And since one of our central principles – critical empathy – requires the ability really to hear and understand the other, without attempting the reshape the other into a mirror of oneself, we looked for a way to represent that listening on the page. (SM)

There is integrity in our process – a method to our madness – that is located in critical empathy. In our discipline, our pedagogy, and our research, knowledge

SOMETHING WICKED THIS WAY COMES

is constructed through the interplay of many voices in various contexts. Our book project involves three different approaches to teaching five plays; however, the book is not merely a collection of distinct interpretations collected together. Instead, as each of us completes her separate chapters, the others write in the margins using Google drive. We deploy two kinds of comments. In one kind, we provide editorial feedback for reframing concepts, revising structure, fixing grammar, clarifying arguments; these are temporary and they become an invisible animating force of the original author's voice. In the other, we offer commentary in the margins that is meant to preserve difference, with curious questions, empathic agreement, respectful disagreement, playful ribbing, and gentle critique (see Figure 9.1).

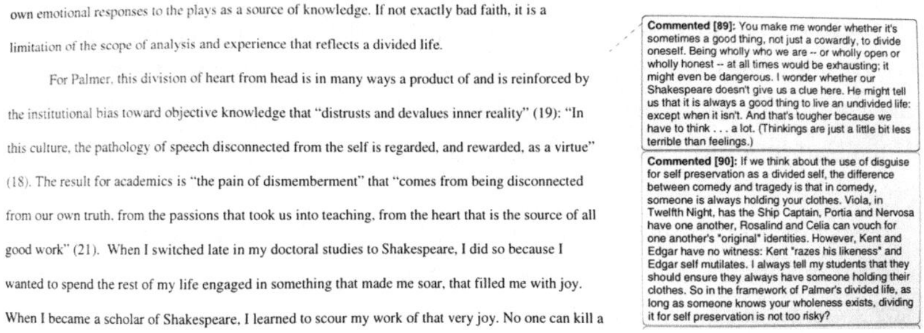

own emotional responses to the plays as a source of knowledge. If not exactly bad faith, it is a

limitation of the scope of analysis and experience that reflects a divided life.

For Palmer, this division of heart from head is in many ways a product of and is reinforced by

the institutional bias toward objective knowledge that "distrusts and devalues inner reality" (19): "In

this culture, the pathology of speech disconnected from the self is regarded, and rewarded, as a virtue"

(18). The result for academics is "the pain of dismemberment" that "comes from being disconnected

from our own truth, from the passions that took us into teaching, from the heart that is the source of all

good work" (21). When I switched late in my doctoral studies to Shakespeare, I did so because I

wanted to spend the rest of my life engaged in something that made me soar, that filled me with joy.

When I became a scholar of Shakespeare, I learned to scour my work of that very joy. No one can kill a

Commented [89]: You make me wonder whether it's sometimes a good thing, not just a cowardly, to divide oneself. Being wholly who we are – or wholly open or wholly honest – at all times would be exhausting; it might even be dangerous. I wonder whether our Shakespeare doesn't give us a clue here. He might tell us that it is always a good thing to live an undivided life: except when it isn't. And that's tougher because we have to think . . . a lot. (Thinkings are just a little bit less terrible than feelings.)

Commented [90]: If we think about the use of disguise for self preservation as a divided self, the difference between comedy and tragedy is that in comedy, someone is always holding your clothes. Viola, in Twelfth Night, has the Ship Captain, Portia and Nervosa have one another, Rosalind and Celia can vouch for one another's "original" identities. However, Kent and Edgar have no witness: Kent "razes his likeness" and Edgar self mutilates. I always tell my students that they should ensure they always have someone holding their clothes. So in the framework of Palmer's divided life, as long as someone knows your wholeness exists, dividing it for self preservation is not too risky?

FIGURE 9.1   Marginalia

That preserved marginalia has become an essential part of our process and our product, which, as in the case of the Shakespearean theatrical model, emulates another form of conversation popular in the Early Modern Period.

> The marginalia are something we are particularly attuned to as Early Modern scholars. Writing in the margins of texts, readers engage with the main text by agreeing, contesting, or expanding in ways that richly enhance the central text. Often multiple readers will respond to one another's annotations. (JR)

In our book project, it was really important to us that we be able to comment on each other's work, to maintain a marginal conversation. That's not easy for most style sheets and conventions of publication, including this one. This commitment made finding an appropriate publisher a challenge. What we did not want was a series monologues to replace the multiplicity of voices and perspectives that animates our research. We wanted to capture the argument, addition, redirection, augmentation that happen in classroom conversations about Shakespeare.

Act V and Epilogue

We'll end by assuring you that, pleased though we are with the process of collaboration, and especially with the Writing Prompts, Retreats, and Marginalia, we recognize that these methods will not suit all collaborators or all projects. It is the very fact that the process we've evolved reflects the subject we work on that makes this work for us. And we get along very well, but we are also temperamentally quite disparate humans, a mix of introverts and extroverts, early risers and night owls, and these differences require negotiation. Extended amounts of time in each other's company could go horribly wrong.

But for us, the intense talking, laughing, writing, brainstorming and dreaming and quoting of Shakespeare at each other for days and days are wonderful and the experience stays with us long after we have gone home. Jessica and Lisa have both said that they hear all our voices in their heads as they teach, and so, whether we are together or not, we find ourselves teaching together. And there are times that Shannon worries that she is starting to sound like the other two.

> In an attempt to discover a more authentic voice, am I just mimicking other originals? In our attempts to maintain polyvocality, are we starting to sound alike? My natural tendency toward mimicry mixed with some lack of confidence in my own scholarship might be leading me astray! Is this the academic equivalent of synchronized menstrual cycles? And is it that bad if it is? (SM)

One of the many things Shakespeare teaches us is that there are many paths to the same end, that we are not all alike, and that our complex contexts matter more than an absolute measure of our productivity. So a final word from each of us.

> Find your kindred spirits. Be open, be yourself, and be prepared to break open rather than to break apart (Palmer, 2015). If we hope to grow and transform then we must be open to a level of discomfort one feels in interstitial spaces between becoming and being. Writing is difficult and challenging and anxiety-producing and makes your brain hurt and your heart despair and YET once we pass through the threshold into a space where we have a thing that feels like us, that reads like us, that is a vehicle of an authentic voice, the joy and delight are boundless. (JR)

> Sometimes I really do need someone to push me into the void, or to ask me a question that I never considered. So much weight is put on us to create things all alone from our own foreheads (like Zeus birthing Athena) or in

SOMETHING WICKED THIS WAY COMES

conversation at a great distance with other texts. It's just so much easier to be wicked when you have a couple of wyrd sisters to back you up. (LD)

I like writing, now. I look forward to my (almost) daily writing hours, and especially to time with the other two. I still have struggles with confidence in my writing, but now I have two others whose judgement I trust who think my stuff makes sense. Alone, I am just weird; together, we are Wyrd Sisters. (SM)

Notes

1 We are using excerpts from our writing prompts for this chapter as our primary text, identifying each of us by our initials.
2 An aside on methodology: This chapter emerged as a meta-collaborative writing experience: we started with 7–8 writing prompts and then identified key themes that emerged from the three perspectives. The common ideas appear mainly in paragraphs like this one; the particular ideas – or even just especially nice turns of phrase – appear in the indented quotations. Then we passed around the draft in rounds until we were happy with the final outcome. Like Graeae, the three Fates who share one eyeball, we trade off "lead" as our multiple projects progress, allowing us to adjust our participation to the complexities of our over-full professional and personal lives.
3 We had hoped, for example, to use the same model of text box conversations that will appear in our book for this chapter, but instead adapted with endnotes, separated quotations, and figures. Incremental progress ("pas de bébé" – babysteps!) here marks our recognition that conditions change only when we change them. We are the system.
4 This is another way in which our practice mirrors the Shakespearean theatre-in-the-round, where someone on the other side of the stage – whom we can also see in the broad daylight of the open-air Globe Theatre – sees the matter on the stage from quite a different angle.

References

Camus, A. (1980). *The myth of Sisyphus, and other essays*. New York, NY: Knopf.
Ede, L., & Lunsford, A. A. (2001). Collaboration and concepts of authorship. *PMLA, 116*, 354–369.

Herrington, A., & Herrington J. (Eds.). (2006). *Authentic learning environments in higher education*. London, UK: Idea Group. doi:10.4018/978-1-59140-594-8

Kuh, G. D. (2008). *High-impact educational practices: What they are, who has access to them, and why they matter*. Washington, DC: Association of American Colleges and Universities.

Palmer, P. J. (2015, June 4). *Naropa University presents Parker Palmer and 'living from the inside out.'* Retrieved from https://www.youtube.com/watch?v=OWRDKNXPq3Y

Shakespeare, W. (2002). *The comedy of errors*. Oxford, UK: Oxford UP.

CHAPTER 10

Writing Wild: Writing Partnerships That Fly

Cecile Badenhorst, Sarah Pickett and John Hoben

Abstract

Writing and publishing in the neo-liberal university can often be challenging for faculty. Hyper-accountability, competitive environments and constant evaluation can wreak havoc on personal writing goals and agendas. In this chapter, we describe our collaborative writing partnership. We use the metaphor of "wildness" and use writing-in-place to explore our experiences. These activities helped us to open our eyes to each other and ourselves, and to shift our writing practices. Using narratives generated through this process, we offer our thoughts on the possibilities writing collaborations can offer.

Keywords

writing partnerships – place – writing – academic writing – faculty writing – publishing – creativity – wildness – writing education

Working in the neoliberal university with multiple competing pressures to perform as excellent teachers, devoted service providers, and exceptional research/writers can be wearying for faculty (Berg & Seeber, 2016). Pursuing the "fiction" of the ideal tenure candidate, while fraught with shame, anxieties, anger and doubt, also divides individuals into winners and losers, and subverts the value of seeking profound relationships (Acker & Webber, 2016, p. 249). In this space of hyper-accountability, evaluation and competition, it is often difficult to slow down, think deeply and reflect on ourselves as scholars, writers/researchers and to recognise our own positionings, both constructing and constructed. Instead of seeing knowledge as relational, knowledge becomes something to be produced and possessed, as we ourselves become lost to an ethic of possession rather than one of care (Fromm, 2011; Gilligan, 1982; Noddings, 1982).

In the frenzy to produce peer-reviewed publications, successful grants and employable graduate students, it is easy to miss "seeing what frames our

© KONINKLIJKE BRILL NV, LEIDEN, 2019 | DOI:10.1163/9789004410985_010

seeing" (Lather, 1993, p. 676). But what if you found an oasis, where, for an hour or so, your imagination snags another's inspiration and attaches to someone else's fantastical vision? What if, in this unusual space, you could work with vulnerability, loss, failure, reflexivity, identity and still perform the academia you are compelled to perform? What if, in this place of peace, writing becomes less of a labour and more of an evocative poetic endeavour, unsettling as that may be? In this chapter, we explore our writing partnership that is infused by a deliberate ethos of relationships-first. We use reflective narratives-as-data interspersed throughout this chapter, to describe our connection and process. We offer suggestions on using metaphor, visuals and other playful prompts to think deeply about our collaboration and our writing and to be productive – but differently productive. We begin with narratives that situate ourselves by what we value in our collaborative process:

> Our collaborative writing group has fostered a space for me to take risks as a writer, learn from others and feel valued. I find that while I'm confident in my knowledge of therapy/counselling practices and associated research, I continue to struggle with finding a writing identity. I'm pulled in several directions as my interests are vast and I don't conceptualize ideas/problems as located within one discipline. I'm excited about participating in and developing research which centres 'arts' as a site of knowledge and yet I'm aware that I don't feel as though I embody an arts-based researcher identity – not as some of my peers do. (Sarah, first narrative)

> Our writing group for me, helps to create a sense of belonging. Something that I value immensely in a job that actually can be quite lonely at times. Writing is such a personal endeavour, especially narrative or poetic writing that it is very important to be able to trust the people you are working with and to feel that they are not going to judge you. In our group I feel like it is ok to fail. (John, first narrative)

> Over the years, I've been schooled as an academic, disciplined into particular ways of thinking and being. When I write a paper, I have a step-by-step process that leads me from beginning to end. What this writing collaboration gives to me is that it turns that writing process upside down and it opens the school doors. I feel like a kid with the whole summer of freedom ahead of me. We have no rules, no system, no organisation to our collaboration. Instead we talk and write. (Cecile, first narrative)

FIGURE 10.1   La Manche, where we went to write-in-place, 53 km south of St John's, Newfoundland

Methodology: I Go, We Go

Our method for this chapter was inspired by the words of Cixous (1994), who states "I go, we go. On the way we keep a log-book, the book of the abyss and its shores" (p. xvi). We met and talked about our collaboration and what it meant to us. The conversation was untamed with interjections and interruptions but also deep listening and recognition of each other. At the end of this intense session, we elected to each write a narrative (*first narrative*) about our experience of being in the group. John also suggested that we move out of our usual academic space (our heads), take a day trip and write in another, more open space (*writing-in-place*) and focus on our bodies. In this way, we sought to move from internal to external, more tactile, spaces. The place we chose for our writing was La Manche, about 53 km south of St John's in Newfoundland. The first fishing community settled here around 1840 and had a population of no more than 55 in its hundred-year history. In 1966, a severe storm washed away most of the houses and the suspension bridge connecting both sides of the harbour, ending the history of settlement. Yet, foundations of houses and other building rubble are still visible. The landscape is wildly beautiful with rugged cliffs and swirling seagulls. It was a perfect place to begin to write "the book of the abyss and its shores" (Cixous, 1994, p. xvi). We included visuals of the place to share our inspiration. In the narratives below, we tease out more about our experience of working together:

> We are also people who are comfortable with uncertainty and tension and we seem to like creating puzzles for each other that we have to "write out" to try and make sense of whatever it is that has intrigued us. I also think that we are all sensitive to how institutions can harm people and we resist this in ways that are persistent and assertive but not aggressive or without dignity. But we are also not 'whiners' and that is important to me. Many of our [writing] pieces have a kind of humility that I see as embodying a type of stubborn grace, I mean that word both in the sense of having a basic quality of human dignity but also in the spiritual sense as well. (John, first narrative)

> I have a long-standing relationship with both of my collaborators. When I first arrived on the university scene as an accidental academic, I met them. Why does the history of these relationship matter for our collaboration ... because I like these people, I've come to know them over time and I trust what I've learned about them. I heard a colleague say when she moved to Newfoundland initially she looked around and thought, so these are the people I will grow old with. In moving across North America and landing at this university I've learned to be discerning about who I want to grow old with – John and Cecile are the kind of people I want to grow old with. I've learned that they care about the whole me, that they are interested in new ideas, they have persevered through hardship and have each taken great risks in life. They are my people, the risk takers, the dreamers, the innovators and creators. (Sarah, first narrative)

> There's a spontaneous rhythm to our collaboration that creates a flow: of ideas, of words, of papers. All this is only possible because with John and Sarah I feel safe from the competition that characterises most academic collaborations. I don't experience the harsh eyes of the peer reviewer in this partnership, or the judging comparisons that often result in notions of deficit. Instead we laugh a lot, talk about our feelings and write. (Cecile, first narrative)

Writing, Collaboration, and Vulnerability

Foucault's (1977) conceptualisation of how subjects become disciplined is useful for understanding how, as academics, we become caught up in practices and behaviours we often do not want to participate in. In *Discipline and Punish*, Foucault (1977) shows how individuals engage in self-surveillance and self-discipline and ultimately become disciplined subjects. Insecure working conditions such as contract-work, or the lengthy process of tenure review, provides an apprenticeship into this self-discipline where we regard ourselves (and others) as worthy or not-worthy (Acker & Webber, 2016). This is important for us as in our group we have one person under contract, one pursuing tenure, and one who has recently become tenured. Being under surveillance, being reviewed, measuring oneself against others creates the conditions for a normalisation of unwritten rules and practices on "how it is to be judged, who is to judge" (Acker & Webber, 2016, p. 236). Hierarchical observations, internal and external surveillance, rewards for conformist behaviour and punishment for deviant behaviour are all hallmarks of the tenure process. Added to this, is the neo-liberal wave of time-pressure, continual auditing, an emphasis on output, productivity, market concerns and a rationality that privileges competition (Hartman & Darab, 2012). Within this environment, writing becomes product-oriented, competitive and focused on publishing outputs. It becomes difficult to slow down, think deeply about how one wants to write and about what kind of scholar one wants to be (Waitere, Wright, Tremaine, Brown, & Paus, 2011).

Yet there has been a wave of resistance to the encroaching structures of neo-liberalism and we join the many other academics who resist normalised practices of being an academic through writing and relationships (Burford, 2018; Handforth & Taylor, 2016; Black, Crimmins, & Henderson, 2017). Like Black et al. (2017), we value personal relationships alongside professional ones and we actively engage in relationships that nurture collaborative processes. Like Handforth and Taylor, we believe that collaboration in our writing is a deliberate refusal to enter into competition. And like Burford (2018), we believe that writing contains the political potential to reflect on and resist the internalisation of disciplinary norms, and a rejection of the desire to be on the "cover of Academic Vogue" (p. 235).

What Are the Tenets of this Type of Collaboration?

There are two tenets to this type of collaboration that we would like to highlight: empathetic life writing and vulnerability. Chambers, Hasebe-Ludt, Leggo, and Sinner (2012) suggest that *empathetic life writing* is one way to counter the grand narratives in academic writing and research. They suggest, like others, that blurring the genres in vibrant and creative ways results in a form of truth-telling (Chambers et al., 2012). A mix of memoir, personal snippets, poetry, prose fragments and reflections help us articulate our experiences. Using a personal lens as the foundation layer, we witness ourselves and each other, while all the time recognising that we are part of the web of relational networks that make up academic life. Our stories are individual but speak to the communal: Individual compositions collecting together in a remixing of lives, both ours and others. This "new reflective turn to the self" (Chambers et al., 2012, p. xxiii) is a turn that comes from the body, the imagination, the heart, and not merely the mind. A close examination of visceral knowing leads us deeper into ourselves. Focusing on the body is a way of claiming the whole person and not just the parts of the person that are acceptable in academic contexts. It is a way of deliberately moving out of the rational space of our minds and embracing the irrational, the emotional, the corporeal and the earthiness and all the accompanying vulnerabilities that we want to own. Written personal fragments, albeit organic and rhizomatic, resonates with our lived experience and opens a further space, an inter-relational space, where we begin to see each other as people who are vulnerable. Here, we attempt to layer the internal, external and inter-relational space. There's an ethos of empathy in this way of writing collectively that is rooted in emotion, passion, imagination and remembrance (Chambers et al., 2012). Empathetic life writing aligns well to Brene Brown's (2006) articulation of *vulnerability*.

Brown's (2006) emphasis on vulnerability draws attention to the "intensely painful feeling or experience of believing we are flawed and therefore unworthy of acceptance and belonging" (p. 45). Importantly her research highlights our embodied experiences of shame, that of being trapped, powerless, and isolated. As academics we often feel trapped by institutional demands, powerless in the face critical interrogation from the peer review and tenure process. Isolation does not result from physically being alone, but rather the perception of being barred from the possibility of human connection and powerless to change the situation. Why does shame matter for our writing collaboration? It matters because according to Brown the antidotes to shame are empathy, connection, power, and freedom. Together as academics, colleagues, and friends we are practicing empathy and connection. Empathy has four cornerstones: (1) to see the world as others see it; (2) to be nonjudgmental; (3) to understand another person's feelings; and (4) to communicate your understanding of that person's feelings (Wiseman, 1996). Writing about ourselves in vulnerable ways creates spaces for ourselves and others to connect. In exposing ourselves as human beings –vulnerable, fallible, full of desires – we connect the personal

WRITING WILD   127

to the social, cultural and historical. We recognise that writing is constitutive: as we write, we are also being written. There is also a pledge here, an intention, that through our writing "we perform our commitment to living with careful intent, critical interrogation, and thoughtful awareness" (Chambers et al., 2012, p. xxvii).

With no formal agreement about this in our collaboration, empathetic life-writing with vulnerability aptly describes our ethos. To have empathy and foster connection, we tacitly knew from the beginning that we must be vulnerable to ourselves and one another. In our collaboration we do not focus a prescriptive research and writing agenda to "fit in" we simply "show up." In "showing up" we create space for innovation and creativity to emerge. Here we refer to the space for our group to grow, the footprint our group leaves behind, and how we fit together in this space, like puzzle pieces, connected and contributing to a beautiful bigger picture. The heart of shame-resilience is vulnerability (Brown, 2006). In allowing ourselves as collaborators to be with others who have had similar experiences and share with people who have been there, we are engaged in acts of radical acceptance. We radically accept that we want something that we do not have and it is not a catastrophe (Linehan & Wilks, 2015). We want relational writing collaboratives. We want to be more than floating heads. The ability to radically accept our circumstances together has fostered a way to embrace connection and foster power. Through this act we create the very kind of meaningful academic life we desire, one that places value on relationally-process focused research and writing. The following narratives were written-in-place and illustrate the transition as we move from internal spaces to external spaces and back again:

Taking the long way around
Twist and turns through stories of past
A peek into another's life rests in a set of stairs standing alone, nestled in the crook of a hill
I imagine my children at play, their bright spirits filling this rough landscape
As we walk together exploring the land as a Newfoundlander and
Come From Aways[1]
Adventure and excitement rustle beneath our feet
With childlike fever, fits of laughter burst between tender moments of care, a pause, the lending of a hand down a steep dip in the rocky trail.
(Sarah, writing-in-place)

There is a bridge here that hangs over a waterfall and a small bay. I'm not sure what it means. If it even has to mean. It is such a tired old metaphor, something inside me wants to burn it away. Maybe it is about distancing ourselves from what came before rather than the connection that I want to see even though I don't feel lonely here. Maybe it is about the fear of falling or feeling more and fully alive than we have ever felt before in that split instant before we hit the cold salt water or a spirit is freed by a jagged rock. (John, writing-in-place)

Like benevolent gods looking down on our worlds we watch a seagull below us catch an updraft and float aimlessly by. Amid the restless wind, the marks made by the many people who have walked these paths, and the stone remnants – relics – of families' lives, we write. We write individually, alone in our thoughts and bodies, but connected together through this experience. We too join in the rhythms of the bay, the water flowing in and then back out to sea. We walk the same footsteps along the paths. We feel the same sun. Then it is time to return, to our computers, our desks, to burrow back into our heads. Yet, I feel like I'm emerging from a long winter and I'm excited to see this new world. (Cecile, writing-in-place)

FIGURE 10.2   La Manche: Visible reminders of other lives on the landscape, we walk where they walked – separated by time but connected

Writing in Place

Most academic places are defined by exclusion and we often fear not-belonging, or even the price of belonging. Security and attachment have meaning only through exile and loss. Walking around La Manche, which is steeped in loss, we attended to the possibilities that the ghost-voices inherent in the place could teach us. It helped us to recognise the parts of ourselves who also participate in excluding others even as we feel the threat of exclusion and not-belonging ourselves.

During our writing-in-place exercise we saw two seals playing and fishing in the cove. They watched us watching them, which evoked thoughts of self-perception and the bridge between conscious and unconscious reality. Seals are associated with many myths and many of the stories about seals have a motif of being trapped by forces outside of one's control that are overcome by transformation or finding something that is lost (Bane, 2013; Couteur, 2015; Houston, 2014; McLeish, 1996a, 1996b;). These are stories of being held against one's will in a strange place and through a form of diminishment or dissolution the self is found and regained. All of these themes resonate with us, since many of our reflective written pieces and our conversations speak about the difficulty of living the way we want, of being free and open and curious, in institutions that seek to possess us in many ways.

This is why we needed to move to a new space. Perhaps these wide-open spaces will help us overcome the sense of being blocked or stuck and unlock the power of self-transformation that we seem to seek in our writing. Like the seals in the myths we use desire to summon other parts of ourselves and in that summoning create something new. In part, this was something we accomplished through our writing-in-place:

> The story privileges a logic of ambiguity through its accounts of interaction. It turns the frontier into a cross, and the river into a bridge. It recounts inversions and displacements: the door that closes is precisely what may be opened; the river is what makes passage possible; the tree is what marks the stages of advance; the picket fence is an ensemble of interstices through which one's glances pass. (de Certeau, 1984, p. 128)

It is the twist and turns, the diversions and the asides that take us to the untrammelled paths that allow us to transform. Looking out over the ocean and up to the sky, we can explore the unseen and hidden unconscious world as well as reflect on the land where our lives are normally lived. Perhaps this was the meaning of us watching the seals from atop the suspension bridge while they watched us. It is the act of recognition that allows us to exist together in the same shared space, something that is powerful in a world where we so often feel that we cannot find recognition for who we are. The narratives below reflect this connection between ourselves and the environment:

> We walk along the path where countless feet have hiked before, admiring the gleaming navy-blue bay and the water-streaked cliffs. We stop at the remains of a structure. A house we wonder? But since it was built high up on the cliff we question the logistics of getting up to the house and down to the ocean to fish. Perhaps it was a church? It seems to be a perfect place for worship. With this view, this vision of the sun on the water, one can be sure of miracles. (Cecile, writing-in-place)

> But listen, these are just images in my mind, like the concrete foundations of those ruined houses, and I am content here on the shore feeling the sun on my skin and a cool breeze that carries something over the sea from miles and miles away. Maybe it brings the spirits that stand and watch us like the seals – their heads peeking just above the surface of everything that lives – taking form out of the far greater world that is just alongside of us, deep and real but just out of sight. Tourists above ground, on the right side of the grave. So many of us here walking seeking release from something, here where it is never fully wild nor tamed, settled and unsettled, this in between place. The walking dream that takes me out of my head. Now even the seals have gone away. (John, writing-in-place)

Seals at play capture our attention amongst discussions of how we move from
surviving in the academy to thriving
I breathe deeply, unafraid to ask questions of my colleagues and friends
Questions which bare the nuances of our thoughts, relationship and
co-existence
I doubt that the ghosts of this magnificence hallow carried themselves with
the competition, independence and righteousness that the academy reveres.
They must have understood deeply that their survival and thriving depended
on relationships. How did we misplace this knowing?
Does it matter, I think not.
What matters is do we seek it now?
Passers-by are unaware of the radical wildness of our actions today
Frolicking, thinking, collaborating, curiously chasing our interests, vast as
they may be

Trusting that sparks of creativity are worth attending to in our pursuits
Radical academia.
(Sarah, writing-in-place)

Collaboration as Wildness

Within our own writing group there is a sense of wildness, of a desire to encounter strangeness, an impulse that is exhilarating and freeing. This impulse opens up spaces – within oneself, with others, with one's writing – for something new and alive. Through walking and talking, we seem to find a ladder or a door that leads somewhere more interesting than our usual conversations around writing within the confines of wall. Connecting to a place, as we did here, created spaces of renewal and generativity. This experience opened us to a sense of wildness. But how can one encounter wildness? Not simply to observe it, or to stand beside it, but to experience the wild from the inside? We wanted to try and catch the wild, being neither fully spectator nor fully author of our own experiences, we wanted to be drawn along by this impulse without fully taming it. Thoughts and images of wildness framed our collaboration in writing this piece: A wildness that captures a restless desire to encounter symbolic death and renewal which is a prospect at once frightening and exhilarating.

FIGURE 10.3   Lunch overlooking the bay thinking about writing, the past, the here and now, the future

During our initial conversations about writing-in-place we tried to come up with reasons for going somewhere else in our bodies. Of course, we eventually realized that our fixation on conscious reasons for connecting with nature were precisely why we needed to go. We needed to claim other spaces outside of institutional spaces and encounter the wild both physically and in our writing. As we walked along the paths and across the suspension bridge, Sarah talked about developmental research that illustrated how important touch and connection were to "normal" human development, giving rise to the thought that simply drawing closer, close enough to "touch" nature, to help each other over boulders and uneven ground was somehow important to our psychic well-being and, in turn, our writing.

But we also recognized that the notion of wildness is also problematic (Prior & Ward, 2016). Is there a true wildness? Do we only see wild in relation to modernity and domesticating otherness? Is it a rationalization of frontier mentality and the inevitable violence that accompanies it (Nash, 1978)? Do we ignore the fact that nature, like wildness exists everywhere, including within ourselves? Inspired by Haila (1997) we see the wild and nature as something that permeates human existence and that yet is not fully contained or controlled within it:

> Thoreau's idea of 'wildness' is in sharp contrast with the standard notion of 'wilderness.' Wildness everywhere present is something totally different from an idea of wilderness as having a concrete referent in some area(s), supposed to be completely outside of human influence. This fixed notion of 'wilderness' gives way to an amorphous mixture of wild, uncontrollable processes which are everywhere present and weave together with human activity which everywhere springs from the same 'wild' processes. (p. 140)

While wildness may be always present, we also have a clear sense that it represents a different kind of internal space where we can encounter ourselves by being distanced from ourselves.

Final Thoughts

In this chapter, we have painted writing in our usual places rather harshly and we have lauded writing-in-place. Perhaps the wonderful spring day after a long winter was to blame. Yet, we feel that although we write well in our offices, writing in a new, different place offered us new ways of being in the academy in addition to our usual ways of writing.

FIGURE 10.4 Walking and talking we find stairs that lead somewhere metaphorically and physically

We offer four suggestions for writing partnerships: (1) *Using metaphors:* In our discussions we latched onto the metaphor of "wild." This seemed to capture our experience of the partnership. Once we had the metaphor, we played with language and ideas to explore it further. This process was extremely generative and exciting. (2) *Using visuals:* In this chapter, we opened our eyes to a new place. Writing-in-place also forced us to attend visually to our surroundings in a way that we often do not do on a regular basis. As many of our written reflections demonstrated, we all felt a little strange at engaging in something so open ended and unstructured but this was precisely what made the experience so valuable to us. It is vitally important to understand this connection between feeling uncomfortable – vulnerable – and being creative. (3) *Using playful prompts*: We use prompts to generate narratives. These include dialogue, metaphors, emotions, and even fiction. For this chapter, we focused on our bodies to remind us that despite the conventional mind-body dualism that has pervaded western thought, our bodies do matter and they inform a large part of our perception and experience. Bodies do not try to explain away tensions, they are shaped and formed by them. (4) *Writing in place*: Taking the time to get away from the walls of our offices and write in places outside that inspire us and invoke us to be in the wild is wonderfully inspiring. Although we are all relatively experienced writers we were challenged and energized by the opportunity to write in place. Often the places we write and think within have a powerful influence upon our frame of mind, one that we often do not examine.

These exercises are meant to be open-ended. There are no model answers, simply a mode of being open to listening, expressing and making associations that can be shared later. It is not the intrinsic value of the finished product that matters but the richness of the process and the experience itself. In a partnership where each person belongs and is cherished, these activities are just a launch-pad to something much more valuable: a wildly exciting writing camaraderie.

Note

1   "Come From Away" refers to people who were not born in Newfoundland.

References

Acker, S., & Webber, M. (2016). Discipline and punish: The tenure review process in Ontario universities. In L. Shultz & M. Viczko (Eds.), *Assembling and governing the higher education institution* (pp. 233–255), London, UK: Palgrave Macmillan. doi:10.1057/978-1-137-52261-0_13

Bane, T. (2013). Selkie. *Encyclopedia of fairies in world folklore and mythology.* Jefferson, NC: McFarland.

Berg, M., & Seeber, B. (2016). *The slow professor: Challenging the culture of speed in the academy.* Toronto, ON: University of Toronto Press.

Black, A. L., Crimmins, G., & Henderson, L. (2017). Positioning ourselves in our academic lives: Exploring personal/professional identities, voice and agency. *Discourse: Studies in the Cultural Politics of Education.* https://doi.org/10.1080/01596306.2017.1398135

Brown, B. (2006). Shame resilience theory: A grounded theory study on women and shame. *Families in Society: The Journal of Contemporary Social Services, 87*(1), 43–52. https://doi.org/10.1080/01596306.2017.1398135

Burford, J. (2018). Sketching possibilities: Poetry and politically-engaged academic practice. *Art/Research International: A Transdisciplinary Journal, 3*(1), 229–246.

Chambers, C. M., Hasebe-Ludt, E., Leggo, C., & Sinner, A. (2012). *A heart of wisdom: Life writing as empathic inquiry.* New York, NY: Peter Lang.

Cixous, H. (1994). Preface. In S. Sellers (Ed.), *The Hélène Cixous reader* (pp. xv–xxii). London, UK: Routledge.

Couteur, P. L. (2015). Slipping off the sealskin: Gender, species, and fictive kinship in selkie folktales. *Gender Forum, 55*(1), 55–82.

de Certeau, M. (1984). *The practice of everyday life* (S. Rendall, Trans.). Berkley, CA: University of California Press.

Foucault, M. (1977). *Discipline and punish: The birth of the prison.* New York, NY: Vintage Books.

Fromm, E. (2011). *To have or to be?* London, UK: Continuum.

Gilligan, C. (1982). *In a different voice.* Cambridge, MT: Harvard University Press.

Haila, Y. (1997). "Wilderness" and the multiple layers of environmental thought. *Environment and History, 3*(2), 129–147.

Handforth, R., & Taylor, C. A. (2016). Doing academic writing differently: A feminist bricolage. *Gender and Education, 28*(5), 627–643.

Hartman, Y., & Darab, S. (2012). A call for slow scholarship: A case study on the intensification of academic life and its implications for pedagogy. *Review of Education, Pedagogy and Cultural Studies, 34*(1–2), 49–60.

Houston, J. (2014). The goddess of the sea: The story of Sedna. *The Canadian Encyclopedia.* Retrieved from http://www.thecanadianencyclopedia.ca/en/article/the-goddess-of-the-sea-the-story-of-sedna/

Lather, P. (1993). Fertile obsession: Validity after poststructuralism. *The Sociological Quarterly, 34*(4), 673–693.

Linehan, M. M., & Wilks, C. R. (2015). The course and evolution of dialectical behavior therapy. *American Journal of Psychotherapy, 69*(2), 97–110.

McLeish, K. (1996a). Proteus. *Bloomsbury dictionary of myth.* London, UK: Bloomsbury.

McLeish, K. (1996b). Sedna. *Bloomsbury dictionary of myth.* London, UK: Bloomsbury.

Nash, R. (1978). The future of wildness: A problem statement. *Bulletin of the American Academy of Arts and Sciences, 31*(8), 18–24.

Noddings, N. (1982). *Caring: A feminine approach to ethics and moral education.* Berkeley, CA: University of CA Press.

Prior, J., & Ward, K. (2016). Rethinking rewilding: A response to Jørgensen. *Geoforum, 69*, 132–135.

Waitere, H. J., Wright, J., Tremaine, M., Brown, S., & Paus., C. J. (2011). Choosing whether to resist or reinforce the new managerialism: The impact of performance-based research funding on academic identity. *Higher Education Research & Development, 30*(2), 205–217. doi:10.1080/07294360.2010.509760

Wiseman, T. (1996). A concept analysis of empathy. *Journal of Advanced Nursing, 23*(6), 1162–1167.

CHAPTER 11

Creating and Sustaining a Community of Academic Writing Practice: The Multi-University Residential Academic Writing Retreat Model

Michelle K. McGinn, Snežana Ratković, Dragana Martinovic and Ruth McQuirter Scott

Abstract

A qualitative case-study narrative documents a series of annual five-day residential academic writing retreats that have brought 39 academics together across universities, fields of study, career stages, and countries since 2007. Inspired by Grant (2008), the retreats foreground goals related to enhancing scholarly writing productivity, fostering participants' identities as academic writers, strengthening peer relationships, and fostering a community of practice. Writers work on independent and collaborative writing projects, provide feedback to one another, participate in workshops, share meals, and prioritize their work as writers. Together the writers form a community involving joint activities and shared resources for individual and collective academic writing practice. The learning value of the community is captured through writers' commitments to advancing their own and others' learning. Evolution, participation, and rhythm sustain the community. The retreat model allows community evolution with attention to individual and social (i.e., private and public) aspects of writing and being writers. Writers engage in different levels of participation, focusing on community values and encouraging open dialogue within and beyond the community. Community activities create a predictable rhythm (i.e., a community heartbeat) that establishes expectations and promotes belonging yet leaves space for diversified rhythms (i.e., a jazz beat) that respect each individual's process and goals. The chapter concludes with reflections intended to inform and inspire academic writers and retreat facilitators.

Keywords

academic writing – residential academic writing retreats – academic writing retreat model – community of practice – qualitative case study – case-study narrative

© KONINKLIJKE BRILL NV, LEIDEN, 2019 | DOI:10.1163/9789004410985_011

CREATING AND SUSTAINING A COMMUNITY OF ACADEMIC WRITING   137

One by one, cars edge up the winding gravel road, leading to a rustic two-storey building. For some of the dozen or so drivers and passengers, it is their first time getting to this rural retreat centre in Ontario, Canada. Others have been coming to the sprawling complex of buildings and cabins for years. All are academic writers who have made time in their busy lives to attend a residential writing retreat. Over the next five days, this gathering across at least two universities of academics, university staff, and senior doctoral students will work on independent writing projects, provide feedback to one another in small "work-in-progress" groups, participate in workshops, share meals, and prioritize their work as writers.

These annual retreats began in 2007 in response to the ever-present pressures on academics to be productive researchers and writers. Time for writing is often scarce, with most academics juggling the demands of teaching and service with the requirement to maintain a consistent output of scholarly papers. Carving out time for writing, especially away from the workplace and home setting, can be a challenge. Furthermore, it is often assumed that academics are skilled and eager writers who do not need further support (Antoniou & Moriarty, 2008). Assistance may be limited to occasional workshops or remedial resources for struggling writers, often in the form of how-to handbooks (Castle & Keane, 2016). In reality, academic writing is frequently a source of anxiety and frustration, and it is usually conducted in isolation (Murray, 2015).

Research shows that academics across career stages can benefit from writing support (Devlin & Radloff, 2014; McGrail, Rickard, & Jones, 2006). Notably, scholars have argued that writing together or alongside other writers can foster a sense of writing as pleasurable activity (Grant & Knowles, 2000; Kiriakos & Tienari, 2018).

Collectively across our institutions, we sought to address these considerations by creating a retreat format that provided space away from our institutional settings, allowed individual writing time, and included group activities designed to support academic writing and research. Scheduling annual writing retreats responds to the recommendations from McGrail et al. (2006) to offer regular, recurring interventions to enhance academic writing practices. As organizers, we wanted to go beyond merely offering time away from distractions for individuals to work independently. We were committed to creating a community of practice (Wenger, 1998, 2010) that would enable members to support and learn from each other and to share mutual respect as writers.

In this chapter, we describe essential elements of this multi-university residential academic writing retreat model, which has been evolving since our first retreat experience in 2007. Although the basic tenets of the model have remained in place, variations have occurred in response to participant feedback and a desire to explore new possibilities. The retreats are a central defining feature of our writing community, but their development and delivery have occurred within the broader frame of ongoing activities and interactions over a span of seven annual retreats. The structure of the retreats is modelled after Grant (2008), who co-facilitated our first two retreats. The approach is also informed by Wenger's (1998, 2010) work on communities of practice.

Our retreats take place at a residential centre approximately one hour from the university where most participants work or study. This location meets our need for a space that is accessible for travel but far enough that people do not feel obligated to return to campus for non-essential meetings. The amenities are simple but comfortable. We are usually housed in one building with 12 individual bedrooms, each equipped with a writing desk. There is also a large common room that we use for workshops and as an optional space for quiet communal work. Internet access and printing facilities are available. Everyone eats together at set times in a dining room elsewhere on the property.

Retreat attendees usually include a mixture of women and men, most of whom are academic writer-participants, along with a group of writer-facilitators who coordinate the retreat activities and engage as writers. Two writer-facilitators (Michelle McGinn and Snežana Ratković) are employees of one participating university and have co-facilitated each retreat. A third writer-facilitator (Dragana Martinovic) is from a partner university and joined the facilitation team after the first two retreats. Prior to the partnership between our two universities, one or two external writer-facilitators from other universities co-facilitated with Michelle and Snežana. Writer-participants have included academics from all ranks, doctoral students, university staff members with research portfolios, and a few community partners. Most attendees are based in Faculties of Education, but there have been writer-participants from a variety of disciplines. Attendance at retreats has ranged from 9 to 18 participants (average = 12). About half the participants have attended multiple retreats, although each year new writer-participants join the mix.

Theoretical Framework

Academic writing retreats are potential sites for communities of practice (Knowles, 2017; Murray & Newton, 2009). Communities of practice take varied forms and are applied across different domains and organizations. Three characteristics define a community of practice: a shared domain of interest, a collective engaged in joint activities or discussion, and a shared repertoire of resources for practice (Wenger-Trayner & Wenger-Trayner, 2015). Members of a

CREATING AND SUSTAINING A COMMUNITY OF ACADEMIC WRITING 139

community of practice are accountable "to what the community is about, to its open issues and challenges, to the quality of relationships in the community, to the accumulated products of its history" (Wenger, 2010, p. 6). In its broadest form, a community of practice presents "a learning partnership among people who find it useful to learn from and with each other about a particular domain. They use each other's experience of practice as a learning resource" (Wenger, Trayner, & de Laat, 2011, p. 9).

The writer-facilitators intentionally designed the retreats to promote sustained learning and practice as academic writers. A shared domain of interest for community members is academic writing, understood broadly to include publications, grant applications, writing routines, and more. We encourage all members to write and support each other as writers. The writer-facilitators work toward creating a sense of community. The annual writing retreats present opportunities to interact and engage in shared activities, to celebrate achieved writing goals, and to inspire the writing and group interactions that occur between retreats.

The design of our community of academic writers attends to Wenger, McDermott, and Snyder's (2002) considerations for developing a successful community of practice. As described in later sections of this chapter, we designed for *evolution* of the community with attention to individual and social (i.e., private and public) aspects of writing and being writers. We invite different levels of *participation* that focus on value and encourage open dialogue across perspectives within and beyond our community. We have established a *rhythm* (a community heartbeat) that embeds familiarity and excitement, and leaves space for diversification (a jazz beat) that respects each writer's process and goals. These three considerations (evolution, participation, and rhythm) inform and shape our ongoing efforts to foster our community of academic writing practice.

Methodological Approach

This chapter is presented as a qualitative case-study narrative (Flyvbjerg, 2006). This method allows for exploration of the community of academic writing practice as a bounded system (Creswell, Hanson, Clark Plano, & Morales, 2007). As three writer-facilitators and a writer-participant, we are members of the community of practice under investigation; hence, this investigation includes an element of self-study (Ellis & Bochner, 2000; Probst, 2016). In-depth data collection includes documents developed for and during the writing retreats conducted from 2007 to 2015. The collected documents include retreat materials, retreat evaluations, testimonials, participants' publication progress reports, and writer-facilitators' reports and funding requests. We secured research ethics clearance to use these documents and participant demographic data for research purposes. We drew upon the entire data corpus to construct a narrative of the retreat structure and the design decisions that have fostered our community of practice. Consistent with Flyvbjerg's (2006) narrative approach, we describe the genesis and evolution of our community of practice, letting readers "discover their own path and truth inside [our] case" (p. 23).

Chronology and Evolution of Writing Retreats

Dr. Barbara Grant (University of Auckland) facilitated our initial retreat in 2007. That retreat was structured around the model she developed for residential academic writing retreats (Grant, 2008). We have maintained the core of her model in subsequent years but modified specifics to accommodate our context and participants' changing desires over time.

Writer-participants receive a multi-page handout in the week prior to the retreat, outlining the retreat structure and the expectation that each person will bring a writing project to work on (e.g., a book chapter, journal article, conference paper). The handout includes instructions encouraging writer-participants to do some initial planning regarding the intended focus, key messages, and audience for their selected writing projects (Brown, 1994/1995). Consistent with Wenger-Trayner and Wenger-Trayner's (2015) defining features of a community of practice, this step confirms that our shared domain of interest is academic writing, and the planning instructions provide an example of a shared resource for our individual writing practices. When participants gather on Sunday evening, they are invited to introduce themselves, and to describe their goals and writing projects. These introductions are the first joint activity and discussion that frames each retreat. At this initial gathering, the writer-facilitators outline the components of the retreat and introduce the basic rules of conduct: respect quiet times for writing, commit to giving and receiving feedback, maintain confidentiality, and work toward their self-identified goals. These are norms that underlie our community practices.

Each of the subsequent four days officially begins with breakfast, followed by a morning of individual writing time. Afternoons are a mixture of quiet writing, workshops presented by writer-facilitators or invited guests, and one-on-one consultations with writer-facilitators or guests. Participants' writing

CREATING AND SUSTAINING A COMMUNITY OF ACADEMIC WRITING   141

projects include journal articles, conference papers, book chapters, books, book proposals, dissertations, play scripts, research grant applications, and other academic tasks. Over the years, participant feedback has led to fewer workshops and more independent writing time. For example, time scheduled for independent writing grew from 17 to 20 hours between 2007 and 2015, while time for workshops decreased in this period from 5.5 to 2.5 hours, including the addition of at least one workshop-free day. Nevertheless, at least two workshops are offered at each retreat, covering topics such as publishing journal articles, preparing book proposals, writing research grant applications, and collaborating and co-authoring.

Scheduled workshops address the three characteristics essential to communities of practice, as outlined by Wenger-Trayner and Wenger-Trayner (2015): a shared domain of interest, joint activities or discussion, and shared resources. Academic writing is a shared domain of interest. As writer-facilitators and writer-participants, we engage in the practice of academic writing. Regardless of academic rank, we learn from experts and each other by attending presentations, sharing information and resources, and reflecting on our own experiences. This social participation enhances our sense of community and strengthens our identities as writers.

Social participation extends to other aspects of the retreat. Writer-participants are assigned membership in small work-in-progress groups (Grant, 2008). These groups are arranged by writer-facilitators to maximize a diversity of background, experience, and university affiliation. Each evening from Monday to Wednesday, two people in each group take turns presenting some aspect of their writing and receiving detailed feedback from others in a structured format. The presenter provides other group members with a few pages of the work about an hour prior to the session, leaving enough time for others to individually read and critique. When it is their turn, presenters begin by describing the purpose of their text and any concerns or questions they would like their colleagues to address. Group members provide concrete, detailed feedback as one member takes notes.

Community continues to build through shared meals, evening social time, walks around the spacious grounds, and impromptu sharing times. The retreat wraps up mid-afternoon on the fifth day with a closing workshop where participants report what they have accomplished and how they intend to sustain their writing beyond the retreat. In addition to sharing success stories, the focus is on giving and receiving support. The writer-facilitators use feedback provided during this discussion and on retreat evaluation forms to inform planning for subsequent retreats.

Participation

The flexible structure of the retreats and the fluctuating roster of attendees allow writer-participants to engage at different levels as core, active, occasional, peripheral, or transactional participants (O'Grady, 2016). Two writer-facilitators from one university (Michelle and Snežana) have organized and attended every retreat. A third writer-facilitator from a partner university (Dragana) joined the facilitation team in 2011 and has participated since. These individuals form the core group as leaders and coordinators of the retreats. They organize the program, facilitate most workshops, invite and encourage writers from their institutions or their wider professional networks to attend retreats, offer to serve as writing consultants for other writers, work to secure institutional funding for writers, and in some years have coordinated the engagement of external writer-facilitators (2007 and 2008) or guest workshop facilitators (2013 and 2014). Importantly, the three individuals are writers and not just facilitators. The three writer-facilitators model active commitment to writing and to their personal writing goals throughout the retreats, and they are thereby perceived as central to the community's shared domain of academic writing. Through their multiple roles, the writer-facilitators are essential to the retreats. Given the longevity of their commitments to the retreats and the community, they are recognized as core participants, and perceived as experts in the domain of writing retreats and writing practice.

Ruth McQuirter Scott is a writer-participant who has attended consistently for five years (scheduling constraints prevented her from attending the earlier retreats). She is clearly an active participant, "closely involved with the focus of the community" (O'Grady, 2016, p. 32). In recent years, she joined the three writer-facilitators in writing about the retreats (including this chapter). Through her transition toward deep engagement in our shared domain, she has now shifted toward core participation in the community of practice.

Other writer-participants are occasional participants, having attended from one to four retreats, dropping in and out as their interests shift and schedules allow. At the retreats themselves, there are also differences in the level of engagement. Writer-facilitators ask all writer-participants to commit to participating fully when they attend a retreat, which includes staying for the full duration and contributing to other writers through work-in-progress groups and ideally all workshops (unless labelled as "optional"). Robust levels of engagement at a retreat have the greatest potential to enrich the reciprocal learning partnership related to writing practice (Wenger et al., 2011). The learning value of our community is captured through participants' commitments to advancing their own and others' learning.

CREATING AND SUSTAINING A COMMUNITY OF ACADEMIC WRITING   143

Most writer-participants demonstrate such commitments; however, not all writer-participants are able to make or fulfill such commitments. Conflicting obligations get in the way for some (e.g., slipping away temporarily for a meeting or convocation ceremony, attending to a family emergency or caring responsibilities). Sometimes writer-participants become so focused on their individual writing goals that they are unwilling to join group activities. Our commitment to respecting each other as writers prompts community members to accept these varying levels of engagement while continuing to encourage all to remain faithful to themselves as writers and, to the extent possible, to our community of practice.

Open dialogue among participants helps everyone foreground the values that inform our community. The writer-facilitators model and encourage all participants to attend to individual and social aspects of writing. Our approach emphasizes the importance and benefits of mutual respect, reciprocity, and generosity in our interactions.

It is evident that many writer-participants value the approach we promote, returning year-after-year or expressing disappointment when other obligations prevent them from attending in a given year. This level of sustained identification and engagement strengthens the sense of community. We also hear regularly from peripheral participants within and beyond the two primary institutions who signal a desire to participate in our retreats or to establish a similar model in their contexts, which affirms the value associated with the retreat model and the corresponding community of practice.

Rhythm across the Community

Each community develops its unique rhythm over time. Wenger et al. (2002) refer to this unique rhythm as the beat of the community. This rhythmic beat is determined by the activities, interactions, practices, and stories that surface across time frames as community members work together.

Our community activities create a predictable rhythm that sets an expectation for members' participation. The community rhythm is created through our annual, weekly, and daily schedules at and between the annual retreats. Developing milestones for our community of academic writing practice (most notably, the scheduling of an annual writing retreat each June) establishes the overall rhythm. At the retreats themselves, the combination of individual writing time, workshops, one-on-one consultations, work-in-progress groups, shared meals, and informal evenings creates familiar rhythms and a sense of belonging for community members. The shifts between whole-group (e.g., workshops and debrief sessions) and small-group activities (e.g., work-in-progress groups and one-on-one consultations) add layers to the community rhythm, as does the individual flow of writing for each writer.

Wenger et al. (2002) argued that a community of practice has multiple and diversified rhythms:

> There are many rhythms in a community – the syncopation of familiar and exciting events, the frequency of private interactions, the ebb and flow of people from the sidelines into active participation, and the pace of the community's overall evolution. A combination of whole-community and small-group gatherings creates a balance between the thrill of exposure to many different ideas and the comfort of more intimate relationships. (p. 63)

As Wenger et al. (2002) further explain, "there is no right beat for all communities, and the beat is likely to change as the community evolves. But finding the right rhythm at each stage is key to a community's development" (p. 63). In our quest to set the right rhythm for our academic writing community, we refer to our community rhythm as a jazz beat, characterized by "an open-ended, multifaceted, ever-changing idea or set of discourses rather than a prescribed and proscribed set of specific musical devices, names, places, or styles" (Ake, Garrett, & Goldmark, 2012, p. 6). Jazz musicians play partly planned and partly spontaneous music. When performing a tune, jazz musicians "create their own interpretations within that tune in response to the other musicians' performances" (Dozier, 2015, para. 4). This unique interpretation of a tune is called improvisation and it represents a defining element of jazz. In similar ways, members of our community play off each other as they are inspired and responsive to others within the midst.

Our community jazz beat is defined by members' responses to their lives as academic writers, replete with "ups and downs, its elation and heart-break, its moments of relaxation and sweaty hard labour, its hate and its love" (McGregor, 2016, para. 11). Similar to jazz ensembles that combine established scales and known passages with improvised melodies (de Bruin, 2015), our community heartbeat is simultaneously rooted in recurring principles and yet open to experimentation, flexibility, and innovation. For example, our community is responsive to emerging and surprising moments in our members' writing lives (e.g., the off-beat and contrasting rhythms in the writing process and among writers).

Writer-facilitators, guest facilitators, and writer-participants create a rhythm together based on respect, reciprocity, balanced communal and individual

CREATING AND SUSTAINING A COMMUNITY OF ACADEMIC WRITING 145

writing time, writer's identity development, and sustainability. Having some predictability ensures that community members stay engaged in community life. However, writer-facilitators negotiate and adjust the pace of activities on a regular basis to meet the diverse and evolving needs of all community members. Our writing retreats provide time and activities for community members to reflect on their writing process, peer feedback, learning, and identities as writers. These reflections encourage members to stay engaged and on track, rather than feel overwhelmed and lethargic. Striking a healthy balance between vigorous engagement and periods of rest has been critical to sustainability for our community.

Community activities evolve according to members' writing projects and preferences, which often pull the focus of our community in different directions. Our community rhythm is modified whenever members identify new goals or preferences, inviting polyrhythmic sensitivity to members' contrasting needs and encouraging new (off-beat) approaches. For example, the annual rhythm of our community remained consistent from 2007 to 2015 (e.g., the writer-facilitators obtained funding each winter, recruited writer-participants each spring, facilitated a retreat each June, and requested participant publication progress reports each fall). However, we have modulated our weekly rhythm during the retreats to address diverse and, at times, contrasting preferences and goals identified by community members (e.g., the shifts in time allocated to workshops vs. individual writing time).

Creating a healthy heartbeat for our community has not been without challenges. Writer-facilitators have experienced distortions in their individual writing goals; they have learned that modelling can be a powerful and difficult pedagogical technique when playing dual roles as writers and retreat facilitators. Sharing their facilitation responsibilities and hosting external facilitators has helped writer-facilitators to balance these dual roles and to increase retreat productivity and satisfaction.

A further challenge for writer-facilitators relates to obtaining funding for the retreats. To keep costs low for writer-participants (often just a $100 facilitation fee), it is critical to ensure annual funding for the retreats. Every winter, the writer-facilitators apply for institutional funding for the retreat. There is a set rental fee for each building at the retreat centre. We need 12 participants to make our stay affordable in our preferred building (and this number also aligns with our ideal of four writers in each of three work-in-progress groups). However, ensuring exactly 12 participants is a challenge, especially when we must pay the deposit so long before writer-participants make their reservations. This recruitment challenge prompted the writer-facilitators to invite writer-participants from other departments, universities, and community organizations (e.g., district school boards), which has diversified our community and is well accepted by retreat participants.

Participant recruitment has become a critical milestone for maintaining a healthy and energizing pulse for our community of academic writing practice, continually adding new elements to the familiar rhythm. Having a group of returning and new writer-participants at each retreat creates a sense of familiarity and novelty, tradition and innovation.

Inspiration for Your Community of Writing Practice

We provide this narrative of our multi-university residential academic writing retreat model as a community of academic writing practice to inform and inspire other academic writers and facilitators. Given intense pressures in the contemporary academic climate, we are convinced that our model has merit across contexts. We conclude this chapter with a few final reflections on what has been most powerful about our approach.

Our model involves writer-facilitators who work alongside writer-participants, encouraging and modelling strategies to prioritize writing and writers. In this way, our retreat model attends to the practice and the practitioners that define our community of academic writing practice (Wenger-Trayner & Wenger-Trayner, 2015). Collaborating in the delivery of the retreats and encouraging all participants to share their knowledge promotes a collective sense of belonging and ownership for the retreats. Such collaboration also fosters collective intentions toward enhancing individual and communal writing practices, as well as collegial relationships within and across institutions. The value of our learning community is realized through these collective commitments (Wenger et al., 2011). Members of our community of practice learn from each other and develop themselves personally and professionally by sharing academic writing knowledge and experience.

Engaging participants from multiple institutions, disciplines, and career stages has contributed positively to the evolution of our retreats and our associated community of practice. Holding strong to the basic tenets of Grant's (2008) retreat model and intentionally changing strategies and welcoming different participants from year to year helps ensure predictable yet fresh content, which strengthens the learning potential of our model. The rural retreat setting where others attend to meal preparation and household chores provides inspiration from nature and seclusion from day-to-day pressures. Finally, we note that our concerted efforts to secure financing from our deans or other research leaders have made it possible to schedule retreats reliably and to entice new and returning participants.

CREATING AND SUSTAINING A COMMUNITY OF ACADEMIC WRITING 147

Acknowledgements

This series of retreats was supported by the Dean's Office in the Faculty of Education at Brock University and a Research Leadership Chair grant from the University of Windsor. Our sincere thanks to Barbara Grant (University of Auckland) for the inspiration and support as we established our residential academic writing retreat model. We are indebted to the writers who have participated with us in the retreats since 2007.

References

Ake, D., Garrett, C. H., & Goldmark, D. (2012). Introduction. In D. Ake, C. H. Garrett, & D. Goldmark (Eds.), *Jazz/not jazz: The music and its boundaries* (pp. 1–10). Berkeley, CA: University of California Press.

Antoniou, M., & Moriarty, J. (2008). What can academic writers learn from creative writers? Developing guidance and support for lecturers in higher education. *Teaching in Higher Education, 13*, 157–167. https://doi.org/10.1080/13562510801923229

Brown, R. (1994/1995). Write right first time. *Literati Newsline.* Retrieved from http://web.archive.org/web/19971014014626/http:/www.mcb.co.uk/literati/write.htm

Castle, J., & Keane, M. (2016). Five writing development strategies to help academics flourish as writers. *South African Journal of Higher Education, 30*(6), 73–93. https://doi.org/10.20853/30-6-721

Creswell, J., Hanson, W., Clark Plano, V., & Morales, A. (2007). Qualitative research designs: Selection and implementation. *The Counseling Psychologist, 35*, 236–264. https://doi.org/10.1177/0011000006287390

de Bruin, L. (2015). Theory and practice in idea generation and creativity in jazz improvisation. *Australian Journal of Music Education, 2015*, 91–106.

Devlin, M., & Radloff, A. (2014). A structured writing programme for staff: Facilitating knowledge, skills, confidence and publishing outcomes. *Journal of Further and Higher Education, 38*, 230–248. https://doi.org/10.1080/0309877X.2012.722194

Dozier, E. (2015, July 7). *"Satchmo" and the spirit of jazz* [Blog post]. Retrieved from http://www.ericdozier.com/blogdashboard/2015/7/7/satchmo-and-the-jazz-revolution

Ellis, C., & Bochner, A. P. (2000). Autoethnography, personal narrative, reflexivity: Researcher as subject. In N. Denzin & Y. S. Lincoln (Ed.), *Handbook of qualitative research* (pp. 733–768). Thousand Oaks, CA: Sage.

Flyvbjerg, B. (2006). Five misunderstandings about case-study research. *Qualitative Inquiry, 12*, 219–245. https://doi.org/10.1177/1077800405284363

Grant, B. M. (2008). *Academic writing retreats: A facilitator's guide*. Milperra, Australia: Higher Education Research and Development Society of Australasia.

Grant, B. M., & Knowles, S. (2000). Flights of imagination: Academic women be(com)ing writers. *International Journal for Academic Development, 5*, 6–19. https://doi.org/10.1080/136014400410060

Kiriakos, C. M., & Tienari, J. (2018). Academic writing as love. *Management Learning, 49*, 263–277. https://doi.org/10.1177/1350507617753560

Knowles, S. S. (2017). Communities practising generous scholarship: Cultures of collegiality in academic writing retreats. In J. McDonald & A. Cater-Steel (Eds.), *Implementing communities of practice in higher education: Dreamers and schemers* (pp. 53–80). Singapore: Springer.

McGrail, M. R., Rickard, C. M., & Jones, R. (2006). Publish or perish: A systematic review of interventions to increase academic publishing rates. *Higher Education Research & Development, 25*, 19–35. https://doi.org/10.1080/07294360500453053

McGregor, T. (2016, April 21). *What is jazz? How is it different from other music?* [Blog post]. Retrieved from https://spinditty.com/genres/What-is-Jazz-Aint-no-other-music-like-it

Murray, R. (2015). *Writing in social spaces. A social processes approach to academic writing*. Abingdon, UK: Routledge.

Murray, R., & Newton, M. (2009). Writing retreat as structured intervention: Margin or mainstream? *Higher Education Research and Development, 28*, 541–553. https://doi.org/10.1080/07294360903154126

O'Grady, A. (2016). Applying educational thinkers to contemporary educational practice. In A. O'Grady & V. Cottle (Eds.), *Exploring education at postgraduate level: Policy, theory and practice* (pp. 25–34). New York, NY: Routledge.

Probst, B. (2016). Both/and: Researcher as participant in qualitative inquiry. *Qualitative Research Journal, 16*, 149–158. https://doi.org/10.1108/QRJ-06-2015-0038

Wenger, E. (1998). *Communities of practice: Learning, meaning, and identity*. Cambridge, UK: Cambridge University Press.

Wenger, E. (2010). Communities of practice and social learning systems: The career of a concept. In C. Blackmore (Ed.), *Social learning systems and communities of practice* (pp. 179–198). Milton Keynes, UK: The Open University.

Wenger, E. C., McDermott, R., & Snyder, W. C. (2002). *Cultivating communities of practice: A guide to managing knowledge*. Cambridge, MA: Harvard Business School Press.

Wenger, E. C., Trayner, B., & De Laat, M. (2011). *Promoting and assessing value creation in communities and networks: A conceptual framework* (Report No. 18). Heerlen, Netherlands: Open University of the Netherlands.

Wenger-Trayner, E., & Wenger-Trayner, B. (2015). *Introduction to communities of practice: A brief overview of the concept and its uses*. Retrieved from https://wenger-trayner.com/introduction-to-communities-of-practice/

CHAPTER 12

Writing about Writing: Collaborative Writing and Photographic Analyses from an Academic Writing Retreat

Kari-Lynn Winters, Natasha Wiebe and Mary Gene Saudelli

Abstract

This chapter discusses an annual residential writing retreat, where members from across various universities gather, for the purpose of supporting scholarly writing initiatives. We developed a method of photo analysis to explore whether the retreat fostered collaborative writing among its participants, interrogating the strengths and limitations of this visual approach. The method not only captured the complexities of participants' stories about their writing experiences – specifically the social, the semiotic, and the critical – but also elicited different perspectives and writing stories from others. Findings suggest that retreats can foster collaborative writing by providing a space for writing teams to meet, offering structured peer feedback, and introducing scholars to each other and planting seeds for shared projects.

Keywords

collaborative writing – writing retreats – photo analysis

This chapter studies an annual academic writing retreat, where members from across various institutions gather, for the purpose of supporting scholarly writing initiatives. Our aim is to use photo analysis to explore whether the residential retreat fosters collaborative writing among participants. Our research questions are:

1. How might an annual academic writing retreat foster collaborative writing among participants?
2. How can photo analyses help inform research about retreats and collaborative writing?

© KONINKLIJKE BRILL NV, LEIDEN, 2019 | DOI:10.1163/9789004410985_012

Writing Retreats and Collaborative Writing

The writing retreat in higher education responds to the challenge of "publish or perish" (Dickson-Swift, James, Kippen, Talbot, Verrinder, & Ward, 2009) by designating time, space, and support for academic writing. While the retreat is championed by scholars in Australia, New Zealand, and the United Kingdom (Grant, 2006; Grant & Knowles, 2000; Moore, 2003; Murray & Newton, 2009), our literature review identified a writing retreat series initiated by the University of Massachusetts-Amherst as early as 1991 (Elbow & Sarcinelli, 2006). Some retreats are residential, with writers staying as many as five days (Farr, Cavallaro, Civil, & Cochrane, 2009; Grant, 2006; Johnson, Blunt, & Bagley, 2017; Oermann, Nicoll, & Black, 2014; Murray & Newton, 2009; Murray, Steckley, & MacLeod, 2012; Price, Coffey, & Nethery, 2015). Alternatively, day-away retreats invite participants to spend several hours in a designated quiet space on campus (Dickson-Swift et al., 2009) or off (Elbow & Sorcinelli, 2006).

Retreat programs range from structured to flexible. For example, the six education scholars who participated in Murray and Newton's (2009) residential retreat in rural Scotland wrote in the same room, following a fixed schedule that interspersed 1.5 hour chunks of individual writing with 15-minute breaks and guided discussions. Conversely, the University of Windsor's interdisciplinary retreat in Ontario offers quiet writing space with optional meals, workshops, and consultations (Wiebe, 2016). Whatever the model, retreats challenge the traditional academic narrative of writing for publication as a solitary, competitive activity by positioning writing as a collegial, community-based one (Grant, 2006; Grant & Knowles, 2000; Elbow & Sorcinelli, 2006; Moore, 2003). Elbow and Sorcinelli (2006) note, "There's a certain energy in the air that helps people be productive and creates a spirit that's collegial and supportive" (p. 222).

Reported outcomes include an increase in writing productivity during retreats (Moore, 2003; Murray & Cunningham, 2011; Price, Coffey, & Nethery, 2015), or increased publication output over time (Dickson et al., 2009, p. 236; Farr et al., 2009). This has been attributed to the state of "flow" that can be facilitated at the event due to the synergy of writing with others (Elbow & Sorcinelli, 2006; Farr et al., 2009; Moore, 2003). Productivity is also perceived to result from designating writing time and space, and minimizing distraction (Dickson-Swift et al., 2009; Moore, 2003). Other commonly-expressed benefits of retreats include positive changes to post-retreat writing practices (Elbow & Sorcinelli, 2006; Grant, 2006; Murray & Newton, 2009; Oermann et al., 2014), such as learning to prioritize writing (Murray & Newton, 2009). Moreover, post-retreat, some participants report that they have begun to identify themselves as writers (Grant, 2006; Murray & Newton, 2009). As one participant

WRITING ABOUT WRITING

wrote, "[Before] I saw myself as an imposter who did not 'belong,' and as a 'wannabe' writer than than one who actually did write .... [Now] I feel more sure of myself as a writer" (Grant, 2006, p. 490).

Retreats may also result in ongoing collaborations of new writing teams and groups (Farr, 2009, p. 18; Grant, 2006, p. 7; Grant & Knowles, 2000, p. 11), as well as shared texts (e.g., Dickson-Swift et al., 2009; Murray & Newton, 2009). During retreats, these teams may engage in *collaborative writing* by thinking and talking about the shared text, and often writing that text together. Scholars from higher education have discussed different structures for collaborative writing, which can be used to describe what happens during retreats. *Lead writing* occurs when one person assumes responsibility for writing the first draft, and then another takes a turn (Ritchie & Rigano, 2007, p. 125). *Turn writing* is "a cooperative rather than collaborative division of labor where contributors negotiat[e] different sections to write" (p. 124). *Side-by-side writing* involves sitting together in a shared writing experience of the same text (p. 132). This last structure may be most commonly experienced at retreats. This is because *side-by-side writing* is not only employed by teams working on shared projects, but also can be experienced during peer consultations about individual projects. The collegial support offered through peer review and discussion are among those factors that help to develop working relationships: "a community of practice that transcends the retreat and translates into continuing collaborative research and writing" (Kornhaber, Cross, Betihavas, & Bridgman, 2016, p. 1217). Kornhaber at al.'s integrative literature review also attributes the development of post-retreat writing collaborations to a sense of shared purpose and connectedness; and to having time and space away from the work of writing to socialize through shared meals and recreational activities during retreats.

Photos and Educational Research

The body of peer-reviewed studies on writing retreats is small. Kornhaber et al. (2016), for instance, located only 11 original peer-reviewed research studies for their integrative literature review. Studies are predominately interviews and surveys of small samples of writing retreat participants. We located no studies using photo analysis to study writing retreats.

Yet, it has been said that a picture is worth a thousand words. Indeed, we live in an image society, where images are commonplace and their meanings (semiotic potentials) can be mediated rapidly. Photos increase readability and engagement and can be processed in as little as 13 milliseconds – much faster than words (Trafton, 2014). Photographs also lend a sense of authenticity and subjectivity to narratives. They offer a "naturalistic modality," resembling reality and showing the context in which the photo is taken (Kress & Van Leeuwen, 1996). More recent research in photographic education (particularly in relationship to brands and branding) argues that photos need to become a priority in our contemporary image-infused culture because they emphasize the relationships among the semiotics (the subjective meanings of the texts), the compositions themselves, and the subject's emotional cues (Morton, 2017). These relationship qualities strengthen narrative research by lending authenticity and subjectivity. Perhaps this is why photographs are used extensively in academic conference presentations and articles to document and bear witness to researched events.

Methods that highlight photos are used in educational research to collect data from research participants. To study particular life experiences, some researchers invite participants to take photographs and then tell stories about the experiences that these photographs depict (Bach, 2007). Bach calls this method *visual narrative inquiry,* and others, *photovoice* (Wang & Burris, 1997). Other educational researchers show photographs to their participants and discuss them to see what stories emerge; this method can be called *photo elicitation* (Wiebe, 2013) or *photo interviews* (Cappello, 2005). Moreover, educational researchers have used photographs to encourage students' writing for critical thinking (e.g., Chonody, 2018; Engblom, 2016) and for developing expository texts (Cummings, 2012). Our study contributes to the small body of educational literature that uses photographs in writing research; it does so by using photo analysis to study the collaborative writing of several education researchers who participated in a writing retreat.

Methodology

The following section describes our qualitative research study, where we (the study participants/retreat attendees) selected several photographs depicting ourselves and others from a larger collection archived by the university that organizes the retreat. To analyze the photographs, we developed a method of photo analysis that invites written analysis from someone in the photo and someone who is not, reasoning that this collaborative approach is appropriate for a study of collaborative writing. Details about the setting and format of this research study, including the three chosen photographs and our framework for analyses, are shared below.

Setting

The setting for this study is an annual academic writing retreat, located at a rural retreat centre in southwestern Ontario, Canada. Inspired by Grant's

WRITING ABOUT WRITING

(2006) biannual retreat for women from three different New Zealand universities, this retreat is a four-day event that routinely brings together writers from several faculties of education for the purpose of supporting scholarly writing initiatives. Approximately 12 scholars share a bunkhouse with separate bedrooms and a common workspace. Retreats began in 2007, and each includes different scholars, workshops, and work-in-progress groups.

During the first evening, scholars participate in a 75-minute orientation, which includes goal-setting and -sharing. At that time, they are also assigned work-in-progress groups of three to four members and introduced to a series of questions adapted from Grant (2008) that are used to guide the group sessions. This introductory session helps to establish norms for newcomers, as well as maintain the "continuity of the retreat culture" (Grant, 2006, p. 484). During the day, participants choose between writing in their own rooms or in the common space. They are invited to attend an optional after-lunch writing workshop (one hour) and required to share a page or paragraph from their ongoing writing with their groups during an after-dinner discussion (one hour). During the evenings, many choose to relax together or independently with walks on nearby trails, board games, novels, et cetera, to recharge from their hard work and the physical discomfort of writing (Farr et al., 2009; Moore, 2003; Murray & Newton, 2009). On the last morning, writers debrief on progress toward their goals, share plans for sustaining writing, and make suggestions for future retreats.

Participants

The participants are the three authors, all of whom attended the retreat, although not necessarily the same year. Kari-Lynn and Mary attended the retreat independently. They came to know each other from supervising a teacher education practicum in South Africa. Discussions of their retreat experience and an invitation to become part of a larger retreat writing team led them to begin this project. Natasha, also a member of the larger research team, joined later. Natasha had attended three retreats with Kari-Lynn; during one, Kari-Lynn provided feedback on Natasha's manuscript. Thus, this study began with all three authors attending the annual writing retreat (although not necessarily the same ones), two authors framing a topic, and a network forming when the third expressed interest in the project. Since the authors are from different parts of Canada, their collaboration relied on Skype and Google Docs for side-by-side writing, and Google Docs for turn writing.

Data Collection

This study is one in the larger *Writing About Writing* project that flowed out of the annual retreat. The data collected for the larger project includes over a decade of retreat photographs, currently stored in an online database by the university that organizes the retreat, alongside other data including progress reports, retreat evaluations, testimonials, workshop materials, and attendance records. For our exploration of collaborative writing, we chose to focus primarily on photographs.

Data Analysis

For this study, we developed a method informed by our previous experience (Winters, 2009; Wiebe, 2013). We call our approach *collaborative photo analysis*, because it invites analysis from someone in the photo (the subject), and someone who is not (the onlooker). Both parties independently answer a series of questions about a photo (summarized in Table 12.1) in the form of a story, a vignette. They then discuss their stories together, looking for themes, gaps, and contradictions. Such collaborative analysis is a fitting method for our study of collaborative writing. Since writing collaborations are rarely linear and never straightforward, we developed an approach that could capture complexity, encouraging analysis of who is in the photo and how they are engaging with each other (the social); the space in which the writers are located, and the resources in the photograph that appear to be supporting their writing (the semiotic); and the different stories about writing that emerge from viewing the photos (the critical). By bringing together the reflections of the subject with the interpretations of the onlooker, our method offers a fuller description of the complexities of writing retreat experience; specifically, how collaborative writing emerges during a retreat.

Each author selected a photograph that was (1) shot at the retreat, and (2) included her image (i.e., she was a subject in the photo). Once two photographs were chosen by each subject author using these criteria, she assigned a photo to each of the others. Then, each subject author analyzed her photographs using Table 12.1 without discussing her ideas with the others. In the meantime, another author – an onlooker – using the same framework, offered a secondary interpretation of the photo.

Findings

For brevity, analyses of three retreat photos are shared below. Though each photo was analyzed using all questions in Table 12.1, the vignettes presented include only some themes from that framework.

WRITING ABOUT WRITING

155

TABLE 12.1   Photo analysis framework

Authorship
- Who is in the photo?
- How many participants are there?
- What do the participants appear to be doing?
- Are there participants present, but outside of the frame?
- Who is taking the photo? Are they a part of the interaction or a passerby?
- Is the angle of the photo low, medium, or high? What does the angle suggest about the photographer (e.g., expertise, power connection to subjects)?
- What is the intention of the photo? Was it posed, or candid (taken without subject knowledge)?

Space
- Where is the scene located? If outdoor, what is in the foreground and in the background? If indoor, what is the nature of the room (e.g., boardroom)? How is the room designed and furnished?
- How is the space lit?
- How are the participants using/interacting with the space?

Structured Routines
- How are the participants engaging with each other?
- Does the photograph indicate a structured routine? (e.g., a "peer critique group" implies two or more writers, reviewing and providing constructive criticism of each other's work)

Embodiment
- Where are the participants directing their gaze?
- How are the participants positioning their bodies?
- What are their facial expressions?
- What is suggested by their body language? (e.g., hand on another's shoulder suggests leadership)

Semiotic Resources and Potentials
- What artifacts (man-made objects) are in the space (e.g., coffee cups, computers)?
- What signs/semiotic resources are being used to communicate: visual, verbal, written, gestural, musical? (e.g., signs of written communication include printed texts, pens, computers)
- What are the semiotic potentials of these artifacts/resources (i.e., what meanings do they hold)?

Emergent Stories
What stories emerge for both subject and onlooker?
- *Story about photo:* A story that describes the circumstances captured by the photo.
- *Story behind photo:* A story triggered by the photo, but which is not actually about the circumstances captured by the photo.
- *Story between photos:* A story that links together several photos under analysis.

FIGURE 12.1
Work in progress group

Discussion

The collaborative analysis of photographs taken at the writing retreats speak to several key elements of collaborative writing. First, the photo analyses invite a conversation regarding how annual writing retreats foster collaborative writing among participants. All three photos depict different ways of being in a moment of writing and different ways of being in a moment of writing collaboration. Second, the photo analyses invite thought about how photos can capture a moment at a writing retreat, informing research about retreats and collaborative writing. Analyses of photos, differing interpretations from the moment, and the authenticity of stories behind the photos provide a nuanced discussion of the experience. Details of these discussions are shared below together with consideration of limitations and strengths of this research.

WRITING ABOUT WRITING

TABLE 12.2   Photo analysis of work in progress

Kari-Lynn (subject):	Natasha (onlooker):

Authorship: Three of the 2015 retreat participants were engaged in an academic peer critique session. Though not seen in the photo, there were several other retreat participants hosting similar in-progress critique groups in the same room.

Space and Semiotic Resources: The make-shift boardroom table between us provided a place to set our computers and notebooks, but it made sightlines to the other's computer screens more difficult since we were across from one another rather than beside each other. Often we would turn the computer around to show what we were working on.

Structured Routines: A "peer critique group" implies two or more writers reviewing and providing constructive criticism of each other's work. As is typical for peer critique groups, three primary modes of communication were highlighted. (1) language (speaking and listening), (2) visual (PowerPoint presentations, computer screen sharing), and (3) printed text (taking notes).

Space and Semiotic Resources: The three participants are sitting quite close together around one end of a makeshift boardroom table, closer than they would sit if working individually on their writing. Kari-Lynn is sitting at the corner of the table, which appears uncomfortable for working, but brings her closer to her peers for conversation. Each participant has a laptop open in front of them; Nicola has an open book by her, and Dragana some paper. A projector is on the table and a screen behind at the head of the table, but the projector is not turned on, indicating this is not a formal presentation.

Structured Routines: Combining my insider knowledge with the participants' body language, their close seating, the open laptops, and the turned-off projector, leads me to conclude that this is the meeting of a work-in-progress-group rather than a formal presentation or individual quiet writing time.

Embodiment: Kari-Lynn is slightly slumped. Her head is on her hands. Is she tired, bored, disengaged, or listening intently?

(cont.)

TABLE 12.2   Photo analysis of work in progress (*cont.*)

Kari-Lynn (subject):	Natasha (onlooker):
Story about Photo: It was a sunny June day and I felt guilty being inside. I remember wishing that we could conduct our meeting outside. The lighting was natural sunlight, as shown in the picture. The room temperature was comfortable. *Story behind Photo*: Though I wished I was outside that day, the critique that I was given by my peers was quite helpful. They helped me narrow down my topic for a book chapter (about body image) and showed me that there were at least two or three more articles that could come from my data set- one about methodology and one about how bodies are implicated in every subject in school. I was grateful for the connections they offered.	*Stories between Photos*: This picture elicited memories of my experiences with work-in progress groups at retreats, and recollections that these groups aren't always effective. I replaced mandatory work-in-progress groups with optional consultations and workshops at the writing retreats I coordinate after participants emphasized that they preferred the quiet writing time.

How Did the Annual Academic Writing Retreat Foster Collaborative Writing among Participants?

The photograph "Work Time" shows several scholars in the shared retreat workspace. They have many writing resources in common (computers, paper, pens). To the onlooker, the photograph might suggest that some participants were engaging in collaborative writing, perhaps side-by-side writing or turn writing. This did happen at the retreats attended by the authors. However, according to Mary, at the time of the photograph, participants were not writing collaboratively; rather, they were respectfully sharing a quiet space while working on independent projects. Yet, this opportunity to write in silence amongst other writers offered Mary the inciting moment of a book collaboration with others outside of the current retreat, as well as this chapter.

Conversely, in the photograph "Nature Walk," collaborative writing was happening even though the image depicts Natasha alone. This photo is framed

FIGURE 12.2
Nature walk

by foliage (not usually a resource associated with writing), yet collaborative writing was occurring behind the scenes, as Natasha and the photographer discussed a grant proposal. This photo offers a unique way to think about writing collaborations – writing while walking! "Nature Walk," although taken outside, and depicting only one person, could be described as side-by-side writing (Ritchie & Rigano, 2007). The analysis of this photo reinforces the observation that time away from the work of writing, to relax and socialize with other retreat participants, can also facilitate "informal dialogue and feedback" (Kornhaber at al., 2016, p. 1221).

The photo, "Work-in-Progress Groups," depicts collaborative writing in action through peer critique (Danielewicz & McGowan, 2005). Here, participants were working together and following a structured routine of peer feedback. Peer groups can have mixed results, depending on such factors as familiarity of participants, personalities, comfort and experience giving feedback,

TABLE 12.3   Photo analysis of nature walk

Natasha (subject):	Mary (onlooker):
Space and Semiotic Resources: In this photo, I am emerging from the lush green woods, walking down the nature trail that is closest to the retreat bunkhouse.	*Space and Semiotic Resources:* I get the sense that Natasha wanted to be alone for this walk as the area seems quite secluded. Directly overhead, the branches high up in the trees seem to have grown entwined. It seems like a long, secluded pathway. The light is diffused.
Embodiment: My arms and hips are swinging, and I am placing one foot in front of the other like I am on the catwalk. The deliberate placement of my feet suggests that I was self-conscious and the photograph was posed, which indeed it was.	*Embodiment:* Natasha's walk seems purposeful – she strides with arm movement. Natasha may be very much enjoying the space and the solitude but not meandering on the walk. Her body positioning indicates the relaxation that may come from a brisk and enjoyable walk. She seems to be taking long strides and swaying her arms. I cannot see the facial expression but I get the sense of calm solitude – a neutral expression perhaps.
Emergent Stories behind Photo: I took this walk at the invitation of another participant, who I met and became friends with during previous retreats. She wanted to discuss an idea for a grant proposal. After our conversation, she took the photo to capture the moment. The photographer subsequently wrote a successful grant proposal.	*Structured Routines:* The photo looks candid; in fact, it looks like Natasha has no idea the photo was being taken.
Emergent Stories Between Photos: I see this photo as a companion to the photo called "Worktime." For me, a good retreat includes writing in synergy with others, as Mary seems to be doing in "Worktime." Good retreats also include relaxing breaks from the hard work of writing; and sharing ideas and advice for writing projects, as I did with the photographer of " Nature Walk."	*Emergent Story about Photo:* I feel like the intention is to capture the moment of communing with nature as a means of quiet thinking while enjoying some exercise. If l were to come upon Natasha in this moment, I would likely smile but would not wish to disturb her as I feel like she is deep in thought.

FIGURE 12.3   Work time

workspaces, and knowledge of each other's writing topics and methodologies. Some of these complexities are captured in the reflections on "Work-in-Progress Groups." Kari-Lynn recalls wishing her group could have met outdoors, although in hindsight, she recognized that an outdoor discussion would not have enabled the same kind of feedback (e.g., bright natural light would have made it difficult to read computer screens). Natasha interpreted Kari-Lynn's body language as possibly bored or disengaged. This reminded Natasha of her own unsatisfactory experiences of work-in-progress groups at retreats. Yet, it is partly because Natasha worked with Kari-Lynn in work-in-progress group that she joined this study. Connections developed during scheduled writing consultations can lead to shared writing projects post-retreat. In fact, for the three authors of this chapter, the retreats have contributed to as many as 14 grant applications, presentations, or publications co-authored with academics we met or collaborated with there, a published academic book, and an additional two publications that received peer review at the retreats.

How Can Photos/Photo Analyses Help Inform Research about Retreats and Collaborative Writing?

Photos lend authenticity and subjectivity to research. Their analyses remind us that events are happening (and writing is flowing) simultaneously within,

TABLE 12.4   Photo analysis of work time

Mary (subject):	Kari-Lynn (onlooker):
Authorship: This was a quiet, individual work on writing time. We were not substantially talking to each other, but there was no real requirement for silence. Participants were sitting together, but distanced, with a space between us. None of these projects were collaborative projects. All seem at ease working in a shared space but not interacting – attention is focused on their laptops with hands on keyboards. I am sitting at the far end of the table, unaware that a photograph is being taken.	*Authorship:* It is unknown who is actually taking this photo as he/she is not seen. I would assume from the medium angle, eye level and long shot framing that the photographer was someone who was trying to archive the event. This picture was not posed.
Space and Semiotic Resources: Eyeglasses are removed, water bottles and coffee cups are present for refreshment during the writing time. Bright sunshine and green trees are visible outside from the window. The room has a "cottage-like" feel to it with the wood paneling, flowered curtain valances, and pictures on the walls. But, it also has a boardroom-like feel like feel with the tables moved together in the centre of the room and chairs surrounding it. There is a windowed door with a wooden rocking chair outside the door on a veranda.	*Space and Semiotic Resources:* Individuals are spread apart in a large well-lit indoor meeting room, where several tables that have been pushed together to make a large rectangle . It appears that each participant has his or her own work-stations. Mary is seated at the end of a long set of tables, hard at work. Though she is sharing the space with the others, everyone seems very busy, working in parallel on their own individual projects. Mary is positioned within the group as a colleague. Six scholars from various universities work individually in a shared meeting room space. Each individual has his/her own computer to use. Artefacts include papers, pens, computers, and cables, coffee cups and water bottles. It would appear that linguistic and digital sign systems (e.g., talking, writing, researching) tend to be the most used within this space, as most of the participants seem to have notes beside them. That said, participants may also be looking at websites and be viewing images.

(cont.)

WRITING ABOUT WRITING

TABLE 12.4 Photo analysis of work time (*cont.*)

Mary (subject):	Kari-Lynn (onlooker):
Story behind Photo: This photograph was taken in the afternoon and while it was sunny outside there was a nip of cold in the air. I was grateful for my favourite yellow cardigan sweater. I was also grateful for my presence at the writing retreat as I was taking the place of Kari-Lynn (who could not be there). I was focused on figuring out the structure of turning my PhD dissertation into a scholarly book as I had just signed a book deal. This photograph shows a form of engagement I welcome—while I enjoy the presence of others in a room, I appreciate quiet focus on my writing in the moment. I do not like a lot of noise or distractions while writing but I love being in beautiful and relaxed spaces while writing. At these moments I find voices unwelcome. Everything about this photograph presents the way I like to work – sunshine, comfortable and soft clothing, calm cottage-like environment, and quiet space. I was feeling happy, productive and grateful.	*Structured Routines:* Though the individuals may have conversations throughout the day, at this point in time they seem to not be engaging with each other, rather they seem invested in their own work. *Embodiment:* The gaze of the participants tend to be focused on their computers. Their bodies are relaxed, but in most cases, hunched over their computers. Facial expressions tend to be neutral.

around, and between retreat participants, even when all participants are not physically present, and photos make tangible even more of the writing collaborations facilitated by the retreat. For example, "Nature Walk," even though it was photographed away from the group, allowed viewers to be present with Natasha as she walked and come to understand how collaborative writing was occurring. Moreover, Natasha's analysis of this photo suggests that writing collaborations happen not only during formal sessions of writing, but also during downtimes. Without Natasha's photo and our analyses, the retreat may have appeared more formal, including only structured tasks like work-in-progress groups or private writing times.

Visualization is an important aspect of writing. Photos and their analyses also aid researchers in seeing (imaging) and remembering retreat moments and settings. For example, in the photo "Work Time," seeing Mary in a yellow cardigan with the bright sun behind her, helps researchers to recognize not only the time of year (e.g., that the retreat may have happened in the summer), but also the feeling of the event (e.g., this rustic, makeshift boardroom might be air-conditioned). Here, through photos and their analysis, viewers/readers have opportunities to visualize particular writing moments and gain more nuanced understandings of these events.

Opportunities for documenting collaborative writing, as well as more nuanced interplays of the social, the semiotic, and the critical, give voice to differing perspectives and encourage richer discussions. For example, while Kari-Lynn was photographed daydreaming about being outside in "Work in Progress Groups," this photo was interpreted by an onlooker as her either being bored or intently engaged. This is often the case with photo analyses, since each person brings their own experiences and background knowledge to the photograph and sees the photo in his/her own nuanced way. Therefore, the onlooker will often see different things than the subject. And the subject will know different things from the onlooker. Natasha's and Mary's analyses of "Nature Walk" demonstrate this idea. While both comment on Natasha's purposeful walk, Mary saw the photograph as spontaneously capturing a solitary and relaxed moment, whereas Natasha recalled it as a posed, self-conscious photograph that commemorated a shared walk-and-talk about writing. Both Mary and Natasha, however, arrive at a similar conclusion: Natasha was enjoying some time away from writing (which Natasha, agreeing with Grant (2006) and Murray and Newton (2009), sees as an important part of a writing retreat). Subjects assume certain positions. Onlookers assign certain positions. Neither is fully complete; rather there is a synergy of truth that runs in and between the photos. Indeed, these multiplicities of truth, when investigated through a researcher's lens, help inform fields of research around critical community collaborations.

Limitations and Strengths

This qualitative study was part of a larger project. Yet, because of the method we created and chose to use – collaborative photo analysis – only certain aspects of the retreat were highlighted and only the aspects of the retreat that included us. Therefore, to some extent, our conclusions about retreats have been generalized.

WRITING ABOUT WRITING

That said, meaningful interplays were evoked. Some were semiotic (based on the meanings of the resources used as well as the settings), social (the ways people gathered at the retreat), and critical (the ways authors assumed and assigned perspectives). This approach led to deeper conversations and more nuanced perspective-taking. Our analyses of the retreat demonstrated that photo analysis creates space for dialogues and discrepancies as well.

Implications

This study explored an annual residential writing retreat, where members from across various universities gather, for the purpose of supporting scholarly writing initiatives. Below, we describe some implications of the research for retreat organizers who wish to support collaborative writing during retreats, and for researchers who are considering adding photo analysis to their approaches for studying writing.

Implications for Retreat Organizers

This study contributes to the research on writing retreats by providing a deeper look at how retreats can foster collaborative writing and develop an ongoing writing community. Our photo analyses suggest that simply providing a space for people to write side by side does not always lead to collaboration. Moreover, scheduling peer discussion groups does not always mean participants will be engaged or that interactions will be useful. However, our study confirms existing evidence that bringing together participants for the shared purpose of writing, and creating space for downtime, does indeed help to develop rapport and encourage spontaneous conversation about writing; in turn, this can help to develop post-retreat collaboration (Kornhaber et al., 2016). Effective writing retreats include time away from writing to honour the "treat" part of the "writing retreat." The paradox is that taking time to play can lead to more writing collaborations.

Implications for Researchers

Our study developed a method of photo analysis that brings together subjects and onlookers of photographs. We used the method to study the phenomenon of collaborative writing at an annual writing retreat. The method offers a different approach to studying collaborative writing and other writing experiences at retreats in a field characterized by surveys and interviews (Kornhaber et al., 2016). The method itself fosters collaborative writing, requiring both subjects and onlookers to analyze each others' vignettes about the photographs and to make sense, together, of the contradictions and commonalities in their interpretations. Photo analysis can give us a better sense of what collaborative writing looks like, literally by offering visuals to go with the textual descriptions of the research studies, and by elucidating the private moments at a writing retreat. Our method of collaborative photo analysis can also be used in other research contexts, such as classroom interactions. It is a way to think about the subjective and onlooker perspective and to explore what these perspectives mean and how they are perceived in an interaction. Moreover, collaborative photo analysis offers an option for member checking (through subject analysis of their own images) and can form a component of triangulation in a mixed-methods study (Hurworth, 2003).

Conclusion

Our work with photos demonstrates some ways annual academic writing retreats can foster collaboration. Findings suggest that that annual academic writing retreats can provide spaces where writing can become collegial, collaborative, and ongoing across time and geographical space. Different manifestations of collaborative writing (e.g., talking about a writing project on a walk, work-in-progress groups, quietly co-authoring texts in the retreat workspace) enable writers to build partnerships and implement different writing practices. Annual writing retreats offer spaces where new collaborations can form, evolve, and network over time. In addition, engaging in photo analyses of retreats offers a unique way to explore collaborative writing. The three authors told different stories of their writing experiences, demonstrating that collaborative writing can occur through different mechanisms created during, and through, retreats.

Analyzing photographs offers a helpful way to inquire about retreat and writing experiences. The photos themselves, as well as the ways they are interpreted by the subjects and the onlookers offer unique assemblages of meaning of how writing and specifically collaborative writing occur in writing retreats. Multiplicities of the social (e.g., Who is in the photo? Where is the photographer?), the semiotic (e.g., Where is the photo taken? What are the artifacts within it?), and the critical (e.g., What perspectives do people assume and assign when writing within a community?) create complex interplays, including structures of cultural routine and the situated contexts in which the writing occurs. Other benefits of using photos for exploring writing experiences include making the public and private aspects of writing collaborations more tangible, and in our case, even more collaborative.

WRITING ABOUT WRITING 167

Acknowledgements

This study is one in a larger *Writing about Writing* project which received research ethics clearance from Brock University (15-035) and the University of Windsor (15-178). According to principal investigator Dr. Snezana Ratkovic, these clearances include permission to use the photographs in this chapter.

References

Bach, H. (2007). Composing a visual narrative inquiry. *The handbook of narrative inquiry* (pp. 280–307). Thousand Oaks, CA: Sage.

Cappello, M. (2005). Photo interviews: Eliciting data through conversations with children. *Field Methods, 17*(2), 170–182.

Chonody, J. (2018). Perspectives on aging among graduate social work students: Using photographs as an online pedagogical activity. *Journal of the Scholarship of Teaching and Learning, 18*(2), 158–173.

Cummings, S. (2012). Teaching for writing expository responses to narrative texts. *The Reading Teacher, 65*(6), 381–386.

Danielewicz, J., & McGowan, J. (2005). Collaborative work: A practical guide. *Symploke, 13*(1–2), 168–181.

Dickson-Swift, V., James, E. L., Kippen, S., Talbot, L., Verrinder, G., & Ward, B. (2009). A non-residential alternative to off campus writers' retreats for academics. *Journal of Further and Higher Education, 33*(3), 229–239. doi:10.1080/03098770903026156

Elbow, P., & Sorcinelli, M. D. (2006). The faculty writing place: A room of our own. *Change, 38*(6), 17–22.

Engblom, C. (2016). Prefabricated images in young children's text-making at school. *Designs for Learning, 8*(1), 37–47.

Farr, C. K., Cavallaro, J. Civil, G., & Cochrane, S. (2009). Taming the publishing beast: The College of St. Catherine Scholars' Retreat. *Change, (May/June)*, 15–19.

Grant, B. (2006). Writing in the company of other women: Exceeding the boundaries. *Studies in Higher Education, 31*(4), 483–495.

Grant, B. M. (2008). *Academic writing retreats: A facilitator's guide.* Milperra, NSW: HERDSA.

Grant, B., & Knowles, S. (2000). Flights of imagination: Academic women be(com)ing writers. *International Journal for Academic Development, 5*(1), 6–19.

Hurworth, R. (2003). Photo-interviewing for research. *Social Research Update, 40*, 1–7.

Johnson, H. A., Blunt, H. B., & Bagley, P. J. (2017). A time and a place to write and hone skills: A writer's retreat for faculty and graduate students. *College & Research Libraries News, 78*(4).

Kornhaber, R., Cross, M., Betihavas, V., & Bridgman, H. (2016). The benefits and challenges of academic writing retreats: An integrative review. *Higher Education Research & Development, 35*(6), 1210–1277.

Kress, G., & van Leewen, T. (1996). *Reading images: The grammar of visual design.* London, UK: Routledge.

Moore, S. (2003). Writers' retreats for academics: Exploring and increasing the motivation to write. *Journal of Further and Higher Education, 27*(3), 333–342.

Morton, H. (2017). The new visual testimonial: Narrative, authenticity, and subjectivity in emerging commercial photographic practice. *Media and Communication, 5*(2), 11–20.

Murray, R., & Cunningham, E. (2011). Managing researcher development: 'Drastic transition'? *Studies in Higher Education, 36*(7), 831–845.

Murray, S., & Newton, M. (2009). Writing retreat as structured intervention: Margin or mainstream? *Higher Education Research & Development, 28*(5), 541–554.

Murray, R., Steckley, L., & MacLeod, I. (2012). Research leadership in writing for publication: A theoretical framework. *British Educational Research Journal, 38*(5), 765–781. doi:10.1080/01411926.2011.580049

Oermann, M. H., Nicoll, L. H., & Block, L. (2014). Long-term impact of an intensive writing retreat experience on participants' ongoing writing behaviors. *Nursing Education Perspectives, 35*(2), 134.

Price, E., Coffey, B., & Nethery, A. (2015). An early career academic network: What worked and what didn't. *Journal of Further and Higher Education, 39*(5), 680–698. doi:10:1080/0309877X.2014.971106

Ritchie, S. M., & Rigano, D. L. (2007). Writing together metaphorically and bodily side-by-side: An inquiry into collaborative academic writing. *Reflective Practice, 8*(1), 123–125.

Trafton, A., (2014, January 16). *In the blink of an eye.* Retrieved from http://news.mit.edu/2014/in-the-blink-of-an-eye-0116

Wang, C., & Burris, M. A. (1997). Photovoice: Concept, methodology, and use for participatory needs assessment. *Health Education and Behavior, 24*(3), 369–387.

Wiebe, N. G. (2013). Mennonite memories of Pelee Island, Ontario, 1925–1950: Toward a framework for visual narrative inquiry. *Narrative Inquiry, 23*(2), 405–423.

Wiebe, N. G. (2016). *Report on the 2015 Writing Retreats at Willistead.* Office of Research and Innovation Services, University of Windsor, Ontario. Retrieved from nwiebe@uwindsor.ca

Winters, K.-L. (2009). *Authorship as assemblage: Multimodal literacies of play, literature, and drama* (Unpublished doctoral dissertation). Brock University, St. Catharines Ontario, Canada.

PART 4

Collaborative Writing Groups

∵

CHAPTER 13

Writing within an Academic Microculture: Making Our Practice Visible

Cheryl Jeffs, Carol Berenson, Patti Dyjur, Kimberley A. Grant,
Frances Kalu, Natasha Kenny, Kiara Mikita, Robin Mueller and
Lorelli Nowell

Abstract

Academics who find themselves institutionally situated in a new or non-traditional discipline with the expectation for scholarship will benefit from the perspectives and learnings of a diverse team of educational developers who share a common scholarship goal. We position ourselves as belonging to a microculture (Mårtensson & Roxå, 2016), as we share a working context in which our collaborative writing norms and traditions are currently in development. In this chapter, we provide examples of, and reflect on, the following collaborative writing activities in which we have been involved at different times: writing in an interdisciplinary team, leveraging a project into scholarly writing, gathering together to write in group settings, fostering writing productivity through retreats, and facilitating a virtual collaborative writing group. We address models, approaches, strategies, strengths, limitations and recommendations that relate to our different experiences. These make visible the assumptions, norms, practices and conventions regarding how we write and publish in the context of our microculture where limited time is allotted to scholarship. Ultimately our narratives converge around the themes of valuing difference, attending to process, and critically reflecting on our writing practice.

Keywords

microculture – educational development – collaborative writing – interdisciplinary – retreats – group settings – non-traditional discipline

We are an academic group of educational developers with diverse backgrounds, roles, and responsibilities. As indicated in our Educational Development Unit's strategic plan (2014), we share a common goal to enhance postsecondary teaching and learning. Within this context, we bring our varied disciplinary backgrounds and interests to bear on individual and collaborative writing projects within and beyond our scholarly group. As with other academics, we face numerous demands on our time and energy that pose challenges to our writing practices and productivity (Jensen, 2017; Olszewska & Lock, 2016). In this chapter, we share and reflect on our practice-based and evidence-based perspectives, experiences, and strategies for strengthening our writing partnerships and commitments to scholarship. As members of an academic unit who individually and uniquely contribute to shared goals, we position ourselves in this discussion as belonging to a microculture. Mårtensson and Roxå (2016) defined microcultures as "local work-contexts where the members over time develop traditions and habits" (p. 177). Microcultures are characterized by high internal trust, intense interactions, collegial support, and rich external collaborations. As the field of educational development evolves and redefines itself on the postsecondary landscape (Gibbs, 2013; Kenny & Taylor, 2017), our roles as educational developers transform from service-providers to colleagues and leaders of change (Gibbs, 2013; Kenny, Popovic, et al., 2017; Knapper, 2016; McDonald et al., 2016; Taylor, 2005). As we navigate this shifting terrain, our local work context can be characterized as a microculture aligned with Mårtensson and Roxå's (2016) features of intensity, collegiality, collaboration, and trust.

In this chapter, we make explicit our microculture's developing traditions and habits with respect to collaborative academic writing, and as such we contribute to educational development as a burgeoning field within academic institutions. Our relatively new academic roles could also be considered non-traditional in comparison to those of many of our institutional colleagues. Therefore, we also hope that academics who find themselves similarly institutionally situated in new and/or non-traditional disciplines with the expectation for scholarship will benefit from the perspectives and learnings of our diverse team. Sword (2017) wrote about the richness of differences in writing practices which we embrace and draw upon in the discussion to follow.

This chapter is the result of a collaboration among nine educational developers. We come from a variety of disciplinary backgrounds including the Arts and Humanities, Sociology, Education, Nursing, Landscape Architecture, and Environmental Science. In the five sections that follow, we offer our perspectives and experiences of: (1) writing in an interdisciplinary team (authored by Kimberley A. Grant, Kiara Mikita, Lorelli Nowell), (2) leveraging a project into scholarly writing (Patti Dyjur), (3) gathering together to write in group settings (Frances Kalu, Lorelli Nowell), (4) fostering writing productivity through retreats (Robin Mueller), and (5) facilitating a virtual collaborative writing group (Natasha Kenny). We address models, approaches, strategies, strengths, limitations, and recommendations that relate to our varied experiences. While there is no single preferred writing method posited here, these narratives converge to make visible the assumptions, norms, practices, and conventions regarding how we write and publish, especially given that we have a limited amount of time allotted to scholarship in the context of our microculture. The features of our microculture are discussed and summarized by Carol Berenson and Cheryl Jeffs in the introduction and conclusion of this chapter.

Writing in an Interdisciplinary Team

A group of three of the authors (Kimberley A. Grant, Kiara Mikita, Lorelli Nowell), all new postdoctoral scholars in novel fellowships within a teaching and learning institute, decided to explore our early experiences through collaborative self-study. We chose this as an approach fitting for a multidisciplinary team – from education, sociology, and nursing – already comfortable with various forms of qualitative research. We aimed to document our transitions from graduate students to postdoctoral scholars, and to contribute to the growing body of knowledge about postdoctoral scholars in non-traditional roles, as we were struck by the resonance and coherence of our ideas. However, as we began to write, we encountered differences between the individual disciplinary microcultures that informed our writing and research practices (Marquis, Mårtensson, & Healey, 2017). We had to navigate our disorientation and persevere in the process to create a unified work that incorporated all our voices.

Most often, the substance of our writing coalesced around similar themes. Challenges, however, emerged early in our writing process. While we were familiar with the variety of styles associated with different disciplinary journals, we found ourselves differing over required research article components and naming conventions associated with those parts. The health researcher defaulted to common qualitative research reporting standards (Tong, Sainsbury, & Craig, 2007) and IMRAD structure (introduction, methods, results, and discussion; for example, see Sollaci & Pereira, 2004). Faced with IMRAD's scientific structure, the sociologist, accustomed to constructivist and discourse analytic research conventions, struggled with notions of 'data collection' and 'findings' in self-produced data, contending instead this amounted to 'data generation' and 'interpretation' (Mason, 2002). We also differed over what should and should not be included in each section. The education researcher wove descriptive and lengthy quotes throughout her writing to honour and highlight cited authors' linguistic choices, while others maintained that references are best brought only into certain article sections and should be mostly paraphrased instead of directly cited. Our differences echoed Poole's (2013) observations that, when "academics from a range of issues collaborate ... they face the challenge of translating disciplinary research languages and of understanding research cultures" (p. 136).

Initially, we found ourselves surprised by our differences, failing to recognize them as assumptions that were rooted in our disciplinary training and experience. We struggled to account for our disparate positions as they seemed *normal* to us. To support the legitimacy of our respective positions, we pointed to work we had defended and published, and to documented journal conventions. As we talked through our conflicting approaches, we realized they emerged from disciplinary differences. By asking and inviting questions about our dissimilarities instead of making declarations about what research articles do and do not include, our conversations began to reflect more curiosity than conflict. We came to embrace the richness of our unanticipated differences, allowing us space to establish content and naming priorities. Where tensions persisted, we deferred to the chosen journal's protocols to arbitrate differences.

On the whole, we were fascinated by how significant and specific our differences could be and by how much we had taken for granted that our disciplinary training and experience were *the norm*. This collaborative process allowed us to become more thoughtful and attentive writers, and we are grateful to one another for broadening our understanding of research dissemination practices. In the end, working closely with colleagues from other disciplines afforded opportunities for learning that we would not have otherwise experienced. Although our initial disorientation was uncomfortable, facing our points of difference with open, respectful dialogue allowed us to more fully explore and articulate our disciplinary norms as well as thoughtfully expand our definitions of *what counts* and *what is normal* in academic research and writing.

Leveraging a Project into Scholarly Writing

As stated by the authors in the previous section, collaborating with colleagues can present challenges if disciplinary differences exist, but adds immense richness as well. I (Patti Dyjur) have found that collaborating with people in my own discipline can present similar challenges and benefits. In my role as an educational development consultant I work with faculties and departments on projects that can take a year to complete. In one such project, the faculty conducted a large, complex review of over twenty programs. The scale of the review required a distributed leadership approach, with three of us working together

WRITING WITHIN AN ACADEMIC MICROCULTURE · 175

closely to coordinate and support groups as they conducted their curriculum reviews. Throughout the process this leadership team learned a great deal about putting theory into practice within a specific context. As a result, we wanted to share what we learned with a wider audience and leverage our successes by writing a journal article (McKenzie, 2008). Three of us worked on the same article, writing different sections and then pulling them together into one publication.

We experienced a number of benefits from writing the article collaboratively. Our collaborative writing effort allowed us to extend the project, leverage its successes, and share strategies with the wider academic community. We met as a group several times during the writing process, which allowed us to reflect on the project together and ask each other questions, ultimately leading to new insights about our work. This in turn improved my understanding of my practice (McKenzie, 2008). We also learned about writing from one another, which was especially important for me as a less seasoned writer; my collaborators had more experience with writing and publishing (Costa & Kallick, 1993). However, I was able to make a unique contribution to the chapter through my knowledge of curriculum review processes and literature in the field. Even though I was less experienced that the others, we all played a role in the article's success. By the time our article was published, one person on the team had moved to a new role at a different institution, so the collaborative writing not only fostered positive working relationships and strengthened collaboration across units, but established ties to other institutions as well.

While the writing process was valuable, it came with challenges too. Although we were from the same discipline, unlike the previous team of postdoctoral scholars, even we used different terms at times as there was a lack of consistency in the existing disciplinary literature. Early on, we had to decide what terms we would use in our chapter as a shared terminology was critical in communicating effectively with one another. Similarly, we each had a unique writing style and tone. For example, one collaborator was accustomed to writing in a passive voice while the others wrote in an active voice. After the initial draft of the article, we worked to knit the different sections of the article together with a similar writing tone so that it was not disjointed to the reader (Marquis et al., 2017). Another challenge was simply the logistics of scheduling meetings with three busy people who all worked in different locations. Even online meetings were tricky to arrange at times. However, we all agreed that the challenges we experienced were overshadowed by the benefits we received from writing the chapter together.

Based on my experiences with the project I would offer the following recommendations for others to consider. First, participating in a collaborative writing project can be an excellent way to reflect on your work, learn from others, and extend your understanding. Second, acknowledge that everyone can make unique contributions to the writing. For example, someone might have depth of experience in communicating with the publisher, proofing, and revising. At such times they can take a leadership role in the writing process (Marquis et al., 2017). Third, even though there can be challenges with collaborative writing, they can be an investment in strengthening working relationships, collaboration, and knowledge, within your department and even across institutions.

Gathering Together to Write in Group Settings

In contrast to the previous sections that discuss collaboration as being about working with others on the same piece of writing, we (Frances Kalu, Lorelli Nowell) frame collaboration in terms of sharing a supportive writing space. We are two recently graduated Ph.D.s who, as graduate students and now academics working in educational development, have come to understand there are considerable expectations to publish and disseminate our work. In working to meet the diverse demands of our roles, time becomes a luxury with regard to scholarly pursuits, making it difficult to write productively and meet scholarly writing expectations (Aitchison, 2009; Olszewska & Lock, 2016). We have sustained our academic writing by participating in and organizing writing groups. Although writing groups are often similar in intention, they can vary substantially in structure to meet the needs of the participants. Below, we describe the three writing group scenarios we have experienced with three different structures. Despite their differences, these groups shared a common goal to create space and opportunities for individuals to come together and be more productive in their writing.

The first writing group was developed to support graduate students campus-wide by offering a quiet space where students could come together weekly to write. Attendance was on a drop-in basis, with students articulating SMART goals (specific, measurable, attainable, relevant, and time-bound) for the session. The goals were shared verbally for accountability, and in written form as a personal reminder. Sessions were three hours in length and served as a space for focused academic writing. Although these sessions were successful based on anecdotal feedback from participants, we learned that the drop-in format presents challenges to creating relationships and forming cohesive and supportive writing groups.

Relationship building was reported as one of the key factors for success within a writing group described by Olszewska and Lock (2016). To address the component that was missing in the first writing group, relationship building was built intentionally into the second writing group facilitated for graduate students within a faculty who shared an interest in completing their dissertations. Sessions were held weekly for two hours every semester with mentorship from academic experts. The dynamics within the group confirm Roxå and Mårtensson's (2015) assertion that microcultures within the same faculty show a high degree of trust between the members. The writing space created became a safe space to share with each other, encourage one another, and build relationships (Olszewska & Lock, 2016). Participants had a 'writing-buddy' within the group that they were accountable to, creating close relationships and fostering collaborative learning.

The third structured writing group was built around Belcher's (2009) *Writing Your Journal Article in 12 weeks: A Guide to Academic Publishing Success.* Participants in this writing group aimed to deliberately set time aside to focus on their writing, set clear and definitive timelines for completing writing projects, and become active contributors within a microculture of like-minded writers. Similar to other writing groups (Olszewska & Lock, 2016), this group set goals to publish individual work by developing collaborative writing practices fostered by trusting, critical, and supportive writing relationships. Participants committed to writing a minimum of fifteen minutes per day for twelve weeks and meeting once per week for one hour to discuss their writing progress and challenges. At the end of each twelve-week session participants committed to completing and submitting their individual manuscripts for publication in peer reviewed journals.

As we reflected on our collective experiences, we recognized that, although increasing scholarly writing output was the main thrust of our writing groups, the learnings gained were much broader. We found regular interaction with our writing group peers allowed for deeper learning, relationship building, and co-construction of knowledge. Through committing to, and participating in, various writing groups we developed a stronger sense of academic accountability to ourselves and to others (Page, Edwards, & Wilson, 2012). As recent graduates and new educational developers, the social and situated practice of partaking in writing groups has helped us as our identities as academics evolve while increasing our self-confidence and self-efficacy in our academic writing. Furthermore, we developed integral skills in balancing the research, teaching, and service responsibilities inherent in academic positions.

Fostering Writing Productivity through Retreats

As with my colleagues in the previous section, my emphasis in this discussion is focused on creating an environment conducive to writing. I (Robin Mueller) struggled with lapses in my writing productivity for many months after launching my academic career – a situation that was stress-inducing, especially given increasing institutional publication demands and expectations regarding high levels of "performativity" (MacLeod, Steckley, & Murray, 2012). My writing productivity woes were due in part to the inevitable struggle a scholar experiences when attempting to find her fit within the postsecondary landscape, but for the most part, it was just really difficult for me to find the time to write. During my doctoral program I had determined that I was the kind of writer who required substantive blocks of time to generate momentum; the practice of daily writing for short periods (Belcher, 2009) was not productive for me. I knew that I valued the benefits of solitary writing, while still longing to be a part of a writing community (Murray & Newton, 2009; Olszewska & Lock, 2016). As a consequence, I have developed a hybrid writing retreat model that allows me to experience writing as a simultaneously individual and collective process. I have structured my individual retreats in a way that mirrors a collaborative model, which enables me to schedule and enact solitary blocks of writing time while still leveraging the feeling, and benefit, of a critical collaborative community.

Murray and Newton (2009) proposed a structured collective writing retreat model that involves: (a) setting, sharing, and reviewing personal writing goals; (b) writing for scheduled periods of time; (c) taking intentional breaks from writing; (d) engaging in short periods of reflection and discussion; and (e) committing to a collective structure for ensuring accountability. The participants in this kind of retreat typically write while in a room together, but there is a significant amount of individual writing time supplemented by shorter periods of dialogue. Retreat participants working in this format have reported that the most valuable collective processes are goal sharing, peer review, collaborative reflection, and the enactment of collective accountability measures.

I have adopted a similar structure for my own individual writing retreats. During these retreats, I travel to an isolated spot away from the office, my home, my family, and society in general! I usually spend four to six days on my own, immersed in writing projects; interestingly, though, the writing I work on during retreat times often includes collaborative projects. Although I am physically isolated from my collaborators one of my requirements for a retreat location is a great wifi connection. This enables me to build in several structured collaborative opportunities during each retreat, including reflective conversations over telephone or Skype, draft sharing, peer review of text and images, and virtual working meetings using platforms such as Google Docs.

Since participants in structured collective writing retreats have identified the structure as an essential aspect to their productivity (Murray & Newton, 2009), I engage in a planning process prior to each retreat to ensure that I have

WRITING WITHIN AN ACADEMIC MICROCULTURE 179

developed goals and a daily structure for myself. Additionally, I share my goals with both my collaborators and supervisors and I create a plan for post-retreat reporting in order to keep myself accountable. The one aspect of Murray and Newton's (2009) model that is difficult to replicate at an individual retreat is the social aspect of intentional writing breaks and collective meals. While I schedule in breaks during my solitary retreats, I do miss the collegiality and generosity that seems to emerge as part of the social conversations during these times.

The pragmatic constraints of our academic roles include those that create obstacles when attempting to host collaborative writing retreats. However, we know that writing retreats contribute to scholarly productivity, motivation, and a sense of well-being for academics (MacLeod et al., 2012; Murray & Newton, 2009). Structuring individual retreats that mirror a collaborative model has enabled me to enhance my writing productivity substantially. When I retreat two or three times per year, I notice a dramatic difference with respect to my ability to manage several writing projects at once, and to contribute in meaningful ways to collaborative writing efforts. I recommend that all academics try such a retreat at least once a year to supplement and enhance their current writing practices. This model offers a reliable approach to ensuring the writing productivity that is expected within our roles, while also enabling ongoing collaborative writing practices.

Facilitating a Virtual Collaborative Writing Group

In this final section, I (Natasha Kenny) bring a different perspective to the discussion by sharing my experience of leading a collaborative writing initiative through a process which occurred mostly in an online environment. I was tasked with bringing together a group of eight colleagues from across the country to complete a peer-reviewed paper, from start to finish, in less than a year. The authors had never worked together, and entered this process with diverse levels of expertise, experience, and perspective on a broadly stated writing topic. I found comfort in using facilitative leadership approaches to guide the way during this project. Through this approach, I focused on providing direction, helping others connect to make meaning, and maximizing each author's strengths to help the group achieve its goal (Cufaude, 2005).

Building trust and encouraging action to *get things done* in a virtual collaborative writing group are imperative to the process. I quickly discovered that trust and intellectual intrigue bond the significant conversations (Roxå & Mårtensson, 2009) that occur both on and off the page in a collaborative writing group. In order to build trust, it is important to create a sense of community, connection, and belonging (Marquis, Healey, & Vine, 2014) for all group members.

I found that the first facilitative leadership strategy to help build trust was to establish collaborative intentions. Although these intentions will look different in each context, the statements below provided a helpful starting point. Our collaborative writing group developed the following statements by drawing upon the work of Lucky and Hoessler (2015) and Adaptive Schools and Cognitive Coaching (n.d.).

- Ensuring positive interdependence and promoting positive interaction;
- Ensuring individual accountability;
- Actively demonstrating positive group approaches;
- Promoting a spirit of inquiry and curiosity;
- Paraphrasing and probing;
- Putting ideas out on the table;
- Being attentive of self and others; and
- Presuming positive intentions.

To create space for writing and dialogue to occur, I intentionally facilitated activities that allowed for collaborative idea generation among all authors. Table 13.1 contains examples of activities that we used during various stages of the collaborative writing process.

As Marquis, Healey, and Vine (2014) suggested, I discovered that leading a collaborative writing group poses both opportunities and challenges given the diversity of expertise, experiences, and perspectives that exist amongst authors. Many challenges are easily overcome through regular communications, creating an inclusive and collaborative community, setting clear timelines, delegating roles and responsibilities, identifying and leveraging the strengths of individual group members, and breaking the process down into actionable tasks (Marquis et al., 2017). I found that much of the stress, anxiety, frustration, and confusion that occurs within a collaborative writing group can be alleviated by intentionally incorporating facilitative leadership strategies to inspire action, meaningful dialogue, and collaboration.

Conclusion

As indicated by the diverse voices represented in this chapter, within our microculture there are a variety of ways to both conceptualize and enact collaborative writing. To reiterate our earlier point, there is no single perspective or method privileged here. Some of our narratives see collaborative writing

WRITING WITHIN AN ACADEMIC MICROCULTURE

TABLE 13.1   Example collaborative writing strategies that can be used at various stages of the writing process

Writing stage	Activity
Introducing group members	Each group member shares their responses to the following questions: Tell us a little about yourself and why you joined this collaborative writing group. What are you most excited about? What sparked your interests related to the theme for our paper? As it relates to our writing theme, what 2-3 specific topics or questions would you be interested in further pursuing through this project? How do you hope to contribute to this collaborative writing group? What are your particular strengths related to research and writing? What would you prefer not to do? What concerns do you have about the process? How might we help address these concerns?
Focusing the scope	Group members break into conversation partners to discuss key themes that they see emerging to help focus our paper. Each pair drafts a brief statement of purpose (e.g. The purpose of this paper is to [WHAT?], in order to [WHY?]). The entire group discusses these statements and prepares a final version based on what resonates with them most.
Literature review	Each group member selects three to four papers that relate to the topic and prepares an annotation for each that contains a brief description of what it is about, how it links to the paper, and any resonant quotations and findings.
Drafting the paper	Writing partners draft manageable (300–500 words) sections of the paper. Each section is reviewed, added to and revised by a partner group.
Reviewing the draft paper	Each group member reviews the draft paper and comments on the following questions: What is the most valuable contribution of our paper? What do you like best? Where are things really coming together? Where is additional clarification needed? What further questions remain? How will we move forward?

as being about working with others on the same piece of work, while others conceptualize collaboration in terms of solitary writers supporting each other in shared space. Some of us embrace a writing everyday approach (Boice, 1989) while others prefer to "binge write" as Sword (2016) affectionately described it. Despite our differences, however, commonalities can be drawn out of these narratives that begin to articulate the traditions and habits of our burgeoning microculture. Specifically, the narratives converge around the following themes: valuing difference, attending to process, and critically reflecting on our writing practice.

The importance of each of us recognizing, drawing upon, and valuing our differences as we collaborate is front and centre in the narratives. Sometimes issues of language, terminology, or disciplinary assumptions about dissemination require working out among collaborators. At other times, discovering and recognizing the varied strengths of team members is on the agenda so that optimal divisions of labour can be established for projects. While working through differences can be challenging, our narratives celebrate opportunities to consider alternative ways of knowing, moments of coming to new insights about our educational development projects, and the gaining of new skills and confidence in our writing abilities that are afforded us through collaboration across differences.

Another theme involves the attention paid to making processes explicit and communicating clearly in order to build relationships and trust with writing colleagues. While our common goal is to produce a product, we recognize that attention to process is key to success in this regard. There is both vulnerability and opportunity in writing with others that makes it important to articulate and communicate our *how* as well as our *what*. Our various processes include clarifying shared expectations, committing to regular communication (whether face to face or virtual), setting individual writing goals and sharing them with colleagues, and reading and commenting on each other's writing. These practices variously create trust and respect, hold us as accountable, support our progress, and ultimately lead to writing productivity.

Finally, our narratives converge around the rich environment for learning that is made possible, not only when we write together, but when we take the time to reflect on our writing. Through this process of making visible some of the norms, assumptions, practices and conventions of writing within our microculture, we have learned more about ourselves and each other, the work that we do in educational development, our writing preferences and proficiencies, and our rich connections and relationships.

Expectations and demands placed on academics to write and publish continue across career stages and levels. These demands can be particularly daunting to faculty in new or non-traditional disciplines. In this chapter we have discussed several perspectives on writing from members of our academic microculture: writing in an interdisciplinary team, leveraging a project into scholarly writing, gathering together to write in group settings, fostering writing productivity through retreats, and facilitating a virtual collaborative

WRITING WITHIN AN ACADEMIC MICROCULTURE

writing group. We hope that what we have offered here are examples, strategies, and reflections that others find valuable and can adapt or adopt in the context of their writing communities.

References

Adaptive Schools and Cognitive Coaching. (n.d.). *Norms of collaboration annotated.* Retrieved November 16, 2018, from http://www.nj.gov/education/AchieveNJ/teams/strat14/SevenNormsofCollaboration.pdf

Aitchison, C. (2009). Writing groups for doctoral education. *Studies in Higher Education, 34*(8), 905–916. doi:10.1080/03075070902785580

Belcher, W. (2009). *Writing your journal article in 12 weeks: A guide to academic publishing success.* Thousand Oaks, CA: Sage.

Boice, R. (1989). Procrastination, busyness and bingeing. *Behaviour Research and Therapy, 26,* 605–611. doi:10.1016/0005-7967(89)90144-7

Costa, A. L., & Kallick, B. (1993). Through the lens of a critical friend. *Educational Leadership, 51*(2), 49–51.

Cufaude, J. (2005). The art of facilitative leadership: Maximizing others' contributions. *Systems Thinker, 15*(10), 2–5.

Educational Development Unit. (2014). *Strategic plan 2015–2018.* University of Calgary: Taylor Institute for Teaching and Learning. Retrieved October 10, 2018, from http://ucalgary.ca/taylorinstitute/sites/default/files/EDU%20Strategic%20Plan%202015-2018.pdf

Gibbs, G. (2013). Reflections on the changing nature of educational development. *International Journal for Academic Development, 18*(1), 4–14. doi:10.1080/1360144.2013.751691

Jensen, J. (2017). *Write no matter what: Advice for academics.* Chicago, IL: The University of Chicago Press.

Kenny, N., Popovic, C., McSweeney, J., Knorr, K., Hoessler, C., Hall, C., Fujita, N., & Khoury, E. (2017). Drawing on the principles of SoTL to illuminate a path forward for the scholarship of educational development. *The Canadian Journal for the Scholarship of Teaching and Learning, 8*(2), 9–17. doi:10.5206/cjsotl-rcacea.2017.2.10

Kenny, N., & Taylor, L. (February, 2017). *Examining the value, outcomes, critical questions, and ideal structure for an interdisciplinary 4-course certificate in educational development.* Educational Developers Caucus of Canada Conference, University of Guelph, Guelph, ON.

Knapper, C. (2016). Does educational development matter? International Journal for Academic Development, 21(2), 105–115. doi:10.1080/1360144X.2016.1170098

Lucky, S., & Hoessler, C. (2015). *Co-authoring take 2: A co-authoring post about co-authoring.* Retrieved October 29, 2018, from http://words.usask.ca/ceblipblog/2015/09/01/co-authoring2/

MacLeod, I., Steckley, L., & Murray, R. (2012). Time is not enough: Promoting strategic engagement with writing for publication. *Studies in Higher Education, 37*(6), 641–654. doi:10.1080/03075079.2010.527934

Marquis, E., Healey, M., & Vine, M. (2014). Building capacity for the Scholarship of Teaching and Learning (SoTL) using international collaborative writing groups. *The International Journal for the Scholarship of Teaching and Learning, 8*(1), 1–36. Retrieved November 8, 2018, from http://digitalcommons.georgiasouthern.edu/ij-sotl/vol8/iss1/12/

Marquis, E., Mårtensson, K., & Healey, M. (2017). Leadership in International Collaborative Writing Groups (ICWG) initiative: Implications for academic development. *International Journal for Academic Development, 22*(3), 211–222. doi:10.1080/1360144X.2017.1291429

Mårtensson, K., & Roxå, T. (2016). Working with networks, microcultures and communities. In D. Baume & C. Popovic (Eds.), *Advancing practice in academic development* (pp. 174–187). Abingdon, OX: Routledge.

Mason, J. (2002). *Qualitative researching* (2nd ed.). Thousand Oaks, CA: Sage.

McDonald, J., Kenny, N., Kustra, E., Dawson, D., Iqbal, I., Borin, P., & Chan, J. (2016). *Educational development guide series: No. 1. The educational developer's portfolio.* Ottawa, ON: Educational Developers Caucus.

McKenzie, M. (2008). You should write that up: Getting practitioners started on writing for publication. *AOTEAROA New Zealand Social Work, 2*, 86–91.

Murray, R., & Newton, M. (2009). Writing retreat as structured intervention: Margin or mainstream? *Higher Education Research and Development, 28*(5), 541–553. doi:10.1080/07294360903154126

Olszewska, K., & Lock, J. (2016). Examining success and sustainability of academic writing: A case study of two writing-group models. *Canadian Journal of Higher Education, 46*(4), 132–145.

Page, C., Edwards, S., & Wilson, J. (2012). Writing groups in teacher education: A method to increase scholarly productivity. *SRATE Journal, 22*(1), 29–35.

Poole, G. (2013). Square one: What is research? In K. McKinney (Ed.), *The scholarship of teaching and learning across the disciplines* (pp. 135–151). Bloomington, IN: Indiana University Press.

Roxå, T., & Mårtensson, K. (2015). Microcultures and informal learning: A heuristic guiding analysis of conditions for informal learning in local higher education workplaces. *International Journal for Academic Development, 20*(2), 193–205. doi:10.1080/1360144X.2015.1029929

Sollaci, L. B., & Pereira, M. G. (2004). The Introduction, Methods, Results, and Discuss (IMRAD) structure: A fifty-year survey. *Journal of the Medical Library Association, 92*(3), 344–357.

Sword, H. (2016). 'Write every day!': A mantra dismantled. *International Journal for Academic Development, 21*(4), 312–322. doi:10.1080/1360144X.2016.1210153

Sword, H. (2017). *Air & light & time & space: How successful academics write.* Cambridge, MA: Harvard University Press.

Taylor, L. (2005). Academic development as institutional leadership: An interplay of person, role, strategy, and institution. *International Journal for Academic Development, 10*(1), 31–46. doi:10.1080/13601440500099985

Tong, A., Sainsbury, P., & Craig, J. (2007). Consolidated Criteria for Reporting Qualitative Research (COREQ): A 32-item checklist for interviews and focus groups. *International Journal for Quality in Health Care, 19*(6), 349–357.

CHAPTER 14

Supporting Writing Collaborations through Synchronous Technologies: Singing our SSONG about Working Together at a Distance

Michelle J. Eady, Corinne Green, Ashley B. Akenson, Briony Supple, Marian McCarthy, James Cronin and Jacinta McKeon

Abstract

Academia in general, and academic writing in particular, are often isolated endeavours (Fergie, Beeke, McKenna, & Crème, 2011). Isolation can hamper academic success – most of us have felt the heightened effects of intense work demands when our support system is not present. This can be even more palpable when collaborative partners are globally located. With the advent of technology, collaborators now have tools to assuage academic isolation and foster rich, productive collaborations. Using synchronous technology, a common passion for SoTL work and collaborative work has led to lasting partnerships across continents that support both personal and professional development. Synchronous and asynchronous technologies offered the authors ongoing opportunities to actively participate in academic dialogue and collaborate on multiple publications, despite being scattered over three continents. This unique academic collaboration is called a Small Significant Online Network Group (SSONG). The name SSONG was modified from work describing "small significant networks" (Roxå & Mårtensson, 2009, 2012; Verwoord & Poole, 2016). The authors included the online component, which provided the apt overarching metaphor of a song, situating song as a collaborative work of art. *Singing our SSONG* has a choral ring to it, underscoring the strength in its collaborative cacophony of voices. The SSONG highlights academic writing's multi-modal elements. The richness of the different author voices in a SSONG bring confidence, encouragement, and personal and professional transformation.

Keywords

academic writing – collaboration – Small Significant Networks – synchronous technology

---

© KONINKLIJKE BRILL NV, LEIDEN, 2019 | DOI:10.1163/9789004410985_014

SINGING OUR SSONG ABOUT WORKING TOGETHER AT A DISTANCE   187

Many of us in the field of academia have come to a point during our careers where we realise that academic writing can often be an isolated endeavour (Fergie, Beeke, McKenna, & Crème, 2011). However, the authors of this chapter found a way to work collaboratively across continents – supporting both personal and professional development. Chance meetings at an international conference and the use of synchronous technology granted the authors the opportunity to engage in academic dialogue and collaborate on various publications to share their experiences despite being scattered over three continents. This chapter represents this unique academic collaboration, which we have called SSONG (Small Significant Online Network Group), in both its process and content. The acronym SSONG was modified from the term, "small significant networks" as described by Roxå and Mårtensson (2009, 2012) and Verwoord and Poole (2016). The group added to the term to include the online component as well as the fact that we were working together as a group. Once the acronym was agreed upon, it provided an overarching metaphor of a SSONG, singing, choir and "the music" of working together that you will find throughout this chapter. Singing our SSONG has a choral ring to it, with a collaborative strength in its cacophony of voices. There is safety in numbers and reassurance, creating even more opportunities to write. The SSONG reminds us that writing is a multi-sensory and a multimedia process. There will be more harmony in the tune the more we can blend the voices and use all the ways of communicating, so that writing informs and transforms discussion (and vice versa).

Many academics relish the opportunity to travel to conferences where they can discuss issues of interest, continue their own learning experiences, and find like-minded individuals who may display passion towards a topic that is important to their own work (Hickson, 2006; Levy, Hadar, Te'eni, Unkelos-Shqigel, Sherman & Harel, 2016; Vega & Connell, 2007). Over time, relationships that begin at conferences can flourish and evolve into potentially co-authoring papers, books, and chapters (Crossman & Clarke, 2010; Hickson, 2006). However, in many cases these "fast friends" and colleagues become lost in the ongoing demands of academic work, as once exciting possibilities of collaboration quickly fade into the everyday teaching, researching, marking, planning, writing, and administration duties that take priority (Baird, 2016).

The academics that make up this SSONG (three from Ireland, two from Australia, and one from the United States) met when they attended an international conference in Los Angeles in 2016. At that conference Gary Poole presented on "small significant networks" as described by Roxå and Mårtensson (2009, 2012) and Verwoord and Poole (2016). In response to this workshop, and other ideas shared at the conference, the new-found friends discussed the possibility of capitalising on their newly formed small significant network to synchronously connect with one another after the conference and continue their discussions throughout the following year. By meeting regularly online and keeping reflective journals, the group maintained their relationships and collaborated on a conference presentation and other publications sharing their experiences of being part of a SSONG.

Technology has a significant role to play in developing these relationships beyond a conference into a sustainable partnership that can lead to further learning as well as collaborative writing opportunities (Baird, 2016; Levy et al., 2016). Synchronous communication is frequently used as a means of connecting colleagues, making collaboration between international colleagues possible (Shu & Chuang, 2012; Smithson, Hennessy, & Means, 2012). Video conferencing sessions through platforms such as Skype®, Adobe Connect® (used by this SSONG), and Elluminate Live!® allow colleagues to collaborate through audio-visual communication, live chat, and digital whiteboards (Exter, Rowe, Boyd, & Lloyd, 2012). Such developments in technology use can connect colleagues from around the world with speed, clarity, and ease, which means that academic writing collaborations can become flexible and fluid (Shu & Chuang, 2012; Strobl, 2014).

This chapter describes how we established our SSONG, starting with the formation of relationships through resulting publications authored online via synchronous (and occasionally asynchronous) technology as a means of collaboration. It explores how participating in the SSONG led its members to try new teaching and learning approaches, as well as the unique conversations and writing opportunities that it afforded.

Challenges of Academic Writing

Academic writing is often associated with several challenges and difficulties. Academics and students face various issues that can affect their ability to commence, continue and complete a writing task. The challenges and difficulties that present themselves in academic writing include, among many factors, time management, motivation, and isolation.

Many academics identify time constraints as a major challenge affecting their ability to undertake an academic writing task (Murray, 2015). The process of academic writing does not just encompass a mere "passive assembling" or a "write up" of all the research and knowledge that has already been achieved. It involves a complex set of processes that overlap considerably with researching itself and, indeed, may contribute dynamically to knowledge making (Badley, 2009). Furthermore, Badley (2009) describes academic writing as a process of "constructing, deconstructing and reconstructing knowledge, connecting, disconnecting and reconnecting concepts, describing and re-describing our views of the world, as well as

SINGING OUR SSONG ABOUT WORKING TOGETHER AT A DISTANCE 189

shaping, mis-shaping and reshaping ideas" (p. 211). The academic writing process is therefore not a small task. The processes that must take place to even begin to write an academic article are complex, time consuming, and multi-faceted.

Time constraints and the multiple responsibilities placed on academics, both in their professional and personal lives, may lead to a lack of motivation to commence, continue, or finish a research or writing task. Motivation is therefore a significant challenge in the academic writing process. A lack of enjoyment and a lack of an individual's belief in his or her innate ability to achieve goals may further lead to a feeling of isolation, challenging an academic in one's writing ability (Surastina & Dedi, 2018).

A Collaborative Approach

To help overcome the feeling of isolation when writing, many academics attempt to write in collaboration with others. Collaboration with like-minded individuals can positively impact upon the academic writing process (Murray, 2015). Collaboration is typically defined as "working with someone to produce something" (Collaboration, n.d.). Reed (2018) called it a "deeply human activity" (para. 3) in which at least two people work with one another toward achieving shared goals. This definition weaves processes and purpose in with the basic requirement of number of individuals involved, presenting in further detail what it means to partake in a collaborative endeavour. Ontological definitions of collaboration discuss the ways of being embodied in a critical collaboration as described by Schuman (2006) and Coleman (2012). Their findings concluded a need to foster trust, equity, compassion, respect, intellectual engagement, and innovation in communication as well as processes as part of the definition of critical collaborations. A human-centered, ontological definition also provides space for critical collaboration to occur, that is, a collaboration that is less production-centered and acknowledges the human connection that makes successful collaborations possible.

Roxå and Mårtensson (2009) have identified the fact that

> most [academic] teachers rely on a small number of significant others for conversations that are characterised by their privacy, by mutual trust and by their intellectual intrigue. Individual teachers seem to have 'small significant networks' where private discussions provide a basis for conceptual development and learning. (p. 547)

This collaboration in small significant networks aids academics in overcoming the challenges of academic writing mentioned above.

Many academics attend national and international conferences to network and collaborate (Hickson, 2006; Levy, Hadar, Te'eni, Unkelos-Shqigel, Sherman, & Harel, 2016; Vega & Connell, 2007). By creating a Small Significant Online Network Group (SSONG), we found that these invaluable small significant networks established at conferences can flourish into meaningful opportunities for collaboration and encourage others to consider creating their own SSONG to sing with others.

Technology Enhanced Writing Opportunities

When collaborations are discussed, the scenario that frequently comes to mind is an in-person group or network that comes together to complete a project or solve a problem. With the advent of technology and the ensuing improvements and innovations, collaborations are no longer limited to people in the immediate local vicinity. With this globalization, opportunities for collaboration abound. Scholars and professionals are not limited to connecting only at conferences or discipline-specific events. We can connect with experts and enthusiasts much more readily and consistently, whether technology facilitates the collaboration entirely, or is used to cement and sustain networks created in person. This access is vital to innovative, productive scholarly collaborations.

Technologies such as email, blogs, Skype, ZOOM, Adobe Connect and Elluminate Live! can play a significant role in developing these relationships beyond a conference into a sustainable SSONG partnership that can lead to further learning as well as collaborative writing opportunities (Baird, 2016; Levy et al., 2016). The use of synchronous forms of technology allow academics and colleagues to connect and collaborate from around the world with speed, clarity, and ease (Shu & Chuang, 2012; Strobl, 2014).

Creating SSONGs supported through the technological applications mentioned above turns individual academic tasks into social tasks, encouraging group collaboration and authoring (Koh & Lim, 2012). These technological platforms allow more group interaction and the development of social relations among team members. This therefore reduces the risk of networks that have been formed at conferences fading into the abyss of everyday life as a busy academic.

Establishing Our SSONG

The members of this SSONG met at the International Society for the Scholarship of Teaching and Learning (ISSoTL) conference in 2016. We were drawn to

SINGING OUR SSONG ABOUT WORKING TOGETHER AT A DISTANCE 191

one another by our shared interests in the Scholarship of Teaching and Learning (SoTL), and a wish to learn from and alongside one another. The two delegates from Australia travelled to the conference together and decided to attend different sessions to gather as much information as possible. In their individual sessions they met the colleagues from Ireland and the United States and ended up not only sharing information but introducing people as well. We all became fast friends and enjoyed the rest of the conference and social activities together. As we each returned home to our respective countries and institutions, the process of fulfilling the 'pinky promise' we made to meet together at least once began. The two Australians in the group were particularly interested in ensuring that previous experiences of conference networking, in which relationships that have been built are quickly forgotten once the conference 'bubble' is burst, were not repeated in this instance. Once returning home, we created journals for each of the SSONG members and glued photographs of our time together at the conference on the covers of the journals. Inside we wrote our first reflection question, the date and time of our first meeting and an encouraging comment about seeing each other the next year at the following conference. These were mailed out to each SSONG member. This was followed by an email with the time and date for the first SSONG meeting.

Because of Michelle's experience and access to Adobe Connect® through her institution, we chose to use that platform for our SSONG meetings (see Figure 14.1). Adobe Connect® supports video conferencing, as well as text chat, whiteboard displays, and file sharing. The audio-visual capabilities of this platform help keep the SSONG anchored in human connection: we don't drift off to become merely disembodied names in an inbox. As a group, we agreed that this was a solution to not being able to meet face-to-face and while we did use asynchronous applications such as emails in between meetings, we wanted the chance to see one another when we held our SSONG sessions. When the time came for us to meet, we each logged on (from three different time zones) and spent some time familiarising ourselves with the platform and catching up with one another. We also discussed our initial reflections, regarding what we learned and had already implemented from the ISSoTL16 conference, and what our goals were for the SSONG.

From that point, the SSONG meetings quickly became a well-harmonized chorus of voices from around the world. One member made sure to send out emails prior to each meeting (every 6–8 weeks), giving new reflection prompts that served as discussion points for the following session. She therefore was responsible for facilitating and guiding the discussions, which helped to ensure we stayed on topic and that everyone had a chance to share. This team member also sent around brief notes after each meeting. These emails ensured

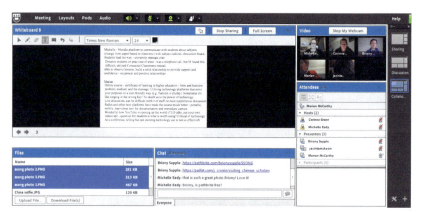

FIGURE 14.1   Screenshot from a SSONG meeting, conducted via Adobe Connect®

everyone was "singing from the same song sheet," as our SSONG member Marian poetically put it, and provided a means of documenting our discussions for future reference (Felten, 2013; Trigwell, 2013).

Our first meeting had established our goals: that the SSONG meetings would provide a space for us to discuss how we can engage in the work of the Scholarship of Teaching and Learning (SoTL) and provide a way to support each other as we venture further into the field. This initial goal setting then guided the discussions in the subsequent meetings, as we talked about connecting with others beyond our own SSONG, implementing SoTL in our work, and discussing the use of technology through a SoTL lens. We also conversed about how meeting together in this way has been beneficial to us, and how significant being a member of the SSONG has been.

A secondary goal of the SSONG that we had established from the beginning involved sharing our process with our peers at the ISSoTL 17 conference. We therefore also spent time throughout the year (both in our meetings and via email) working on the conference abstract and presentation, as well as laying the foundation for a journal article about the SSONG. These discussions ensured that we were all making contributions that matched our expertise, and meeting deadlines proposed by the group. Using both synchronous (video conferencing) and asynchronous (email, Google Docs®) technology tools for this purpose, meant that we could be certain that our expectations and meanings were aligned without misinterpretation, while keeping the time-commitment manageable.

To prepare for these dissemination opportunities, we divided the workload into smaller chunks (e.g., writing up the logistics of the SSONG or teasing out the benefits of the SSONG from our journal reflections). In one of our meetings, we established who would be responsible for each section, and created a

GoogleDocs® so that we could collaboratively plan both the conference presentation and journal article. This formed the basis of our ISSoTL17 conference presentation, which was given in a 'tag-team' approach so that each team member could communicate their perspective. As we prepared for the conference presentation, each person wrote up their section for the journal article. This work was continued after ISSoTL 17, with a team member being responsible for ensuring that the article was coherent and clear. In our online collaborations we identified a need for specific pieces to be added such as a clearer discussion of our theoretical framework underpinning the SSONG approach, and we worked together as a team, each writing a section to fulfil this need. Draft versions of the article were regularly emailed around to the team, with tracked changes and comment functions utilised to keep track of what had been, and what should be, amended. The penultimate version was then emailed to the team for final edits prior to submitting it to the journal chosen as most appropriate by the team in one of the SSONG meetings.

In this way, every member of the team was able to contribute in a significant way to the journal article, and it reflected our varied perspectives and experiences. Our voices shone through, thanks to frequent use of quotes drawn from our reflections as well as the shared process of writing. Having one member of the team conducting the article helped it to be focused, coherent, and completed in a reasonable amount of time. A similar procedure was put in place when writing this book chapter, however the job of conducting this piece was shared to another team member.

Practice Makes Perfect

Our SSONG's collaboration is a deeply human endeavour in which a group of individuals share purposefully and relate critically, compassionately, creatively, and respectfully to one another on a variety of levels. Whether individually, the group as a whole, the collaborative process itself, or the agreed-upon outcomes, the SSONG enabled us to collaborate at every stage. Our varied levels of professional experience and SoTL expertise created an opportunity for collaboration; for us to sing together. It was in this space that we engaged in a dynamic, interactive, non-linear process of learning by doing, shifting continually between thinking, discussing, and writing.

With members on three continents, our SSONG would have had little chance of survival without our shared commitment and the opportunities provided by technology. With these new avenues to promote international collaboration, our SSONG has evolved into the supportive, productive collaboration we all enjoy. Synchronous technology allows us to interact as if we shared a physical location; we are able to see facial expressions and hear changes in tone and inflection. Supplementing these interactions with asynchronous technology has enabled us to have richer, more comprehensive discussions and writing opportunities. We collaborate in a unique space that is both group and individual space. We can be responsive to the interests, expertise, and excitement of the group as a whole and to individuals. This supports the fluid nature expected for successful collaborations.

Writing – as both a process and a product – remains at the core of our productive international collaboration. We have used reflective journals to explore ideas and bring those insights to our online meetings, where they can help shape others' current and future projects. When SSONG members have needed to be absent from a meeting, they have used writing (through emails) and other application (such as premade videos to show in the meeting or using Padlet and Pathbrite) to share ideas with the group. As we prepared to share our experiences as a SSONG with others through a conference presentation and journal article, our writing (separately and together) solidified our ideas and clarified our understandings of how our collaboration had impacted us. Each of these written expressions, from the spontaneous to the deliberate, supported the distillation of meaning and enabled a SoTL approach that facilitated the documentation of practice through the naming, sharing, and critiquing of its parts.

Our collaboration injected energy and vibrancy into our writing, removing the oft-felt sense of isolation in academia. Having a synchronous deadline, and close colleagues to keep us accountable, motivated us to write. Knowing that it would be first read by those whose opinions we valued, and who we knew cared, opened us up to peer review at all stages of the process. Writing is an act of confidence that needs to take us beyond the blank page and is intermingled with discussion and commentary. The informal nature of our SSONG breeds good writing, for it comes from within, arising out of authentic conversations about meaningful issues. Our SSONG meetings built ideas as well as confidence in our abilities to contribute. This was further supported by our division of labour into bite-sized chunks, allowing us to participate in "snack writing" (Murray, 2015, p. 50) rather than becoming overwhelmed by the work required.

At the same time, writing has kept the collaboration whole and alive. As the collaboration thrives, so do our chosen projects. We become energized by our individual and group participation. We are intellectually stimulated through one another's contributions as a paper takes shape, and we find new connections within the literature and embodied experience. Our work as individuals propels our collaborative efforts in an engaging and supportive way.

Discordant Harmonies: Challenges in SSONG

Time for academics (or lack thereof) has been identified as a major barrier to implementing changes in the work that we do whether in curriculum development, establishing relationships or growing one's profile. This is demonstrated by a plethora of studies that show how academics feel under increasing time pressure within their roles (Allmer, 2018; Antony, 2015; Brew, Boud, Crawford, & Lucas, 2017; Carter, Kensington-Miller & Courtney, 2017; Martins & Nunes, 2016) to name but a few. This lack of time and time pressure were the major bumps in the road for this SSONG. We each needed to make the time to meet and, with those meetings occurring across three time zones, some of us invariably needed to stay up late or get up early.

There is no doubt that a strong commitment to the team and the ideals of the SSONG helped alleviate stress around making the time and logging on outside working hours; it became less about work and more about building common ground across continents and SoTL practices (Van Waes et al., 2016; Williams et al., 2013). The relationships were underpinned by a shared passion and interest in SoTL and a curiosity around the added value of a SoTL community to our individual and institutional contexts (Wenger-Trayner & Wenger-Trayner, 2015). This also helped to sustain levels of motivation in terms of knowing that there were upcoming online meetings planned to which we each wanted to contribute.

There were occasions when one of the team members might have been unavailable given the other elements of our lives outside academia (e.g., Ph.D. completion, family commitments, travel, sickness, and so on). However, we worked hard to overcome anyone's apparent missing voice in the synchronous meetings by calling on other asynchronous means. These included sharing a short video of reflections, emailing notes of reflections, or using other online platforms such as Pathbrite®.

Our SSONG was powered by knowledge sharing, rather than being task driven (Wenger, 1998). It existed and was sustained because of the fundamental aspect of knowledge sharing, which was in turn was only possible through a commitment to being present. This facilitated a range of collaborative activities, including the co-construction of a conference presentation, journal article, and this book chapter. Being familiar with each other in both social and academic contexts made this process of task negotiation much easier.

As dissemination opportunities arose, so too did challenges related to their associated deadlines. The best laid plans can run awry, and other pursuits may interrupt time that was set aside for collaboration and writing. Various members of the SSONG have had to change or reduce their contributions as deadlines encroached and time ran short. The strong relationships that we have created have enabled us to realign and recalibrate the harmonies, supporting one another as needed. In all cases, we have enabled each SSONG member to contribute as much as possible, to ensure fully representative input.

Conclusion and Final Encouragement

It is clear that academics face many challenges and difficulties when it comes to beginning and completing an academic writing task. These challenges may include time management, motivation, and isolation. Our experience indicates that collaboration with like-minded, passionate academics significantly reduces the challenges and difficulties faced throughout the academic writing process and therefore enhances the productivity and quality of an academic's work. In order to meet and collaborate with like-minded individuals, we propose the formation of a Small Significant Online Network Groups (SSONGs). The formation of SSONGs incorporates the use of technology to facilitate regular online group meetings to ensure that collaborations and friendships formed at international conferences and via various networks do not fade away. SSONG will enhance the cognitive performance of those undertaking an academic writing task in any field, as communication and collaboration among like-minded individuals boosts motivation and enjoyment and increases one's interest and desire to complete a difficult writing task which is multi-layered, time consuming, and thought provoking.

Despite our distance, we succeeded where many stumble. We shared in collaborative discussions that deepened our engagement with topic area that was a passion for each of us (in this case, SoTL), and successfully authored papers and presentations. Our process involved each member volunteering for a particular part of the workload, writing individually, and then coming together to assemble the pieces into a whole and revise the product. This isn't a new way of collaboration, yet through our commitment to SSONG, consistency, trustworthiness, and use of writing as both communication and product, we were able to create and meet deadlines even though we do not share physical space. Our accountability emerges from our genuine interest in our topic and care for each member. Our use of synchronous and asynchronous technology to support our interactions has kept our SSONG vibrant, responsive, and fruitful.

References

Allmer, T. (2018). Precarious, always-on and flexible: A case study of academics as information workers. *European Journal of Communication, 33,* 381–395. https://doi.org/10.1177/0267323118783794

Antony, J. (2015). Challenges in the deployment of LSS in the higher education sector: Viewpoints from leading academics and practitioners. *International Journal of Productivity and Performance Management, 64*(6), 893–899. doi: 10.1108/IJPPM-12-2014-0192

Badley, G. (2009). Academic writing as shaping and re-shaping. *Teaching in Higher Education, 14*(2), 209–219. doi: 10.1080/13562510902757294

Baird, D. (2016, October 13). *How to easily stay connected after a conference (using Facebook)* [Web log post]. Retrieved April 9, from http://daniellebaird.com/stay-connected-after-conference/

Brew, A., Boud, D., Crawford, K., & Lucas, L. (2017). Navigating the demands of academic work to shape an academic job. *Studies in Higher Education, 43*(12), 1–11.

Carter, S., Kensington-Miller, B., & Courtney, M. (2017). Doctoral supervision practice: What's the problem and how can we help academics? *Journal of Perspectives in Applied Academic Practice, 5*(1), 13–22. doi:10.14297/jpaap.v5i1.235

Collaboration (2018). In *Oxford English living dictionary* online. Retrieved July 3, 2018, from https://en.oxforddictionaries.com/definition/collaboration

Coleman, A. (2012). The significance of trust in school-based collaborative leadership. *International Journal of Leadership in Education, 15*(1), 79–106. https://doi.org/10.1080/13603124.2011.578755

Crossman, E. J., & Clarke, M. (2010). International experience and graduate employability: Stakeholder perceptions on the connection. *Higher Education, 59*(5), 599–613. doi:10.1007/s10734-009-9268-z

Exter, K. D., Rowe, S., Boyd, W., & Lloyd, D. (2012). Using Web 2.0 technologies for collaborative learning in distance education – Case studies from an Australian university. *Future Internet, 4*(1), 216–237. doi:10.3390/fi4010216

Felten, P. (2013). Principles of good practice in SoTL. *Teaching and Learning Inquiry, 1*(1), 121–125. doi:10.20343/teachlearninqu.1.1.121

Fergie, G., Beeke, S., McKenna, C., & Creme, P. (2011). "It's a lonely walk:" Supporting postgraduate researchers through writing. *International Journal of Teaching and Learning in Higher Education, 23*(2), 236–245.

Hickson, M, III. (2006). Raising the question #4 why bother attending conferences? *Communication Education, 55*(4), 464–468. doi:10.1080/03634520600917632

Koh, E., & Lim, J. (2012). Using online collaboration applications for group assignments: The interplay between design and human characteristics. *Computers & Education, 59,* 481–496. doi:10.1016/j.compedu.2012.02.002

Levy, M., Hadar, I., Te'eni, D., Unkelos-Shpigel, N., Sherman, S., & Harel, N. (2016). Social networking in an academic conference context: Insights from a case study. *Information Technology & People, 29*(1), 51–68. doi:10.1108/ITP-09-2014-0220

Martins, J., & Nunes, M. B. (2016). The temporal properties of e-learning: an exploratory study of academics' conceptions. *International Journal of Educational Management, 30*(1), 2–19. https://doi.org/10.1108/IJEM-04-2014-0048

Murray, R. (2015). *Writing in social spaces: A social processes approach to academic writing.* New York, NY: Routledge.

Reed, E. (2018, March 15). *What collaboration really means* [Web log post]. Retrieved July 4, 2018, from https://www.thoughtfarmer.com/blog/what-collaboration-really-means/

Roxå, T., & Mårtensson, K. (2009). Significant conversations and significant networks exploring the backstage of the teaching arena. *Studies in Higher Education, 34*(5), 547–559. doi:10.1080/03075070802597200

Roxå, T., & Mårtensson, K. (2012). How effects from teacher training of academic teachers propagate into the meso level and beyond. In E. Simon & G. Pleschova (Eds.), *Teacher development in higher education: Existing programs, program impact, and future trends* (pp. 213–233). London, UK: Routledge.

Shu, W., & Chuang, Y. H. (2012). Wikis as an effective group writing tool: A study in Taiwan. *Online Information Review, 36*(1), 89–103. https://doi.org/10.1108/14684521211206980

Schuman, S. (2006). *Creating a culture of collaboration.* San Francisco, CA: Jossey-Bass Publishers.

Smithson, J., Hennessy, C., & Means, R. (2012). Online interaction and "real information flow": Contrasts between talking about interdisciplinarity and achieving interdisciplinary collaboration. *Journal of Research Practice, 8*(1), 1–19.

Strobl, C. (2014). Affordances of Web 2.0 technologies for collaborative advanced writing in a foreign language. *CALICO Journal, 31*(1), 1–18. doi:10.11139/cj.31.1.1-18

Surastina, & Dedi, F. S. O. (2018). Examining academic writing motivation of prospective Indonesian language teachers using exploratory factor analysis. *International Journal of Instruction, 11*(2), 15–24. https://doi.org/10.12973/iji.2018.1122a

Trigwell, K. (2013). Evidence of the impact of scholarship of teaching and learning purposes. *Teaching and Learning Inquiry, 1*(1), 95–105. doi:10.20343/teachlearninqu.1.1.95

Van Waes, S., Moolenaar, N. M., Daly, A. J., Heldens, H. H. P. F., Donche, V., Van Petegem, P., & Van den Bossche, P. (2016). The networked instructor: The quality of networks in different stages of professional development. *Teaching and Teacher Education, 59*, 295–308. Retrieved from http://dx.doi.org10.1016/j.tate.2016.05.022

Vega, R. D., & Connell, R. S. (2007). Librarians' attitudes toward conferences: a study. *College & Research Libraries, 68*(6), 503–515. https://doi.org/10.5860/crl.68.6.503

Verwoord, R., & Poole, G. (2016). The role of small significant networks and leadership in institutional embedding of SoTL. *New Directions for Teaching and Learning, 146,* 79–86. doi:10.1002/tl.20190

Williams, A. L., Verwoord, R., Beery, T. A., Dalton, H., McKinnon, J., Strickland, K., ... Poole, G. (2013). The power of social networks: A model for weaving the Scholarship of Teaching and Learning into institutional culture. *Teaching and Learning Inquiry, 1*(2), 49–62. http://doi.org10.20343/teachlearninqu.1.2.49

Wenger, E., & Wenger-Trayner, B. (2015). *Communities of practice: A brief introduction.* Retrieved from http://wenger-trayner.com/introduction-to-communities-of-practice/

Wenger, E. (1998). Communities of practice: Learning as a social system. *Systems Thinker, 9*(5), 2–3. https://doi.org/10.1177/135050840072002

CHAPTER 15

Growing the Canadian SoTL Community through a Collaborative Writing Initiative

Elizabeth Marquis and Nicola Simmons

Abstract

Recognizing the challenges that often attach to writing for publication, this chapter describes a Collaborative Writing Groups (CWG) initiative that supports scholarly writing about teaching and learning in higher education. This model, which sees groups of scholars from multiple institutions working together virtually and face-to-face to co-author manuscripts on topics of shared interest, has been shown to contribute to building scholarly capacity, community, and collaboration, while also leading to the development of manuscripts that contribute meaningfully to the literature. We describe the model, which was initially developed by the International Network for Learning and Teaching Geography in Higher Education and subsequently modified for the International Society for the Scholarship of Teaching and Learning, outline some of the evidence demonstrating its efficacy, and reflect on our experiences adapting the initiative to support collaborative writing in the Canadian context. While the CWG process was originally developed for individuals working on the scholarship of teaching and learning (SoTL), it is also applicable to those in other fields and disciplines. Thus, we situate our discussion within the SoTL literature that shaped the initiative, but also offer considerations and recommendations for those wishing to adapt and apply the model in other contexts.

Keywords

collaborative writing groups – writing group facilitation – Scholarship of Teaching and Learning

Publication is a fundamental component of research across most disciplines, but it can also be a challenging endeavor (MacLeod, Steckley, & Murray,

© KONINKLIJKE BRILL NV, LEIDEN, 2019 | DOI:10.1163/9789004410985_015

2012). As noted in the introduction to this volume, many recommendations for faculty writing position the scholar as an isolated author. In this chapter, we describe an innovative Collaborative Writing Groups (CWG) process that was created to support scholarly writing about teaching and learning in higher education, and which has also been shown to contribute to building scholarly capacity, community, and collaboration (e.g., Marquis, Healey, & Vine, 2014; Matthews, Marquis, & Healey, 2017). We describe the model, outline some of the evidence in support of its efficacy, and reflect on our experiences adapting the initiative to support and develop collaborative writing in the Canadian context. While the CWG process was originally developed for individuals working on the Scholarship of Teaching and Learning (SoTL), it is also broadly applicable to those in other fields and disciplines. Thus, we situate our discussion of the CWG within the SoTL literature that originally shaped the initiative, but also offer considerations and recommendations for those wishing to adapt and apply the model in other cases and situations.

Background: The SoTL Canada-CJSoTL Collaborative Writing Groups

Within the Scholarship of Teaching and Learning (SoTL), the notion of 'going public' – that is, disseminating the results of one's inquiries into teaching and learning – has long been positioned as a defining element of the field (e.g., Hutchings & Shulman, 1999; Hutchings, Huber, & Ciccone, 2011; Trigwell, Martin, Benjamin, & Prosser, 2000; Felten, 2013). Nevertheless, conducting, presenting, and publishing SoTL work can be difficult for scholars, particularly when teaching and learning inquiry constitutes new and unfamiliar scholarly terrain for many (Kelly, Nesbit, & Oliver, 2012; Simmons et al., 2013; Tremonte, 2011). Efforts to support SoTL scholars' writing thus stand to contribute in significant ways to the ongoing growth and development of the field.

At the same time, many within the SoTL community have called for teaching and learning inquiry to become increasingly collaborative and inter-institutional (Gale 2007; Higgs, 2009; Marquis, 2015), and/or have considered the significance of conducting and supporting SoTL work at multiple levels, including the national scale (e.g., Poole, Taylor, & Thompson, 2007; Simmons, 2016). In the Canadian context, SoTL Canada – a constituency of the Society for Teaching and Learning in Higher Education (STLHE) – has engaged in a range of efforts to support and grow a national SoTL community, including promoting collaborations and connections amongst SoTL practitioners and sharing a variety of resources. The CWG initiative described in this chapter was another venture supported by SoTL Canada, in partnership with the Canadian Journal for the Scholarship of Teaching and Learning (CJSoTL), intended to foster national SoTL collaborations, promote the development of new SoTL scholarship, and contribute to building the capacity of Canadian SoTL scholars.

This initiative was modeled closely after a similar program first developed by the International Network for Learning & Teaching Geography in Higher Education (Healey, Foote, & Hay, 2000; Healey, 2006), and subsequently adapted for the International Society of the Scholarship of Teaching and Learning (see Healey, Marquis, & Vajoczki, 2013; Marquis, Healey, & Vine, 2014, 2016; Healey & Matthews, 2017). The model involves bringing together diverse teams of SoTL scholars, including individuals from a variety of disciplines and locations and with a range of SoTL experience, to co-author teaching and learning articles on topics of shared interest. In most cases, groups develop papers that are conceptualizations of the given topic – that is, typically no empirical data are collected, though some groups may draw on other work in progress or on their own experiences. As with previous iterations, group facilitators and broad topic areas were selected for the SoTL Canada CWG in advance, with particular attention paid to selecting facilitators who have "the ability to lead and encourage participants to write collaboratively and complete the articles on time" (Marquis, Healey, & Vajoczki, 2013, p. 4). SoTL Canada members were then invited to apply to participate via an open call, and groups (seven groups of 4–9 participants each) were formed by the initiative leaders.

The work of the CWGs subsequently proceeded in four distinct phases: virtual planning and writing, in person meeting and writing, virtual writing and editing for publication, and submission of manuscripts and journal peer review. We show timelines of each phase, with the specifics of our initiative in parentheses. Further detail about each of these phases is provided below and illustrated in Figure 15.1.

1. Virtual Planning: 6 months (January–June)
   a) Facilitators invite group members to connect virtually
   b) Groups discuss the direction of their paper, initially brainstorming ideas around the topic, and ultimately narrowing a focus
   c) Groups work virtually to write an extended abstract (2000 words) for peer review
   d) Other groups' members comment on two papers (one assigned, one of their choice) and offer feedback on flow, clarity, and suggested resources
2. Groups come together in person for 2.5 days writing retreat (June, immediately following the 2016 STLHE Conference)

GROWING COMMUNITY THROUGH COLLABORATIVE WRITING GROUPS? 203

a) Groups work on facilitated writing of papers in progress
b) Several mini sessions bring all groups together to discuss work in progress and issues arising, with peers acting as "critical friends" (Carr & Kemmis, 1986)
c) Several mini sessions allow groups to work on their own on the further planning and writing of papers
d) Collective meal times are an important part of the process to build trust and relationships as part of the collaborative process

3. Virtual Writing: 4 months (July–October)
a) Groups continue to work virtually to complete the paper by the deadline
b) Further critical friend peer review occurs
c) Groups edit their papers and submit initially to initiative facilitators, who act as final editors

4. Submission of Manuscript and Journal Peer Review: 6 months (October–March)
a) Groups submit manuscripts to the journal for formal blind peer review
b) Groups revise and resubmit in response to reviewer feedback
c) In conjunction with initiative facilitators, journal editorial team makes decisions about articles to be accepted for publication in a special issue

For the SoTL Canada CWG, all groups submitted articles that passed successfully through CJSoTL's peer review process and were published in a special issue in June 2017 (Simmons & Marquis, 2017).

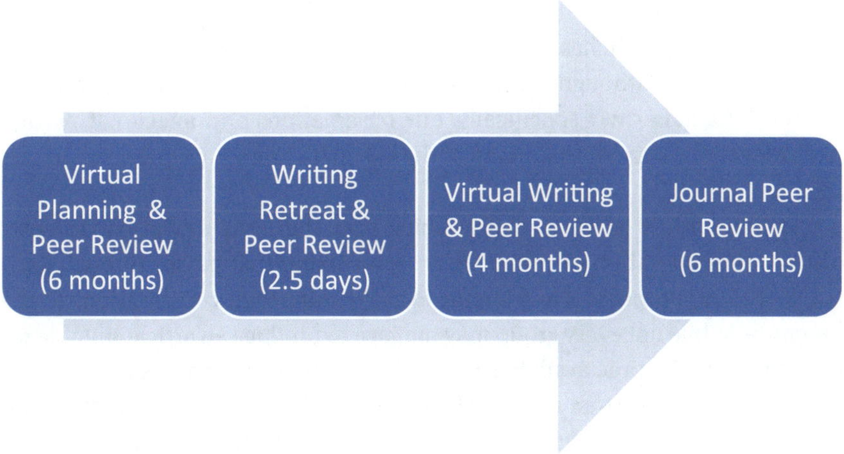

FIGURE 15.1   Collaborative writing group process timeline

Why this Model? Evidence from Previous Research

While the CWG model is not without its challenges (including its scope and the commitment required from participants, facilitators, and initiative organizers), previous research (conducted largely in conjunction with the ISSoTL CWGs on which this initiative was based) demonstrates that the approach can have a number of benefits for participants and for the broader scholarly community. Participants in the 2012 ISSoTL CWGs, for instance, suggested that the initiative's collaborative, large-scale approach to supporting writing for publication contributed to growing their capacity as SoTL scholars in several ways (see Marquis, Healey, & Vine, 2014, 2016). Participants who identified as junior scholars and/or as newer to the field reported the benefits of gaining access to mentors and collaborators through the CWG process, while those who were more experienced described appreciating the opportunity to mentor in this novel context.

Similarly, participants made comments illustrating the ways in which the initiative helped to create a sense of scholarly community and helped them feel part of that community, noting that participation contributed to the development of their scholarly identities and established connections and collaborations that, in some cases, extended beyond the boundaries of the eighteen-month initiative itself. The opportunity to be facilitated through a process of collaborative writing and publication was also described by participants as promoting beneficial experiential learning; many described feeling that their capacity to give and receive feedback, write for publication, and/or work in or facilitate large, diverse groups had been enhanced.

Participants likewise suggested that the range of people involved in the CWG supported the growth of their scholarly capacity, exposing them to new perspectives and approaches, and leading to the generation of novel ideas and understandings. Although we did not conduct research in conjunction with the SoTL Canada CWG specifically, our observations and anecdotal participant reflections suggest that many of these benefits may have persisted in this iteration.

Furthermore, it is worth emphasizing that the CWG model consistently leads to the generation of collaborative scholarship that passes through journal peer review processes and stands to make important contributions to the literature. While not every group may manage to produce an article suitable for publication in the time available during the initiative, most do, as is evidenced by both the special issue of CJSoTL arising from the SoTL Canada CWG and by earlier examples (e.g., Healey & Marquis, 2013; Matthews & Healey, 2016; Healey, Pawson, & Solem, 2010).

Given these successes, individuals and groups have begun to adapt the CWG model to a range of other cases and contexts. An adaptation of the process was used for a SoTL Canada special journal issue (Simmons, 2016). In this instance, self-selected groups comprised authors from the same institutions. There was no facilitated in-person session. The similarity with CWGs was the extensive peer review throughout the process and the overall process coordinator who maintained timelines towards publication. Others have considered applying the model in a manner closer to its initial form to facilitate collaborative writing in an institutional context (one institution asked us to be consultants on their adaptation). It has also been adapted as an experiential learning opportunity for students in an undergraduate glacial sedimentology and geomorphology course (Maclachlan & Lee, 2015), demonstrating its flexibility and applicability to varying disciplinary contexts. Like Healey (2017), we believe there is potential benefit to further adapting and refining the model in a range of contexts and offer the following recommendations for others interested in deploying the CWG process, drawn from our own experiences and from existing research.

Reflections on Key Features

Alongside demonstrating the benefits of the CWG model, existing research highlights a number of challenges attached to the approach and a series of key factors that underpin its success given these challenges. Many participants in the ISSoTL CWGs have noted the difficulty of virtual collaboration, for instance – particularly early in the process and when participants do not know each other well (or, in many cases, at all). The face-to-face workshop was thus seen as essential to group formation and progress; as one participant in the 2012 ISSoTL iteration put it, "once we got together, it was just easier to do everything" (Marquis, Healey, & Vine, 2016, p. 536). In addition to providing focused, structured time to work collectively in the same space, the face-to-face component of the CWG model was also positioned as important for facilitating informal, social connections amongst participants, which were in turn seen as fundamental to effective group functioning and the development of trust, a finding which is echoed in Chapter 16 in this volume by Motley, Divan, Lopes, Ludwig, Matthews, & Tomljenovic-Berube and Chapter 17 by Kensington-Miller, Oliver, Morón-García, Manarin, Abrahamson, Simmons, and Deshler. The significance of the 2.5 day residential workshop thus cannot be overstated. Of course, to some extent, virtual collaboration is an unavoidable component of the model, so thinking carefully about when the face-to-face components happen, and what guidance and support are given to participants in advance, is important. For example, for the SoTL Canada CWG, we met with group facilitators in advance to discuss possible ways of facilitating group formation online early on, including taking time to encourage getting to know one another as individuals before turning to the practicalities of the work too emphatically. Nevertheless, given the significance of the face-to-face component of the initiative, we also elected (as have others running CWGs) to mandate commitment to attending the face-to-face workshop. While some participants had to back out or Skype in due to unanticipated last-minute issues, our expectation was that everyone would take part in the face-to-face session. We would strongly recommend continuing with this approach as the model is adapted and perhaps exploring other opportunities for incorporating face-to-face components.

We have had the experience of hosting the facilitated workshop before a conference (as was done with the ISSoTL international collaborative writing groups) and after a conference (as was done with the Canadian version because of space limitations). We strongly recommend the former. Writing in this way and participating in the depth of peer review and group discussion activities during the retreat takes a great deal of energy; after a conference may prove too taxing!

Another essential element corroborated by our own experiences is the necessity of strong, facilitative leadership for each writing group. Participants in the 2012 ISSoTL CWG highlighted the centrality of the group leaders to the initiative's success, for instance, and in follow up research (Marquis, Mårtensson, & Healey, 2017) emphasized the following features as particularly important components of an approach to leadership in the CWG context:

– Connecting group participants with relevant literature
– Creating an inclusive, welcoming environment
– Encouraging/ensuring group members' active participation
– Allowing others to lead
– Delegating responsibilities
– Setting timelines and keeping the group on track
– Assuming responsibility for final decisions

Leading a writing group within this model thus seems to require a delicate balance between facilitative, distributive approaches that encourage and support others to take action and share responsibility, and strong organizational and time management skills that help to shepherd people through the difficult task of writing in a large, dispersed group on a relatively short timeline.

Effective leaders are also essential to helping groups navigate one of the other primary challenges of the CWG model discussed in the literature: the difficulty of bringing together the range of perspectives and ideas generated by a large and diverse group of co-authors into a single, coherent manuscript.

GROWING COMMUNITY THROUGH COLLABORATIVE WRITING GROUPS?

This challenge should not be underestimated, but our experience suggests that strong leaders can play a key role in helping groups navigate it by making space for diverse perspectives and insights, while ultimately working to emphasize the need to synthesize, integrate, and prioritize ideas. We thus strongly recommend that careful attention be paid to selecting group leaders in advance and that the criteria used in this selection process draw from the research findings synthesized above. Given the complexity and significance of this role, it is also important to inform leaders in advance about the approaches they will be expected to take and the challenges they might encounter and to consider ways of supporting them throughout the process. Indeed, Healey and Matthews (2017) note that in the 2015 ISSoTL CWG some group leaders reported feeling stressed – a feeling that was reiterated by some leaders in the SoTL Canada version of the initiative. More explicit discussion of expectations and processes in advance and throughout might help to mitigate these feelings and further study of such stresses is recommended.

Finally, in their reflections on the 2015 ISSoTL CWG, Healey and Matthews (2017) note that the CWG model may not be for everyone, particularly given its requirement to commit to a messy, open-ended process of both online and in-person collaboration with a diverse group of people one might not know at the outset. We would agree. In observing the groups' progress in our role as initiative facilitators throughout the SoTL Canada CWG, it became clear that some participants had different expectations for the process and that group dynamics varied considerably from one group to the next. We would echo Healey and Matthews (2017) in suggesting that it would be beneficial to make explicit to potential participants in advance the approaches to participation that are most likely to make for a rewarding experience, including "willingness to collaborate on a journey that has an uncertain outcome," "empathy for others from different cultures and contexts that affect how they collaborate," and "willingness to make time and space for collaboration using online tools" (p. 5). More overt discussion of such features should serve to clarify expectations for participants and smooth the process throughout, while also underlining the challenges that do exist and the limitations of the model.

We thus propose four foci for success, as outlined in Figure 15.2. A face to face component (F2F) seems to be critical and should come in the middle of work in progress. The timing of this retreat needs to take into account participants' energy (for example, we would not again host it following a conference). We also have found that explicit advance conversations to help frame expectations positively support the process – expectations of the role of group facilitators (including what they should not do) and expectations of participant roles and engagement.

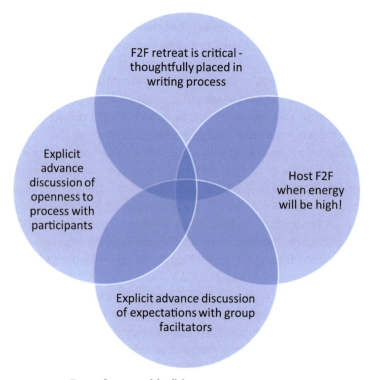

FIGURE 15.2   Factors for successful collaborative writing groups

The Collaborative Writing Group process, especially the face-to-face component, requires careful advance planning, and is well worth it in terms of successful outcomes.

Final Thoughts

In this chapter we have described our experiences with the process of facilitating collaborative writing groups of strangers working to produce publishable manuscripts over 16 months. We have outlined key features that we see as requirements for a successful process and have represented those in Figures 15.1 and 15.2 as frameworks we believe could be applied to other settings.

Participants in the Collaborative Writing Group process continue to express that they did not feel they would otherwise have had a completed manuscript within the time frame. We see it building confidence in those who participate and are delighted to see that some continue to work on other projects, often in subgroups of the original group. It is this support for academic colleagues at all career stages, including students, and the generative nature of the initiative that contributes to growing a Canadian SoTL community and is a compelling reason to continue this work.

References

Carr, W., & Kemmis, S. (1986). *Becoming critical: Education, knowledge and action research*. London: Falmer.

Felten, P. (2013). Principles of good practice in SoTL. *Teaching and Learning Inquiry: The ISSoTL Journal, 1*(1), 121–125.

Gale, R. (2007). Points without limits: Individual inquiry, collaborative investigation, and collective scholarship. *To Improve the Academy, 26*, 39–51.

Healey, M. (2006). From Hawaii to Glasgow: The International Network for Learning and Teaching Geography in Higher Education (INLT) five years on. *Journal of Geography in Higher Education, 30*(1), 65–75.

Healey, M. (2017). Reflections on the development of International Collaborative Writing Groups (ICWGs) about teaching and learning in higher education. *The Canadian Journal for the Scholarship of Teaching and Learning, 8*(2). https://doi.org/10.5206/ cjsotl-rcacea.2017.2.3

Healey, M., & Matthews, K. E. (2017). Learning together through international collaborative writing groups. *Teaching & Learning Inquiry, 5*(1). Retrieved from https://tlijournal.com/tli/index.php/TLI/article/view/176/156

Healey, M., & Marquis, E. (Eds.). (2013). Writing without borders: 2013 international writing collaborative. *Teaching and Learning Inquiry, 1*(2).

Higgs, B. (2009). The Carnegie catalyst: A case study of internationalization of SoTL. *International Journal for the Scholarship of Teaching and Learning, 3*(2). Retrieved from http://digitalcommons.georgiasouthern.edu/ij-sotl/vol3/iss2/4/

Healey, M., Foote, K., & Hay, I. (Eds.). (2000). International perspectives on learning and teaching geography in higher education, set of nine papers. *Journal of Geography in Higher Education, 24*(2), 217–298.

Healey, M., Marquis, E., & Vajoczki, S. (2013). Exploring SoTL through international collaborative writing groups. *Teaching and Learning Inquiry, 1*(2), 3–8. https://doi.org/10.20343/teachlearninqu.1.2.3

Healey, M., Pawson, E., & Solem, M. (Eds.). (2010). *Active learning and student engagement: International perspectives and practices in geography in higher education*. London: Routledge.

Hutchings, P., & Shulman, L. S. (1999). The scholarship of teaching: New elaborations, new developments. *Change: The Magazine of Higher Learning, 31*(5), 10–15.

Hutchings, P., Huber, M. T., & Ciccone, A. (2011). *The Scholarship of Teaching and Learning reconsidered: Institutional integration and impact*. San Francisco, CA: Jossey-Bass.

Kelly, N., Nesbit, S., & Oliver, C. (2012). A difficult journey: Transitioning from STEM (Science, Technology, Engineering and Mathematics) to SoTL. *International Journal for the Scholarship of Teaching and Learning, 6*(1). Retrieved from http://academics.georgiasouthern.edu/ijsotl/v6n1.html

Kensington-Miller, B., Oliver, C., Morón-García, S., Manarin, K., Abrahamson, E., Simmons, N., & Deshler, J. (2019). An international interdisciplinary writing group: Perspectives on building partnerships and developing community. In N. Simmons & A. Singh (Eds.), *Critical collaborative communities: Academic writing partnerships, groups, and retreats* (pp. 228–241). Leiden, The Netherlands: Brill Sense.

Maclachlan, J. C., & Lee, R. E. (2015). Student collaborative writing groups: Mapping glacial geomorphology and glacial sedimentology. *Cartographica: The International Journal for Geographic Information and Visualization, 50*(3), 163–164.

Macleod, I., Steckley, L., & Murray, R. (2012). Time is not enough: Promoting strategic engagement with writing for publication. *Studies in Higher Education, 37*(6), 641–654.

Marquis, E. (2015). Developing SoTL through organized scholarship institutes. *Teaching & Learning Inquiry, 3*(2), 19–36.

Marquis, E., Healey, M., & Vine, M. (2014). Building capacity for the Scholarship of Teaching and Learning (SoTL) using international collaborative writing groups. *The International Journal of the Scholarship of Teaching & Learning, 8*(1). Retrieved from http://digitalcommons.georgiasouthern.edu/ij-sotl/vol8/iss1/12/

Marquis, E., Healey, M., & Vine, M. (2016). Fostering collaborative teaching and learning scholarship through an international writing group initiative. *Higher Education Research and Development, 35*(3), 531–544.

Marquis, E., Mårtensson, K., & Healey, M. (2017). Leadership in an International Collaborative Writing Groups (ICWG) Initiative: Implications for academic development. *The International Journal for Academic Development, 22*(2), 211–222.

Matthews, K. E., Marquis, B., & Healey, M. (2017). International collaborative writing groups as communities of practice. In J. McDonald & A. Cater-Steel (Eds.), *Implementing communities of practice in higher education* (pp. 597–617). Singapore: Springer.

Motley, P., Divan, A., Lopes, V., Ludwig, L. O., Matthews, K. E., & Tomljenovic-Berube, A. M. (2019). Collaborative writing: Intercultural and interdisciplinary partnerships as a means of identity formation. In N. Simmons & A. Singh (Eds.), *Critical collaborative communities: Academic writing partnerships, groups, and retreats* (pp. 212–227). Leiden, The Netherlands: Brill Sense.

Poole, G., Taylor, L., & Thompson, J. (2007). Using the scholarship of teaching and learning at disciplinary, national and institutional levels to strategically improve the quality of post-secondary education. *International Journal for the Scholarship of Teaching and Learning, 1*(2). Retrieved from http://academics.georgiasouthern.edu/ijsotl/issue_v1n2.htm

Simmons, N. (Ed.). (2016). The scholarship of teaching and learning in Canada: Institutional impact. *New Directions for Teaching and Learning, 146*, 1–102.

Simmons, N., Abrahamson, E., Deshler, J. M., Kensington-Miller, B., Manarin, K., Morón-García, S., Oliver, J., & Renc-Roe, J. (2013). Conflicts and configurations in a liminal space: SoTL scholars' identity development. *Teaching and Learning Inquiry: The ISSoTL Journal, 1*(2). Retrieved from https://tlijournal.com/tli/index.php/TLI/article/view/46/20

Simmons, N., & Marquis, E. (Eds.). (2017). SoTL within Canadian contexts and communities: The collaborative writing groups initiative. *Canadian Journal for the Scholarship of Teaching & Learning, 8*(2).

Tremonte, C. M. (2011). Window shopping: Fashioning a scholarship of interdisciplinary teaching and learning. *International Journal for the Scholarship of Teaching and Learning, 5*(1). Retrieved from http://academics.georgiasouthern.edu/ijsotl/v5n1.html

Trigwell, K., Martin, E., Benjamin, J., & Prosser, M. (2000). Scholarship of teaching: A model. *Higher Education Research & Development, 19*(2), 155–168.

CHAPTER 16

Collaborative Writing: Intercultural and Interdisciplinary Partnerships as a Means of Identity Formation

Phillip Motley, Aysha Divan, Valerie Lopes, Lynn O. Ludwig,
Kelly E. Matthews and Ana M. Tomljenovic-Berube

Abstract

This chapter describes the collaborative writing experiences of a multidisciplinary group of educators brought together through an International Collaborative Writing Group (ICWG) initiative originally organized by the International Society for the Scholarship of Teaching and Learning (ISSoTL) in 2012. Our ICWG writing partnership helped us develop our scholarship in ways that might not have otherwise been accomplished, had we worked alone or even with colleagues in our same institution or country. Through an analysis of a collection of individual reflective narratives about our collaborative writing experiences, we describe opportunities, affordances, inhibitors, and enablers for this approach to collaborative writing. We delineate the community of practice that we have successfully developed and how it has helped each of us develop our Scholarship of Teaching and Learning (SoTL). We share the mechanisms that we have used to facilitate our work; the types of choices we have made about what research areas to explore that fit with our interests and the constraints of distance-based collaboration; and, most importantly, the ways in which our writing partnership has developed a stronger understanding of what SoTL is, and can be, moving forward.

Keywords

collaboration – writing partnership – relationships – identity – discourse community

The story of our writing partnership began in Canada in 2012, through the *International Collaborative Writing Groups* (ICWG) project convened at the *International*

© KONINKLIJKE BRILL NV, LEIDEN, 2019 | DOI:10.1163/9789004410985_016

COLLABORATIVE WRITING

Society for the Scholarship of Teaching and Learning (ISSoTL) conference. The ICWG aimed to develop writing capacity in the Scholarship of Teaching and Learning (SoTL) by bringing together scholars from different countries, contexts, disciplines, and degrees of experience in higher education, to work together for a year on a collaborative writing project. The ICWG was a structured, formal approach for collaborative writing centered on a two-day face-to-face workshop. In our specific case, the members of our collaborative group come from a range of disciplinary backgrounds (Biosciences, English, Chemistry, Communications, and Education), countries (Australia, Canada, Trinidad and Tobago, us, and uk), institutional contexts (small, private liberal arts; large, comprehensive public; research-intensive; metropolitan; regional), experiences in SoTL (0–10 years), positions in universities (students, tenured faculty, student-staff, casuals), and evolving life stories that unfold around work (e.g., families, caring responsibilities, religious identities). Matthews, Divan, John-Thomas, Lopes, Ludwig, Martini, Motley, and Tomljenovic-Berube (2013) worked together for a year to produce a scholarly publication. Following the completion of the ICWG, a subset of our initial group, consisting of Divan, Ludwig, Matthews, Motley, and Tomljenovic-Berube (2017), continued to work together on a second paper. Thus, while our initial collaborative writing arose from the structured ICWG model, it continued informally and outside of the ICWG structure.

In this chapter, we reveal how our writing partnership helped us develop our scholarship in ways that might not have otherwise been accomplished had we worked alone or even with colleagues in our same institution or country. We reflect on how engagement in this initiative allowed us to build professional relationships and identities as SoTL scholars and teachers, we share our insights regarding the factors that have facilitated our work, focusing on strategies that have enabled us to sustain our writing interactions over a period of six years, despite the constraints of distance-based collaboration.

Communities of Practice and Writing Groups

SoTL is concerned with enhancing the instructors' teaching practices and students' learning experiences through evidence-based inquiry. Scholars working in the field of SoTL are commonly trained in discipline-specific research and writing approaches and many experience challenges when engaging with SoTL. Hutchings, Huber, and Ciccone (2011) found these challenges include unfamiliarity with SoTL research methodologies and isolation, as SoTL practitioners often work as lone individuals within their disciplines. Structured writing groups and writing retreats can bring together communities of individuals to write and publish on topics of shared interest. Kornhaber, Cross, Betihavas, and Bridgman (2016) explain that the benefits of such writing groups are well-documented, including building communities that can act in providing mentorship, opportunities for networking, supporting academic writing competence, and increasing publication outputs.

Typically, writing groups are comprised of multiple writers meeting for mutual support and feedback whilst working on their own articles. Numerous researchers, specifically, Kahn, Goodhew, Murphy, and Walsh (2013) and MacKenzie and Myers (2012), have found that bringing together individuals from different disciplines, institutions, and/or countries to foster collaborative writing in learning and teaching, occurs with less frequency in comparison to discipline-specific collaborative work. Marquis, Healey, and Vine (2014) emphasize that the ICWG is one of the few examples of collaborative writing initiatives bringing together individuals from around the globe and across disciplines, where participants write about SoTL, resulting in publications informed by international perspectives. Matthews, Marquis, and Healey (2017) explain that the values of these large scale, team-based collaborative approaches have been reviewed through the lens of communities of practice (CoP) discourse. Wenger, McDermott, and Synder (2002) define CoP as "groups of people who share a concern, set of problems or a passion about a topic, and who deepen their knowledge and expertise in this area by interacting on an ongoing basis" (p. 4). Matthews et al. (2017) describe how the ICWG initiative can act as a vehicle for supporting the development of CoPs through interactions that enable shared learning. These, in turn, can build participants' capacity in SoTL. Opportunities to engage in dialogue with others, collegial support, and mentorship provided by group members whilst working towards a shared goal are all identified as valued components of writing groups (Marquis et al., 2014, 2015; Kornhaber et al., 2016; Kent, Barry, Budds, Skipper, & Williams, 2017).

Challenges to the Development of a SoTL Identity

The quest for identity for SoTL practitioners is an ongoing concern; if we stay the course and remain involved with SoTL, most of us must eventually confront the dilemma of SoTL research versus disciplinary research. Disciplines are often characterised by particular ways of thinking and doing (Bercher, 1989) and thus, discipline-specific specialisation leads to induction in the norms of that discipline and accordingly, the formation of a discipline-specific identity.

A number of studies have explored the anxieties that arise when discipline-based scholars engage with the inter-disciplinary area of SoTL. Simmons,

COLLABORATIVE WRITING

Abrahamson, Deshler, Kensington-Miller, Manarin, Moron-Garcia, Oliver, and Renc-Roe (2013) report how a group of SoTL scholars from different disciplines all described experiencing doubt and insecurity when they first engaged with SoTL. Support provided through interactions with a SoTL community was highlighted as key factor in developing their identities as practitioners of SoTL. Reasons for discomfort can be due to epistemological differences between the participants' disciplines and that of SoTL. Miller-Young, Yeo, and Manarin (2018) explored the epistemological tensions that arise when academic staff (faculty) engage in a multi-disciplinary community designed to support their SoTL. These authors found that scholars from stem disciplines were uncomfortable with the perceived subjectivity of SoTL whilst scholars from cognate disciplines were uncomfortable with the interdisciplinary nature of SoTL. Some participants also reported disruption in their sense of identity, causing them to question themselves as a teacher, a researcher, and a member of their disciplinary community.

Developing a SoTL Identity through Collaborative Writing

The role of ICWGs in building a SoTL identity is relatively unexplored. In this chapter, we present an analysis of reflective narratives written by six members of our ICWG originally formed in 2012. Each member responded to the following three questions, designed to explore how engagement in the ICWG initiative had supported the development of their professional identities as SoTL scholars:

1. How has involvement in our ICWG shaped how you see yourself as a scholar? Consider how the collaborative experience contributed to your growth/development as a SoTL practitioner and ways it may have created opportunities in terms of professional identity.
2. How has involvement in our ICWG contributed to your sense of being a part of a SoTL discourse community? How has involvement in our ICWG shaped how you work/engage with others in the SoTL community?
3. Thinking about your ICWG experiences, what guidance or advice would you give to others about collaborative writing for publication?

Key themes extracted from the reflective narratives are presented below. We include relevant quotes from the six scholars to help explain our analysis. Out of these themes arise a series of recommendations for effective and successful collaborative writing for publication, especially when that writing is primarily done by a team working remotely, at great distances from each other.

Results of Thematic Analysis

We collected and analyzed our narrative reflections and found emerging themes that touch on several benefits of the collaborative writing process.

Strengthening Identity through Community

Collaborative writing can provide opportunities for shared experiences that then help form community and encourage a sense of belonging that promotes confidence and certainty as a teacher, researcher, and scholar. Several members reflected on how participating in the collaborative writing process enabled them to develop a new understanding or appreciation of their value as scholars. Valerie's experience with our group was transformative in terms of developing her confidence as a scholar and building her identity as a contributing member within the SoTL discourse community. She has since carried the collaborative writing ethos into other projects. She stated,

> The collaborative experience grounded me and was pivotal in my growth, development, and interest to be seen as a SoTL practitioner.

She expressed a sense of coming into the SoTL community of practice through the collaborative writing process from a place of initial uncertainty – an outsider position. For her, the shared writing process nurtured a sense of acceptance and belonging within our collaborative writing group and, by extension, the SoTL discourse community.

Extension of Scholarship

The discourse of process, more than writing to produce a product, reveals an underlying thread of relationships within the group and beyond, ones that stretch into the broader academic community and speak to a notion of collegiality that we all hope to experience as scholars, teachers, and professionals in higher education. Aysha's experience with the group was one of joining a new scholarly community and coming to learn and belong through the co-writing process. Her confidence and efficacy grew from feeling like something of a novice at the beginning to quickly becoming a leader who has translated her SoTL collaborative writing experiences to other institutional contexts. In point of fact, Aysha led the development of our second published article. She reflected:

> I was fairly new to SoTL research. Involvement in the collaborative writing experiences exposed me to colleagues at different stages of their SoTL

COLLABORATIVE WRITING

journey ... which enhanced my understanding of what SoTL is and how SoTL research is communicated and disseminated.

Aysha's participation in our writing group enabled her to consider the ICWG structure as a model of something that could be implemented in other areas of the academy for research and scholarship. She has since translated her experience into creating new collaborative writing opportunities to engage with professionals in other discourse communities, both locally and internationally.

Power of Social Learning

Many members of the group referenced a deeper understanding of SoTL, as well as related discourse communities, that arose from the ongoing collaborative writing process. This shared observation highlights the power of social learning where writing together is a relational learning endeavour in contrast to a transactional interaction. Phillip speaks about his experience with our writing group as one of coming into, and feeling a part of, the broader SoTL discourse community. He signals how the shared writing experience fostered empathy – an important emotional component underlying academic collegiality – that revealed new insights into his own professional context and practice and created new opportunities for other collaborations. He stated,

> It has been helpful for me to understand the constraints that each person's specific higher education situation demands of them, as a teacher, and as a researcher and scholar. This knowledge better enabled me to address the challenges I face at my own university, and to also better appreciate some aspects of my position that, before the ICWG, I had taken for granted.

Importantly, the ICWG experience also affirmed his identity as a collaborative scholar, one who thrives in creative team-based working relationships where he can both contribute to, and learn from, the members of a group.

Developing Self-Efficacy

Collaborative writing can bolster and develop a teacher's values, identity and effectiveness through participation in a discourse community; it can also provide access to a deep resource that can be used to extend and enhance one's approach to teaching and scholarship. Echoing others concerning a sense of belonging, Lynn illuminated the affective dynamic arising from the collaborative writing process. She wrote:

I feel that I will be a lifelong member of the SoTL community, and the experiences I have had not only give me confidence as a teacher and a scholar, but the added gift of like-minded professional colleagues, and friends, from all over the world.

Feeling able to sense and seize new opportunities to apply research learned through the collaborative writing experience to her own practices as a teacher and scholar were a strong component of Lynn's reflection and further enhanced how she views herself as a professional educator. The collaborative experience enabled her to view her role as a teacher in a more inquisitive way, with a greater focus on evidence-based practices. She continued,

My work with our ICWG has greatly influenced how I approach my lesson plans and my evaluation of student success in all of my classes. I am more discerning in finding ways to improve my teaching and providing multiple ways to enable my students to learn.

The shared experience and opportunity to learn how others approach their professional work directly impacted her identity as a teacher, and as a productive scholar.

Safe Opportunities for Mentorship

Collaborative writing can provide opportunities for direct and indirect mentorship and can thus act as a vehicle for developing research and scholarship in new areas. Ana has also been able to translate her experience in our collaborative writing group into other collaborative efforts and develop her identity as a professional working in higher education along the way. As a Ph.D. student when we first started writing together, Ana felt overwhelmed and "in the deep end," yet supported and safe to learn. The collegiality of the members of the group, as well as the intentionally designed structure of the ICWG program, where each collaborative group had at least one student member, helped provide a constructive and facilitative system for all to work within. For those members newer to SoTL, this was an ideal opportunity to tread into this territory. Ana reflected:

The writing group provided an excellent opportunity to get my feet wet in SoTL with the support of a team, rather than attempting to enter this field on my own with very little guidance.

The potential for early mentoring of an emerging scholar through collaborative writing was a valuable aspect of the ICWG experience for Ana. Her

COLLABORATIVE WRITING

participation helped set her on a pathway that has influenced her professional identity as a scholar, and a teaching and research academic.

Shaping Professional Identities

The ICWG program offered members the potential for extending and shaping scholarly identities by creating opportunities for leadership and guidance in the face-to-face aspect of the collaborative writing, but also, and perhaps more significantly, through the separated and digitally-mediated collaboration that was ultimately the bulk of our research and writing process. Kelly discusses how her capacity as a writer, a vital aspect of being an academic, was developed through the collaborative writing process. Echoing others, she acknowledges how the shared writing experience shaped her stance and identity as a professional and a scholar. Concerning the ICWG, she wrote:

> The experience affirmed the type of colleague I want to be within the academic community and my notion of leadership through collaboration and dialogue.

Members of the writing group helped create a sense of belonging for Kelly by creating a judgement-free space for her to figure out her process as a writer and as a leader.

Discussion

The themes shared above from our narrative reflections highlight many of the overlapping and distinct ways that collaborative writing shaped our professional identities. Our collaborative process was defined by relational interactions embodying collegiality. Of course, the value of our diversity was often mentioned, along with material gains (e.g., publications and promotions); nonetheless, we continued to come back to relationships, as Phillip succinctly captures, "One of the smartest things we did initially was to simply take the time to get to know each other." Finding ways to understand and empathize with the members of our group was key to our productivity. Ana expands on this idea further:

> In the five and half years that our writing group has worked together, there have been many personal and professional changes in each member's life. Our perseverance has pushed us through the birth of children, promotions, illnesses, and job changes. I think our longevity is a

testament to the bond we struck at the start of our collaboration when we met face-to-face at the ICWG workshop, which I believe was an invaluable part of the process.

Ana's statement illustrates that we were able to effectively write together as a group because we cared for and looked out for each member. The human relationships we created helped us define the boundaries and procedures for our collaborative writing activities; they also helped enable us to individually and collectively shape our professional identities through the experience. Her thoughts also illuminate the unique challenges of the temporal and geographical locations of our co-writing. In five and half years of working as a group, we have only once all been together in person, and that was for two days. Yet, that time spent together, combined with a commitment to a shared objective, was enough to cement a bond that has carried us forward through several collaborative writing projects. The time demands, and the emotional work of co-writing, are not to be underestimated. A strong dedication to collaborate online is fundamental to success, particularly given the busy nature of academic work when participating in international writing groups. So, what fueled our shared commitment?

We believe that the relational bonds that grew from a place of empathy and a shared starting point with the work, where many of us were coming into the discourse community from a place of uncertainty, helped initially strengthen our relationships. Our academic roles at our respective institutions were quite varied and different, as were our experience levels within the academy. Ironically, those differences were an asset: What we all shared in common was the fact that we each came to the ICWG experience from a unique starting place.

The writing group structure enabled us to engage in a shared journey into the SoTL discourse community as fellow travelers. Our path was paved through collegiality, which Aysha defines as she offers advice to others considering collaborative writing with international peers:

> Our willingness to share responsibility and support colleagues is also important. It is likely that the group has different levels of experience and that workloads and time commitment to the project at any given stage of the process will vary. Acknowledging this is important. Balancing within the group, to meet any impending deadlines may be challenging at times and stepping up stepping in, and supporting may be required to deliver on tasks and function successfully, as a group.

Lynn expands upon the realities where collegiality can guide a way forward: Collaborative writing projects require a firm and unwavering commitment

COLLABORATIVE WRITING 221

to all members of the team. While you probably feel that way when you join, life's complications (both good and bad) may challenge you, at some point, in the project's duration.

Simple activities, such as learning together about SoTL by sharing our varying perspectives, providing mentoring opportunities or chances to step into leadership roles, developing new research skills borrowed from teammates, and learning about how we each approach our roles in higher education are all factors that have contributed to enhancing our sense of identity within the SoTL discourse community and beyond.

Recommendations

In the almost six years since we first met and started working together, we have successfully published two journal articles. We've learned many things, along the way, about best practices for remote collaborative writing. Concerning the value of collaborative writing groups, Valerie stated: "The richness and vast knowledge and different experiences that the collaborations bring to the table outweigh any challenges." Our experience clearly indicates that in our case, this was true. We believe that collaborative writing, for others, can be similarly effective. To that end, drawing on our own perspectives of writing together, we offer a set of recommendations for collaborations where the bulk of the work is done at a distance, through means other than face-to-face interactions.

Relationship Building

The emotional and affective aspect of our experience as a writing group may be the most important to our success. The initial opportunity to meet and work face-to-face for two full days at the ISSoTL conference in Canada allowed our group to get to know each other, build initial relationships, and develop the collegiality needed to successfully work together from afar. Since then, we've not only collaborated to publish two articles, we've been witness to the ups and downs of each other's lives.

We have occasionally been able to meet face-to-face beyond our initial time together at the ICWG in 2012, gathering at conferences and the like, but our ongoing relationships with each other have mostly continued and grown at a distance. Although we've spent only small amounts of time in the presence of one another, we feel a strong bond and commitment, in ways that transcend time and place. We believe that the chance we were afforded to work directly together, at the start of our first paper, was an essential step that initially helped form our sense of community. To that end, Kelly suggested that the "structure of [the] ICWG was vital and brought us together." The chance to work collaboratively on a SoTL publication was a strong lure for participants. She continued by advising new writing collaborators to

> take advantage of such opportunities and encourage your discourse community to create them if they do not currently exist. If a formal structure is not likely, then use conferences and events, within the discourse community, to meet new colleagues and form writing partnerships.

We strongly suggest new writing groups and partnerships begin the process by finding ways to develop these types of relationships. Creating opportunities for associated members to begin a new collaboration, by meeting face-to-face, can be important and helpful to the long-term success of the endeavor. Phillip expressed how getting to know the collaborative team

> allowed us to realize the interests, objectives, and experiences we shared in common, and to some extent, minimize the aspects of our professional selves that were inherently different, such as our academic disciplines. We were able to figure out who we were, as individuals and as scholars and not just to get to know each other better but also so that we could collaborate as effectively as possible.

Without empathy and awareness of each member's professional – and sometimes personal – lives and obligations, success may be harder to reach, especially when the work becomes difficult or tedious. Becoming involved in new working relationships and becoming familiar with the different ways that academics approach research and scholarship can be rewarding, exciting, and instructive, with rich opportunities to extend the range of what is possible. Maintaining an awareness of, and openness to, difference may lead to greater productivity and also to greater professional satisfaction by creating pathways and opportunities that extend beyond one's typical disciplinary or institutional structures.

Collaborative Structure

When the bulk of the research and writing will happen with team members who are dispersed and not able to work directly together, it will be necessary to develop a detailed plan for the writing project. A structured plan will likely benefit any collaboration but becomes even more important when the members of the group will work remotely.

We believe an important step in the planning process is for the group to select a topic for research and writing that is conducive to the work being done

COLLABORATIVE WRITING 223

independently by members. Furthermore, settling on a topic that can be sub-divided in workable and equitable ways will help ensure that all members of the group have responsibility for tasks that contribute to the overall progress and success of the project. Phillip stated,

> The other smart thing – I believe – that we did with both papers was to choose a topic that we were all interested in, but also one that we would be able to manage when we were not able to work together face-to-face.

Our research, including data collection and analysis, had to occur before any real writing could begin. We were deliberate about what we thought we could manage separately and then share via digital tools. With the two papers we've published so far (Matthews et al., 2013; Divan et al., 2017), this awareness led us to focus on a document analysis approach where we could review large num-bers of SoTL publications in an attempt to learn from a broad corpus of pub-lished writing. Dividing up a set number of papers and establishing an analysis protocol has not only proved to be doable by each member, it has also allowed us to take advantage of the distributed intelligence of the group (Matthews et al., 2013; Divan et al., 2017).

Another important structural recommendation is to establish clear dead-lines over the duration of the project. Lynn had very clear thoughts on this aspect of planning:

> If someone asked me about joining a large-scale collaborative writing project, I would emphasize that it requires a serious consideration of the entire project's time commitment. The work environment of a col-laborative publication requires hard deadlines that must be met so the incremental handoffs are on time, and this relay process occurs over a substantial period. It can be very difficult to plan long-term, but it must be factored into the decision to participate.

In our case, for both papers, we chose to set up many small deadlines during the course of the project, rather than fewer large deadlines. Being late on a small deadline is less of a hazard to the success of the project than doing the same with a larger deadline. Nonetheless, as deadlines are important to any project, being late with one can be a challenge for the group to handle. In our case, the supportive and collegial nature of our writing group was often able to absorb any delays without too many problems. For example, over the course of our collaborative writing, several team members have brought children into the world, which created situations where they needed support.

Leadership Designation

Our initial endeavor, as a writing team and the paper we ultimately published, was made possible by having a designated leader. This person was part of the initial ICWG planning and was the appointed organizer and leader of our group. Because of how effective that arrangement was for our work with our first publication, and because of how effective this member was at managing our collective research and writing, we elected to appoint a leader from the group to spearhead our second project. In both cases, communication and task delegation were important jobs that the project leader facilitated. According to Aysha, "Good communication is essential. Especially since there are differences, globally, in the use of certain terminology and that communication is often on-line." She goes on to say that

> leadership responsibility has been rotated amongst the group members which has worked well. It also provides the opportunity for additional skills-building in a supportive environment and distributes the workload, making engagement with the writing easier.

The writing of this chapter marks the third published project for our group, and again we elected to designate a specific member, to lead the project. With the second and third projects, the choice of who to lead was ultimately made based on who stepped forward to do so, and not based on any notion of title, rank, or other external marker of hierarchy.

Having an assigned point person to lead the group can be beneficial in many ways, including: delegation of specific tasks, management of team members and also of deadlines and project requirements, setting up the technologies used (see more on this below), and facilitating and maintaining continual communication to ensure that the project progresses. As Phillip states,

> this kind of management is especially beneficial when the participants are working in different countries, across many time zones ... though we have all participated in both papers, having one person essentially manage the creation of the paper – from research to data collection and analysis and, ultimately, the actual writing – made our work much more efficient than it would have been otherwise. Having someone manage the process, especially in collaborations that span institutions or countries, can be of great value to the process.

Having all team members buy into, and respect, the role that the leader inhabits is an essential ingredient that must be in place for this type of structure to work.

COLLABORATIVE WRITING

Useful Tools

The use of digital technologies made our collaborations possible. Without technologies like *Basecamp* and *Skype*, that we took advantage of for organization and communication, and the various cloud-based applications available in the *Google Drive* suite of tools (that we used to share and analyze data, and to write collaboratively), we would have had a more difficult time making progress with both publications. According to Ana

> our group used and continues to use an online project management tool that allows us to virtually "meet" and share our documents, provide comments, set goals and deadlines. This tool, *Basecamp*, has been invaluable in ensuring that all members are on the same page and that we have a central location for our team to exchange information.

Most of these tools are freely available and easy to get started with and use. Several in our group were not entirely comfortable with these types of digital applications, but as Valerie explains, they are usually very accessible and easy to learn: "I would let them know they don't have to worry at all, even if they have never used them before … as they are easy to use and seamless." Beyond the tools described above, there are many other inexpensive, or free, tools that can help facilitate and manage collaborative projects, such as *Trello* (project management), *Dropbox* (file sharing), and *Slack* (digital communication and collaboration).

Conclusion

Our collaborative writing has produced published scholarship, but perhaps more importantly, it has nurtured our professional identities as SoTL scholars who are better able to write alone and collaboratively. Miller-Young, Yeo, and Manarin (2018) suggest that bringing together researchers from differing backgrounds and disciplines can initiate challenges around epistemology. In our specific case, the members of our collaborative group come from a wide range of disciplinary backgrounds, institutional contexts, university positions, experience with SoTL, and lives. Rather than hinder us, the formation of our varied group challenged us to navigate our inherent epistemological differences through direct communication, open dialogue, and sharing early in the process such that we were able to understand and value what each of us brought to the project's tasks and goals from our specific backgrounds. Marquis, Healey, and Vine (2016) suggest that a commitment to mutual satisfaction with the goals of the work can be advantageous for the team when participants

> expressly discuss members' interests, situations and needs, and adapting to account for this diversity wherever possible, are thus potentially vital strategies for effective collaboration, particularly in diverse, international groups" (p. 540).

The richness of the multidisciplinary and multicultural structure of our group has enabled us to grow as SoTL practitioners alongside our disciplinary work and to develop our individual scholarly identities, as well as that of our team.

We argue that collegial, collaborative writing can be a significant component of SoTL identity formation and that writing partnerships should attend to more than writing tips, tricks, and strategies in ways that conceive of writing as a process of becoming a member and belonging to a scholarly academic community. We believe that the insights we have shared about how we facilitate our work can extend beyond SoTL, with implications for other scholarly discourse communities. We also believe that our writing partnership has contributed intellectually to advancing SoTL through our contributions to the literature as well as to our own identities as SoTL scholars by developing a stronger understanding of what SoTL is and can be moving forward.

References

Bercher, T. (1989). *Academic tribes and territories: Intellectual enquiry and the culture of disciplines.* Buckingham: Open University Press/SRHE.

Divan, A., Ludwig, L., Matthews, K., Motley, P., & Tomljenovic-Berube, A. (2017). Survey of research approaches utilised in the Scholarship of Teaching and Learning publications. *Teaching and Learning Inquiry, 5*(2), 16–29.

Hutchings, P., Huber, M. T., & Ciccone, A. (2011). *The Scholarship of Teaching and Learning reconsidered: Institutional integration and impact.* Hoboken, NJ: Wiley.

Kahn, P., Goodhew, P., Murphy, M., & Walsh, L. (2013). The Scholarship of Teaching and Learning as collaborative working: A case study in shared practice and collective purpose. *Higher Education Research & Development, 32*(6), 901–914.

Kent, A., Barry, D. M., Budds, K., Skipper, Y., & Williams, H. L. (2017). Promoting writing amongst peers: Establishing a community of writing practice for early career academics. *Higher Education Research & Development, 36*(6), 1–14.

Kornhaber, R., Cross, M., Betihavas, V., & Bridgman, H. (2016). The benefits and challenges of academic writing retreats: An integrative review. *Higher Education Research & Development, 35*(6), 1210–1227.

MacKenzie, J., & Myers, R. A. (2012). International collaborations in SoTL: Current status and future directions. *International Journal for the Scholarship of Teaching and Learning, 6*(1), 1–8.

Marquis, E., Healey, M., & Vine, M. (2014). Building capacity for the Scholarship of Teaching and Learning (SoTL) using international collaborative writing groups. *International Journal for the Scholarship of Teaching and Learning, 8*(1).

Marquis, E., Healey, M., & Vine, M. (2015). Fostering collaborative teaching and learning scholarship through an international writing group initiative. *Higher Education Research & Development, 35*(3), 531–544.

Matthews, K. E., Divan, A., John-Thomas, N., Lopes, V., Ludwig, L., Martini, T., Motley, P., & Tomljenovic-Berube, A. (2013). SoTL and students' experiences of their degree-level program: An empirical investigation. *Teaching and Learning Inquiry, 1*(2), 75–89.

Matthews, K. E., Marquis, B., & Healey, M. (2017). International collaborative writing groups as communities of practice. In J. McDonald & A. Cater-Steel (Eds.), *Implementing communities of practice in higher education* (pp. 597–617). Singapore: Springer.

Miller-Young, J., Yeo, M., & Manarin, K. (2018). Challenges to disciplinary knowing and identity: Experiences of scholars in a SoTL development program. *International Journal for the Scholarship of Teaching and Learning, 12*(1).

Simmons, N., Abrahamson, E., Deshler, J., Kensington-Miller, B., Manarin, K., Moron-Garcia, S., Oliver, C., & Renc-Roe, J. (2013). Conflicts and configurations in a liminal space: SoTL scholars' identity development. *Teaching and Learning Inquiry, 1*(2), 9–21.

Wenger, E., McDermott, R. A., & Synder, W. (2002). *Cultivating communities of practice: A guide to managing knowledge.* Boston, MA: Harvard Business Press.

CHAPTER 17

An International Interdisciplinary Writing Group: Perspectives on Building Partnerships and Developing Community

Barbara Kensington-Miller, Carolyn Oliver, Sue Morón-García, Karen Manarin, Earle Abrahamson, Nicola Simmons and Jessica Deshler

Abstract

In this chapter, we describe our international collaborative writing group (ICWG), which came together in 2012 and reconvened in 2017 to share experiences, renew friendships, and reflect on past memories and expectations. This group formed a micro-community of practice that has celebrated successes while simultaneously being cognisant of differences in views, direction, and output. While we initially only 'signed up' for a writing collaborative project five years ago, we discuss what keeps us coming together – in small groups as well as the whole – for further writing projects. Using Personal Construct Theory (PCT), we discuss how we have built a learning culture for our group. We reflect on what aspects of the collaboration, including ways the initial writing group was structured and supported, have invited us to continue to come back to the wellspring of collaborative work. We bring international perspectives on what being part of a writing group means beyond the simple output of scholarly work to interrogate what has allowed us both to be a community of practice, and to practice as a community.

Keywords

international writing group – collaboration – community of practice – George Kelly – Personal Construct Theory (PCT) – academic identity

What are the traits of a successful international interdisciplinary writing group? Why do we continue to write together? We locate answers to these questions in

© KONINKLIJKE BRILL NV, LEIDEN, 2019 | DOI:10.1163/9789004410985_017

examining the inception, early development, dynamics, and key processes of our writing group, formed in 2012 and still going strong in 2018.

Our writing group formed at a conference in Hamilton, Canada (2012) as part of the International Collaborative Writing Groups (ICWG) project (Healey, Marquis, & Vajoczki, 2013; Motley, Divan, Lopes, Ludwig, Matthews, & Tomljenovic-Berube, 2019). Scholars and students from different disciplines and countries, with a shared interest in different aspects of the conference theme of researching teaching and learning, applied to participate and jointly write an academic article for submission in early 2013. A call for participants indicated a list of topics along with a named leader/facilitator for each topic. Each prospective participant had to submit a brief statement, pitching for a place in up to two groups, indicating why we would benefit from involvement and what we could contribute. If successful we would be selected for one of these groups.

Those of us who were selected received a "welcome to the project" e-mail in mid-March 2012; this obliged us to make contact with fellow topic group members and co-produce a 2000-word outline of our article that was to be uploaded to a virtual site. Our communication at this point was via email as we were working across time zones and needed a quick and efficient way to message each other.

We met face-to-face for the first time two days before the conference. We spent the two pre-conference days together, reviewing and revising our ideas, writing narratives and addressing peer feedback from the other groups. Following the conference, we continued to work remotely from our home countries for another two months and successfully submitted the article (Simmons et al., 2013).

In 2017 we reflected on the strength of our relationships and longevity of our collaboration. We wondered what it was that happened in our group's early years to enable us to continue, producing conference contributions (in 2014 and 2017), an article, a chapter, and to give rise to two spin-off partnerships. We met to discuss our experience and then wrote and analysed individual narratives responding to a series of prompts outlined in the methods section below.

Collaboration within an International and Interdisciplinary Writing Group

There is emerging evidence of the value of structured writing groups within academia. Healey and Matthews (2017) tell us they "create time to continue meaningful collaborations" (p. 2). Literature on communities of practice (Wenger,

1998) confirms the function and purpose of collaborative spaces as a place for enhancing the learning process. The ICWGs attract members from diverse backgrounds and disciplines who co-create scholarly outputs on key issues important to those members (Healey et al., 2013; Marquis, Mårtensson, & Healey, 2017).

These groups can, however, be troublesome. According to Healey and Matthews (2017), some ICWG members were discomforted by diversities within the groups. This is not surprising as Becher and Trowler (2001) famously describe academic disciplines as tribes defending territory against each other. Many scholars (Kelly, Nesbit, & Oliver, 2012; Kensington-Miller, Renc-Roe, & Morón-García, 2015; Manarin & Abrahamson, 2016; Simmons et al., 2013) describe the challenges of moving beyond one's primary disciplinary identity to develop the cross-disciplinary perspectives necessary for success in interdisciplinary settings. Disciplines also have diverse attitudes towards collaborative writing (O'Brien, 2012; Wasser & Bresler, 1996).

How, then, do members of disciplinary diverse writing groups develop the coherence and confidence to collaborate? Kezar (2005) identifies relationships and networks as "key levers" (p. 857) for collaboration within higher education institutions. Walsh and Kahn (2010) highlight the importance of planned and emergent working, strategies to promote exchange and inclusion, engagement, and stable patterns of social interaction. International collaborative writing groups like the ICWG, however, operate outside of the context of a particular department, institution or discipline, suggesting that their success depends on internal group factors.

Method

This chapter is based on an analysis of narratives provided by seven of the eight participants of our ICWG group (one member had passed away by the time we reconvened in 2017). We decided to focus on what had established our relationship in 2012. The authors represent diverse disciplines, countries, and academic roles (see Table 17.1). Prompt questions included: Why did you get involved or what did you hope to get from participating? What was your experience of and learning from the initial group process? Why did you go on (or not) to further collaborations? What advice would you give to anyone else considering this type of collaboration? The narratives ranged in length from approximately 700 to 1300 words. Three participant-authors took the lead on the thematic analysis (Braun & Clarke, 2006), which was then presented to the whole group for verification (Lincoln & Guba, 1985). Emerging themes

AN INTERNATIONAL INTERDISCIPLINARY WRITING GROUP

TABLE 17.1   Author demographics

Author	Country	Primary academic role	Disciplinary background
Barbara	New Zealand	Academic Developer	Mathematics
Carolyn	Canada	Independent Scholar Student member in 2012	Social Work
Sue	England	Academic Developer	Education, Languages
Karen	Canada	Faculty Member	English
Earle	England	Faculty Member	Sport Science
Nicola	Canada	Faculty Member Leader/Facilitator	Higher & Adult Education
Jessica	U.S.A	Faculty Member	Mathematics
Joanna†	Hungary	Academic Developer	Higher Education

described factors related to the group's development and the personal and professional impact of participation.

Theoretical Lens

In their analysis of the ICWG project, Healey and Matthews (2017) identify being open to question and revising personal cognitive schema as important to success. They contend that members of the group must share a "willingness to collaborate on a journey that has an uncertain outcome" (p. 4). The journey, they explain, needs to be understood in the context of exploration and experimentation that embraces co-creation with diverse scholars.

Success also depends on good leadership and the effective management of group processes, especially when the group is diverse. In their review of literature on leadership and identity, Epitropaki, Kark, Mainemelis, and Lord (2017) note that leadership is a dynamic and hierarchical construct dependent upon context. While leadership within a collaborative academic endeavour like a writing group can be shared, relationships are not equal as faculty members bring different experiences and confidence to any collaboration (Manarin, Carey, Rathburn, & Ryland, 2015). Leibowitz, Ndebele, and Winberg (2014) note that academic identities "change over time as participants position and reposition themselves" arguing that "collective identities depend on how individuals perceive themselves, as well as how they are perceived and positioned by others" (p. 1266). They emphasize the need to pay attention to intersubjectivity in the group, including issues of expertise, belonging, value, and participation.

As we were analysing the narratives, the appropriateness of Kelly's (1955) Personal Construct Theory (PCT) as a theoretical lens through which to view our group experience became apparent. PCT describes people constructing their identity in interaction with their immediate context through an "anticipatory rather than reactive system" (Kelly, 1955, p. 119). Simmons (2011) explains: members bring to the group 'anticipations' or constructs developed through their past experiences, following Kelly's (1955) notion that experience can only be understood with the passing of time. These constructs frame their investment in, and are tested by, the group experience through a cycle of anticipation, investment, encounter, confirmation/discomfort, and revision of anticipations (see Figure 17.1). Members enter a state of disequilibrium and discomfort when these existing constructs do not adequately account for the situations they encounter; Kelly refers to this as "being caught with one's constructs down" (Simmons, 2011, p. 229). Finding a solution leads to the development of new constructs and revised anticipations of future events. While members encountering the same experience will interpret it differently in accordance with their existing cognitive schema, shared experiences can lead to a similar framing of events and promote connections within the group.

Results

We divided our results into three thematic interrelationships: expectations, experience, and evolution/impact, as illustrated in Figure 17.2. These are

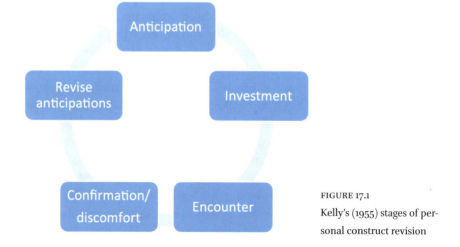

FIGURE 17.1 Kelly's (1955) stages of personal construct revision

interdependent as each informs and influences the others, and through the process, the group (re)develops and recognises its identity and voice. We begin the results with our expectations prior to meeting and then coming together as a group.

FIGURE 17.2
Thematic interrelationships

Expectations

We had varied reasons for participating in the writing project and mixed anticipations. Some were seeking something new. Barbara reflected: "at that stage in my career, five years in, I was looking for new areas." Karen wanted a different experience: "The ICWG was such a different model that I wanted to try it." Nicola, our facilitator, "had been thinking about ways to build the … literature." Others were hoping to extend connections. Earle pointed to how the group "served as a network for international scholarship, a purposeful community of practitioners," while Sue "hoped to make connections that would enable [her] to continue writing."

Curiosity about the group process motivated members to engage. Barbara said "I was curious as to how Nicola would work with a group of strangers …. How would seven other academics connect and share when none of us had met before." Karen "wanted to experience the process … even if it had been a miserable experience (it wasn't) or we hadn't been able to write something publishable, my goals would have been met." Seven out of eight members believed that simply participating in the process would increase their knowledge of the field or of their place within it or would enhance skills of direct benefit to their work.

A shared motivation for participating in the group was a concrete desire to see a paper published from its work. The reasons for this varied. Sue acknowledged "a big motivator was working towards a published article (academic kudos)," while Nicola noted this was "an area of great interest to me and one where I saw possibilities for literature." The group valued that there was "a definite end goal (and timeline) in mind from the start – which provided structure to the project" (Karen) and that participants could "combine passion with publication" (Earle).

All group members brought with them some uncertainty and "fear of the unknown" (Jessica). Earle noted that "the thought of working with an international scholarly group was daunting. Images of fear and possible imposter syndrome crept into my thoughts." Several described a self-perception of inadequacy linked to past experiences of academic marginalization. Carolyn, for example, said "I approached the process with trepidation. As a student in a group of seasoned academics ... I was very aware of my inexperience." Others worried about not matching up. Nicola said, "I remember feeling like I was a novice amongst very seasoned company in the fellow facilitators of other groups" and Barbara thought "I wouldn't have anything much to offer when I heard the background of the rest of the group ... I had that imposter feeling."

There were concerns about the feasibility of the initial endeavour. Karen wondered: "How could we write a single piece with so many voices? ... I went into it feeling like I didn't know what we were doing or how we were going to come up with something worth publishing." Nicola worried "about how I was going to facilitate a group of people I'd never met on a tight timeline towards publication."

Group Experience

Although invested in the process, the feelings of uncertainty and self-doubt continued when the group met face-to-face for the first time. Sue described "flipping between wondering if I could contribute fruitfully, feeling a little stressed/silenced when favourite ideas were dropped or side-lined." Jessica recalled "I mostly remember feeling very out-of-my-element during the meeting." Despite the discomfort, however, writing in a group of relative strangers provided safety to address a topic that could otherwise make people feel exposed. Barbara mused that "it was the perfect opportunity to give it a go with nothing to lose and everything to gain." This felt like an acceptable level of risk, as Jessica noted: "Like it's ok for me to not know what I'm doing as long as my 'regular' colleagues don't know that I don't know what I'm doing." Trust was

AN INTERNATIONAL INTERDISCIPLINARY WRITING GROUP 235

important: "Without my own knowledge of each person's area of expertise, I had to trust that each person knew what they were talking about," wrote Carolyn, while Sue felt "relief to be among such a competent bunch of colleagues and feeling protected by collective responsibility."

Participating in the writing group, both during the initial two days and over the subsequent months, was invigorating. Sue recalls "feeling energised by the discussions" while for Jessica "one of the things I valued most was just being around people who inhabit a different scholarly world than I do." Members learned from each other, and the diversity of the group was important to this. As Earle noted, it "meant that novice worked with experienced, and experienced members cultivated new ideas through interaction with newcomers." Karen felt that "often we collaborate with people like ourselves; this collaboration brings together really different people with really different ideas or assumptions. I value that immensely." While each member felt they "could speak the same [disciplinary] language as at least one person" as expressed by Jessica, the group's combination of what Karen called "its oddity and its diversity" made interactions productive.

The group's diversity also presented a challenge. It demanded time and patience; as Carolyn expressed, "differences in culture and language and discipline created an unusual demand on us to thoughtfully listen to every contribution." Karen talked of spending "a lot of time circling around the topic … it was important that a lot of different ideas be put out there." A great deal of negotiation was required. Sue expressed "the necessity of ceding some ground in support of the overall project." Karen noted "we had to be willing to give up sentences or phrases or tone that we were happy with" and "some elements we were really interested in."

The group unanimously commended the excellent group facilitation by "a fearless leader in Nicola who kept us on track and took our individual contributions and made sure the group product was on target for the program" (Jessica). She elicited and acknowledged each person's contributions: "There seemed to be room for everyone to contribute something" (Sue). Barbara noted that "the brainstorming was good and the respect everyone had for the others was evident, which I put down to Nicola establishing good groundwork." Carolyn said: "Our group was characterised I think by that willingness to listen. Nicola modelled it beautifully with her very facilitative style." This extended to the writing process; "we have very different writing styles, but Nicola was able to weave our pieces together" (Karen).

Nicola described her strategy: "I distributed the leadership role as much as possible, and increasingly stepped back so the group could self-direct and self-propel towards the final publication." She recalled, "I remember thinking about group dynamics throughout the retreat – and explicitly drawing the group's attention at one point to the fact that we weren't disagreeing ... and richer conversations resulted .... One of the most important things for our group happened a bit by happenstance. I was absent for quite a bit on the last day .... I left my group with a task .... When I came back to the room, they were done – and had assigned me the role of weaving together the voices for the final editing. I would have chosen some reason to leave the room to finalize transferring the leadership to them – but this worked out very well." Nicola's absence was identified as an important factor in ensuring that roles were distributed throughout the group. Barbara said, "I loved the way she kept handing the decisions back to us and at times walked out of the room forcing us to decide what we wanted." Nicola continued this approach in the months leading towards the publication of the first article. As Sue summarized, "the way Nicola corralled us and left us to work things out at strategic points really helped us bond and work our way through tricky points. There was a strong motivation to succeed: we wanted to please our leader!"

Evolution

Writing together in order to produce that first article had an impact on the academic identity of every group member. Sue had "been struggling with [her] academic identity for a number of years, having been 'othered' as an academic developer and researcher" and now "felt more like the ... scholar [she] wanted to be." Jessica "was still developing [her] own scholarly identity with the pressures of tenure and reputation attached to it." Earle described how The Sound of Music lyrics: "When you know the notes to sing, you can sing most anything" resonated with his growing interdisciplinary identity as it "illustrates the need to develop an appreciation for individual notes prior to forming symphonies."

Additional smaller collaborations sprung up after the publication of the first article: Sue was inspired "to look for other partners for research: working together is a learning experience, spurs you on, provides checks and balances and means you don't need to be good at everything." She related the difficulty of knowing "how best to contribute, [being] aware of stronger voices and those who had more successful writing experience. ... I think that's why the additional side project with Barbara and Joanna was important." Karen shared that "having built these working relationships in the first project, Earle and I were able to continue on with less external structure ... exploring ideas that ... weren't part of that paper." For Carolyn, "I have been left with a belief that the unlikeliest partners can help each other move forward, enrich thinking, expand perspectives and simply make the journey more enjoyable."

AN INTERNATIONAL INTERDISCIPLINARY WRITING GROUP 237

Strong connections developed amongst group members. Carolyn reflected: "I was immensely struck in Calgary by how easy it was to pick up the conversation and how comfortable we appeared to be with each other. I was surprised by my genuine feeling of caring about our group members and by the sense that I would feel able to call on them if need be, although I probably never will." This was echoed by Nicola:

> What a gift – that people who worked together on arguably a single project, should be able to come together (most of us) four years later and sit down to dinner and pick up deep conversations about our journeys as if we had never left our initial table from 2012. The connection is like family – we don't always see each other, sometimes subsets of the group get together, work together, or just meet at conferences, and while some of us do so less often, the family ties of that small, intrepid, and firmly connected social and professional network are still as strong.

As Barbara noted, we began as a "group of strangers [but are] now family."

During this time, the group lost Joanna, a dear and valued member, to cancer. This affected us differently depending on the closeness of the relationship and whether we had been working with her on a tangential project. Barbara lamented that "we were all gutted by her passing and it really felt like losing a family member." Nicola noted "life has a way of throwing things at us ... the loss of our dear colleague Joanna seemed only to bond us more tightly. We have certainly laughed together a lot, but I think we have also shed tears together."

Discussion

As the whole group looked at the themes, we were struck by the resonance with Kelly's (1955) Personal Construct Theory. The data illustrated our anticipations, the ways we invested in the writing group, our encounter with the process of writing together, our constructs being confirmed or unsettled, and anticipations revised to increase group coherence.

Our initial *anticipations* parallel the findings of Healey and Matthews (2017) that participants sought new opportunities to share practice and extend collaborations beyond the local. We came seeking new experiences and ways of working, international connections, research collaboration and writing support. We anticipated that collaboration would increase our knowledge or be of direct benefit to our academic work. Everyone was curious as to how the process would unfold and looked forward to our goal of publishing a paper: creating something tangible and with academic currency.

Underlying these anticipations were deeper concerns about what would take place: fears of being exposed and trepidation about the process of co-authoring. We wondered whether the endeavour was feasible and whether it was possible to weave together so many voices. Not knowing other group members, we feared we would not match up. We were invested in the group's outputs; the learning and academic publication promised through participation were important to us all. However, entering the group also required considerable *investment* in the group's process. We had to bring curiosity, a willingness to experiment, and a trust in the competence of group members who were initially strangers.

The *encounter* with the writing group enriched us via energising discussions, new relationships and ideas from diverse disciplines and levels of experience. This diversity was one of the keys to success as it meant we had to actively engage with different ideas and assumptions, explaining what we meant and thereby taking discussion to deeper levels. In navigating this diversity, our group could not rely on leveraging the pre-existing institutional networks and relationships (Kezar, 2005) or the stable social patterns (Walsh & Kahn, 2010) identified as important supports for collaboration. We did, however, have many of the other characteristics noted by Walsh and Kahn (2010), including a focus on process, strategies to promote engagement, recognition of both planned and emerging output, and strategies for building capacity.

The encounter brought *discomfort*. There was frustration with decision-making; involving everyone slowed a process that relied on timely contributions and meeting tight timelines. The biggest challenge was overcoming differences in culture, language, and discipline. This required respect and courtesy, to thoughtfully listen to everyone's contribution, and to negotiate and *revise anticipations*. Members had to be willing to give up different styles of writing and topics or themes that resonated with them but not others. Like others in the ICWG, we had to be open to experiment and adjust (Healey & Matthews, 2017; Motley et al., 2019). This was part of a shared process of academic identity development. As Brew (2008) notes, academic identities are context-dependant. Our disciplinary identities and ways of doing things became unsettled by our group experience and required negotiation and revision. Gradually a coherence developed within the group and our SoTL or cross-disciplinary identities emerged or were strengthened as we saw both ourselves and our work approached differently.

The unexpected loss of a group member forced us again to *revise anticipations*. She was family. We grieved and became closer as we realised the importance of staying connected. We found we had more to give as a group and four years later picked up the threads of where we left off, eager to explore the value of our ongoing collaborations. Smaller collaborations have sprung up from the thoughts and ideas relinquished for the benefit of the larger project; these have added to the richness of our connections.

As described by Marquis, Mårtensson, and Healey (2017), good leadership was essential. Our leader did early groundwork to establish rules of engagement so that everyone respected each other's contribution and was safe to proceed through Kelly's (1955) phases. She interwove our different voices and writing styles. She distributed leadership as much as possible, continually handing decisions back to the group to encourage shared ownership and move towards fluid leadership. As discussed by Leibowitz, Ndebele, and Winberg (2014), we respectfully talked about issues of power, expertise, and authority throughout the collaborative process. This honesty contributed to our deep bonds and the following recommendations, which we humbly offer to other writing groups:

- Bring your expertise but park your ego (explicit conversations about group process can help)
- Appoint a leader/facilitator who leads as a guide on the side; be prepared to share leadership as required
- Listen carefully, ask for explanations, offer thoughts and clarify (leave nothing unsaid)
- Embrace discomfort and uncertainty as part of the process
- Stay connected and responsive (silence helps no one)
- Revise and review timelines as needed to accommodate the above

What has been particularly pertinent to us during this process has been our evolution as a group, made possible only because we have created a safe space in which we can continually revise anticipations, take risks by being open to new experiences, and engage with our diversity. Through the writing group process and the time following it, how we have seen ourselves has shifted and how we approach our work has shifted. Our anticipations approaching this current writing project, for example, were positive and energetic.

Conclusion

In writing this chapter we have reflected upon the investment and discomfort that has characterised our journey and continued to explore together what it is about our international collaborative writing group that works so well. We have offered advice to others contemplating a collaborative writing group and suggested why the leader of such a group might wish to develop their facilitative skills to set up the conditions for shared leadership. As Sue recently summarised:

> I think what's happened is that we are not afraid of harsh judgement from each other and so willingly contribute fearlessly; it has become a true collaboration in which everyone can and does offer something. We give each other space, we have some phenomenal organisers who are confident in their own ability to produce academic output (I am learning lots) and we carefully consider what each other offers. That trust has built through original conversations, ongoing collaboration and willingness and ability to renew those connections.

We continue to evolve. We gathered our descriptions several years after the group's initial formation, which allowed us insights gained over the passing of time that might not have been available to us closer to the event. In the process of writing this chapter, our leadership has become increasingly fluid as members have taken turns to step up in accordance with our group's shifting capacities. The difficulty of deciding authorship order reflected this. For us, the rewards for these efforts have been great: real relationships, deep learning, and interdisciplinary identity development alongside the publications.

References

Becher, T., & Trowler, P. R. (2001). *Academic tribes and territories* (2nd ed.). Buckingham, UK: Society for Research into Higher Education and Open University Press.

Braun, V., & Clarke, V. (2006). Using thematic analysis in psychology. *Qualitative Research in Psychology, 3*(2), 77–101.

Brew, A. (2008). Disciplinary and interdisciplinary affiliations of experienced researchers. *Higher Education, 56*(4), 423–438. doi:10.1007/s10734-007-9102-4

Epitropaki, O., Kark, R., Mainemelis, C., & Lord, R. G. (2017). Leadership and followership identity processes: A multilevel review. *Leadership Quarterly, 28*(1), 104–129.

Healey, M., Marquis, B., & Vajoczki, S. (2013). Exploring SoTL through international collaborative writing groups. *Teaching & Learning Inquiry: The ISSoTL Journal, 1*(2), 3–8.

Healey, M., & Matthews, K. E. (2017). Learning together through international collaborative writing groups. *Teaching & Learning Inquiry: The ISSoTL Journal, 5*(1), 1–6.

Kelly, G. A. (1955). *The psychology of personal constructs. Volume 1: A theory of personality.* New York, NY: WW Norton and Company.

Kelly, N., Nesbit, S., & Oliver, C. (2012). A difficult journey: Transitioning from STEM to SoTL. *International Journal for the Scholarship of Teaching and Learning, 6*(1), 18.

Kensington-Miller, B., Renc-Roe, J., & Morón-García, S. (2015). The chameleon on a tartan rug: Adaptations of three academic developers' professional identities. *International Journal for Academic Development, 20*(3), 279–290. doi:10.1080/13601 44X.2015.1047373

Kezar, A. (2005). Redesigning for collaboration within higher education institutions: An exploration into the developmental process. *Research in Higher Education, 46*(7), 831–860.

Leibowitz, B., Ndebele, C., & Winberg, C. (2014). 'It's an amazing learning curve to be part of the project': Exploring academic identity in collaborative research. *Studies in Higher Education, 39*(7), 1256–1269.

Lincoln, Y. S., & Guba, E. G. (1985). *Naturalistic inquiry*. Beverly Hills, CA: Sage Publications.

Manarin, K., & Abrahamson, E. (2016). Troublesome knowledge of SoTL. *International Journal for the Scholarship of Teaching and Learning, 10*(2), 2.

Manarin, K., Carey, M., Rathburn, M., & Ryland, G. (2015). *Critical reading in higher education: Academic goals and social engagement*. Indiana, IL: Indiana University Press.

Marquis, E., Mårtensson, K., & Healey, M. (2017). Leadership in an International Collaborative Writing Groups (ICWG) initiative: Implications for academic development. *International Journal for Academic Development, 22*(3), 211–222.

Motley, P., Divan, A., Lopes, V., Ludwig, L. O., Matthews, K. E., & Tomljenovic-Berube, A. M. (2019). Collaborative writing: Intercultural and interdisciplinary partnerships as a means of identity formation. In N. Simmons & A. Singh (Eds.), *Critical collaborative communities: Academic writing partnerships, groups, and retreats* (pp. 212–227). Leiden, The Netherlands: Brill Sense.

O'Brien, T. L. (2012). Change in academic coauthorship, 1953–2003. *Science, Technology, & Human Values, 37*(3), 210–234.

Simmons, N. (2011). Caught with their constructs down? Teaching development in the pre-tenure years. *International Journal for Academic Development, 16*(3), 229–241.

Simmons, N., Abrahamson, E., Deshler, J., Kensington-Miller, B., Manarin, K., Moron-Garcia, S., Oliver, C., & Renc-Roe, J. (2013). Conflicts and configurations in a liminal space: SoTL scholars' identity development. *Teaching and Learning Inquiry: The ISSoTL Journal, 1*(2), 9–21.

Walsh, L., & Kahn, P. (2010). *Collaborative working in higher education*. New York, NY: Routledge.

Wasser, J. D., & Bresler, L. (1996). Working in the interpretive zone: Conceptualizing collaboration in qualitative research teams. *Educational Researcher, 25*(5), 5–15.

Wenger, E. (1998). *Communities of practice: Learning, meaning and identity*. Cambridge, MA: Cambridge University Press.

CHAPTER 18

Creation, Critique, Consolidation

Nicola Simmons

Abstract

This synthesis chapter outlines the common themes of the collaborative writing groups in the book. Prevalent themes include writing retreat pragmatics such as how positive processes are supported by setting and negotiating goals and having a dedicated space. They also include the *soul work* that comprises trusting and successful writing partnerships that help avoid isolation and support the development of scholarly identity as an academic writer.

Keywords

synthesis – consolidation – soul work – goals – negotiation – dedicated writing space – trust – self-authorship – avoiding isolation

The chapters in this volume illustrate a variety of autoethnographic approaches to the collaborative writing process – that often messy exploration of understanding from within. From that exploration, the authors have crafted lucid descriptions and recommendations to guide others contemplating everything from writing partnerships to groups and retreats of both small and larger groups.

In this synthesis chapter, I use the chapter authors' words to illustrate the common themes that appear throughout the volume. These themes comprise two key areas: (1) the pragmatics of writing retreats, such as setting goals, negotiating those goals and participant roles, and the importance of a dedicated space for writing; and (2) the *soul work* that is supported by trust, leads to self-authorship as writing scholars, and helps scholars avoid the challenges of always writing in isolation.

Process Logistics

Authors brought different approaches to goal-setting, sharing approaches that were all grounded in clear communication. They outlined how they negotiated

© KONINKLIJKE BRILL NV, LEIDEN, 2019 | DOI:10.1163/9789004410985_018

CREATION, CRITIQUE, CONSOLIDATION 243

specific aspects of the process and how they benefited from a dedicated and often offsite place for their writing. In this section I expand on each of these themes.

Goals

Throughout the volume, authors note the importance of clear goals and creating a "program of work" (Chapter 2). Many referred to the value of a transparent process and recommend taking time to "set the tone" (Chapter 5). Chapter 14 authors pointed to the ways "initial goal setting then guided the discussions in the subsequent meetings." Authors noted the value of "regular contact, setting short term goals (Chapter 3). Shorter deadlines towards a final product helped: "We chose to set up many small deadlines during the course of the project, rather than fewer large deadlines" (Chapter 16).

Leaders can support that process, as noted in Chapter 17: "Our leader did early groundwork to establish rules of engagement so that everyone respected each other's contribution and was safe to proceed." The leadership role was acknowledged in facilitated writing retreats: "At this initial gathering, the writer-facilitators outline the components of the retreat and introduce the basic rules of conduct: respect quiet times for writing, commit to giving and receiving feedback, maintain confidentiality, and work toward their self-identified goals" (Chapter 11).

At the same time, it is important to note that not all writing groups are as prescriptive: "In our collaboration we do not focus a prescriptive research and writing agenda to 'fit in' we simply 'show up'" (Chapter 10). Chapter 1 authors similarly noted "ours was a leaderless writing partnership. Neither of us assumed responsibility for keeping each other on track nor for organizing in-meeting activities."

Authors throughout the book described the importance of keeping each other on track, noting that their self-regulation was easier in the group, upon which they depended for social support as well as to augment their own commitment. Each group has its own dynamic; what seems to be important is having initial conversations about expectations for the writing process and negotiating any aspects of disagreement. "Attention paid to making processes explicit and communicating clearly in order to build relationships and trust with writing colleagues" (Chapter 13). Similarly, Chapter 15 authors recommend "explicit advance conversations to help frame expectations positively support the process." Communication that is "timely, friendly, supportive (yet challenging)" (Chapter 3) is appreciated by all.

Negotiation

While some chapters are about scholars in the same or similar disciplines "learning with and from" (Chapter 5) each other, "faculty, even outside of their own discipline, can support each other's writing efforts through sharing goals, offering successful strategies, and discussing challenges' (Chapter 7). Many note the value of these critical partners coming from other disciplines, saying they appreciated the alternative perspectives that academics from other fields brought to their work. Chapter 17 authors acknowledged that "our disciplinary identities and ways of doing things became unsettled by our group experience and required negotiation and revision." Similarly, these approaches affect the details of writing: "While we were familiar with the variety of styles associated with different disciplinary journals, we found ourselves differing over required research article components and naming conventions associated with those parts" (Chapter 13).

Disciplinary differences are not the only kind requiring negotiation: "We get along very well, but we are also temperamentally quite disparate humans, a mix of introverts and extroverts, early risers and night owls, and these differences require negotiation" (Chapter 9). Ongoing conversations are important to mitigate challenge that may arise from these differences: "We respectfully talked about issues of power, expertise, and authority throughout the collaborative process" (Chapter 17).

Dedicated Writing Space

Many chapters discuss the challenges inherent in trying to write from one's office and refer to the notion of dedicated writing space as important to their processes. Chapter 6 authors note that "place is certainly not the only but often one of the most difficult parts of the writing equation" and value that "it has been a safe quiet space."

Some groups held their retreats in places well away from the campus, noting "perhaps these wide-open spaces will help us overcome the sense of being blocked or stuck and unlock the power of self-transformation that we seem to seek in our writing" (Chapter 10). Chapter 9 authors said "these retreats provide us with intense and very productive time together, unencumbered by other responsibilities. Long hours, meals, walks, and naps punctuate talking, sketching, whiteboarding, and writing." Chapter 11 authors found "the rural retreat setting where others attend to meal preparation and household chores provides inspiration from nature and seclusion from day-to-day pressures." This sense of 'getting away' was important: "During these retreats, I travel to an isolated spot away from the office, my home, my family, and society in general!" (Chapter 13). There was also the sense of the importance of balancing work and play: "Effective writing retreats include time away from writing to honour the 'treat' part of the 'writing retreat.' The paradox is that taking time to play can lead to more writing collaborations" (Chapter 12).

CREATION, CRITIQUE, CONSOLIDATION   245

The groups' focus on setting goals, negotiating the writing process, and setting a space away from the pressures of day to day work worked to enable a space for the individual processes that helped them develop their identity as writing scholars, which I outline in the next section.

Soul Work

While the authors provide pragmatic recommendations for others wishing to create writing groups, whether that be with a writing partner, in a small group that continues to meet onsite or offsite, in annual retreats, in organizing such events for others, or in one time collaborative writing groups, there is a theme that runs throughout the book of the "soul work" that Dirkx (2008) refers to as "hard, emotional, messy, uncertain, ambiguous, and ill-structured process, with no pat strategies, methods, or specific models to guide the way" (p. 66).

What does help with that messy soul work, however, are the kinds of approaches that appear as thematic threads throughout the book: *trust* is seen as an important support to the *self-authorship* that most authors experienced. They also value the relationships that help avoid the typical isolation of the academic author.

Trust

Perhaps the most pervasive theme in these chapters is about trust and its importance in the collaborative writing process. All authors mention trust – that "intense presence, careful listening, and a willingness to go where your partner leads" (Chapter 2) and being open to unexpected outcomes. They outline the necessity of creating it with writing partners and of its value to the writing process. As Chapter 13 authors explained, they

> quickly discovered that trust and intellectual intrigue bond the significant conversations (Roxå & Mårtensson, 2009) that occur both on and off the page in a collaborative writing group. In order to build trust, it is important to create a sense of community, connection, and belonging (Marquis, Healey, & Vine, 2014) for all group members.

Trust is thus a precursor to collaborative work: "We need to be able to share our vulnerabilities and feel like we can ask questions without the fear of being ridiculed" (Chapter 5). Likewise, Chapter 10 authors felt that "in our group I feel like it is ok to fail."

This trust was often strongly linked to empathy: "There is integrity in our process – a method to our madness – that is located in critical empathy" (Chapter 9). Chapter 10 authors also noted that "together as academics, colleagues, and friends we are practicing empathy and connection." Chapter 9 authors unpacked this notion further: "Empathy is only possible when there is a multiplicity of selves, each looking at and confirming the reality of the others."

Groups spent time getting to know each other: "One of the smartest things we did initially was to simply take the time to get to know each other" (Chapter 16). At the same time, as noted by Chapter 17 authors, there had to be trust of the unknown: "We had to bring curiosity, a willingness to experiment, and a trust in the competence of group members who were initially strangers."

Trust that allows group members to be honest with each other also allows them to ask critical questions: "Querying and writing keeps us honest, and guards against any tendency to be swept away in a pleasing and energetic groupthink" (Chapter 9). Trust thus led directly to being able to critically support the work of academic writing. Chapter 4 authors noted that

> The feedback we were able to provide each other during our weekly meetings proved to be invaluable to our growth as academic writers but would not have occurred had we not established relationships with each other and created a safe social space for writing.

All chapters outline the benefits of their writing partners as *critical friends* (Carr & Kemmis, 1986) to help interrogate ideas and writing in a supportive way, noting the importance of "having a critical friend that can push you" (Chapter 3). The encouragement (and sometimes pushing) of the informal peer mentoring seemed to create the ideal conditions for personal growth.

Self-Authorship

Although the partnerships outlined in this volume are about writing, it is also clear that significant self-authoring (Baxter-Magolda, 1999) occurs. Authors described their changing perceptions and ways in which their identity as an academic writer developed. "The writing retreat seemed to build up the faculty members' view of themselves as writers" (Chapter 7). This is also echoed in Chapter 8: "One unanticipated benefit of the boot camp has been the influence it has had on faculty members' sense of self as writers and scholars."

The collaborative nature seems to support individual development: writing partnerships "provide individual self-efficacy as a writer by developing confidence and helping members overcome obstacles" (Chapter 4) and "our

CREATION, CRITIQUE, CONSOLIDATION

collaborative writing group has fostered a space for me to take risks as a writer, learn from others and feel valued" (Chapter 10).

As Chapter 16 authors noted, "collaborative writing can provide opportunities for shared experiences that then help form community and encourage a sense of belonging that promotes confidence and certainty as a teacher, researcher, and scholar." This is echoed by Chapter 4 authors, who observed that "through consistent feedback we began learning about ourselves as academic writers, as well as the rules of academic writing within our respective fields." Similarly, Chapter 17 authors found that "cross-disciplinary identities emerged or were strengthened as we saw both ourselves and our work approached differently."

Writing partnerships and retreats, through the collaborations, fostered environments where scholars could develop self-efficacy as authors. Chapter 15 authors observed that the groups "supported the growth of their scholarly capacity, exposing them to new perspectives and approaches, and leading to the generation of novel ideas and understandings, which is echoed in Chapter 11: "This social participation enhances our sense of community and strengthens our identities as writers." Ultimately, these groups "nurtured our professional identities as ... scholars who are better able to write alone and collaboratively" (Chapter 16).

Avoiding Isolation

One of the common themes was the notion of scholars as 'lone academics' writing in solitude and how the writing partnerships overcame the inherent challenges of that image. Collaborative writing "helped faculty feel they did not have to struggle alone and that others also have challenges" (Chapter 7). Writing retreats mitigate isolation: "Retreats may play an important role in interrupting the habits of writing in isolation, which can be more damaging than productive" (Chapter 8). As Chapter 9 authors noted, "It is striking how many times the word 'lonely' appears in our writing about this topic." Chapter 1 authors found that "while we did not identify social support as a key goal for our group, we both agree that it has emerged as a very important outcome." Chapter 2 authors, preparing a course together, discovered that "by asking questions together, by reading together, and by writing together, we try to escape the pitfalls of knowledge that exist in parallel and disconnected spaces." Similarly, Chapter 6 authors found "it creates the opportunity to network with other tenure track faculty whose drive, techniques, and simple compassion have been invaluable to maintaining the focus and momentum necessary to finish projects."

Chapter 14 authors noted how "our collaboration injected energy and vibrancy into our writing, removing the oft-felt sense of isolation in academia"

(Chapter 14). That lift was felt in professional as well as social ways: "The family ties of that small, intrepid, and firmly connected social and professional network are still as strong" (Chapter 17). There is importance in "having time and space away from the work of writing to socialize through shared meals and recreational activities during retreats" (Chapter 12).

Clearly, the emotional support is critical: "The strong relationships that we have created have enabled us to realign and recalibrate the harmonies, supporting one another as needed" (Chapter 14). Chapter 1 authors noted how "writing with others can foster motivation through mutual encouragement, accountability, or healthy competition." As one participant in Chapter 8 remarked, "After a very stressful term, I entered this retreat on the verge of demoralized burnout. Now I feel strengthened and reaffirmed."

Summary

What stands out in this book is the authors' stance on the value of writing partnerships. While authors have outlined the challenges that they overcame and necessary negotiations, they also point to the ways in which "working in partnership allows individuals to glimpse behind the curtain and share the mechanics of academic writing" (Chapter 3). They also comment on specific skills that were developed through the process: "Many described feeling that their capacity to give and receive feedback, write for publication, and/or work in or facilitate large, diverse groups had been enhanced" (Chapter 15). Chapter 12 authors summarized that "academic writing retreats can provide spaces where writing can become collegial, collaborative, and ongoing across time and geographical space."

Figure 18.1 indicates the common elements outlined by the authors for successful collaborative critical communities: Setting goals, negotiating processes, and having a dedicated space can lead to group trust, enhanced self-authorship, and avoiding isolation in the writing process.

Modelling the Collaborative Process

All authors referred to the meta-cognitive aspect of reflecting on their writing process. The process of this book followed a path that parallels many of the writing collaborations that form its chapters. Author groups wrote their own chapters (*creation*). Peer-review was incorporated to address the challenges of writing in isolation (*critique*). Each lead author reviewed two other papers and recommendations were integrated into the final chapters (*consolidation*) (see Figure 18.2).

FIGURE 18.1   Elements of successful collaborative writing groups

Through this process, chapter authors were able to benefit from reading each others' work, and chapters were tweaked in the re-writing stage, in some cases to refer to other work within this volume. The result, we feel, is a cohesive collection of collaborative writing models.

Healey and Matthews (2017) offer that participants in collaborative writing groups must bring certain qualities for the groups to be successful:

1. Willingness to collaborate on a journey that has an uncertain outcome.
2. Adventurousness that embraces a journey of co-creation with unknown, diverse scholars.
3. Open mindedness to question what one thinks [the topic] is.
4. Empathy for others from different cultures and contexts that affect how they collaborate.
5. Willingness to make time and space for collaboration using online tools (pp. 4–5).

With somewhat less attention to the last point (though one could replace 'online' with the notion of other face-to-face approaches) all of these appear in chapters throughout this book. The co-authors' willingness, adventurousness, open-mindedness, and empathy have very much been the qualities that made this project possible.

Collaborative writing depends on the dedication and commitment of all involved, and nowhere has that been truer than in the production of this volume. Thanks are due to all who submitted proposals, conferred with writing

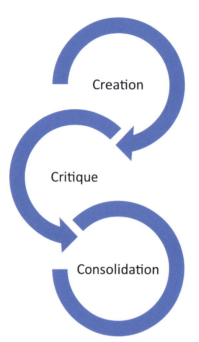

FIGURE 18.2   Collaborative writing process: Creation, critique, consolidation

partners, wrote and submitted on time, provided strong and supportive critique of others' chapters, and revised their papers to address peer feedback. I am extraordinarily grateful to all authors for their excellent chapters and recommendations about collaborative writing partnerships.

References

Baxter Magolda, M. B. (1999). *Creating contexts for learning and self-authorship*. Nashville, TN: Vanderbilt University Press.

Carr, W., & Kemmis, S. (1986). *Becoming critical: Education, knowledge, and action research*. London, UK: The Falmer Press.

Dirkx, J. M. (2008). Care of the self: Mythopoetic dimensions of professional preparation and development. In T. Leonard & P. Willis (Eds.), *Pedagogies of the imagination* (pp. 65–82). Dordrecht, The Netherlands: Springer.

Healey, M., & Matthews, K. E. (2017). Learning together through International Collaborative Writing Groups. *Teaching and Learning Inquiry, 5*(1) 1–6. https://doi.org/10.20343/5.1.2

Printed in the United States
By Bookmasters